CUSTER AND THE FRONT ROYAL EXECUTIONS OF 1864

ALSO BY JAY W. SIMSON

Crisis of Command in the Army of the Potomac:
Sheridan's Search for an Effective General (McFarland, 2008)

CUSTER AND THE FRONT ROYAL EXECUTIONS OF 1864

Jay W. Simson

McFarland & Company, Inc., Publishers
Jefferson, North Carolina, and London

LIBRARY OF CONGRESS CATALOGUING-IN-PUBLICATION DATA

Simson, Jay W., 1953–
    Custer and the Front Royal Executions of 1864 / Jay W. Simson.
      p.   cm.
    Includes bibliographical references and index.

    ISBN 978-0-7864-3973-7
    softcover : 50# alkaline paper ∞

    1. Shenandoah Valley Campaign, 1864 (August–November)
2. Custer, George A. (George Armstrong), 1839–1876.
3. Executions and executioners — Virginia — Front Royal —
History — 19th century.   4. Front Royal (Va.) — History,
Military —19th century.   5. United States — History — Civil War,
1861–1865 — Atrocities.   6. Confederate States of America. Army.
Virginia Calvary Battalion, 43rd.   7. Mosby, John Singleton,
1833–1916.   I. Title
    E477.33.S56   2009
    973.7'37 — dc22   2008041730

British Library cataloguing data are available

On the cover: General Philip H. Sheridan, 1864 (Corbis Images);
The Army of the Potomac Marching Up Pennsylvania Avenue, 1891
(Pictures Now)

Manufactured in the United States of America

*McFarland & Company, Inc., Publishers
  Box 611, Jefferson, North Carolina 28640
  www.mcfarlandpub.com*

To the members of the
Western Ohio Civil War Roundtable
for all of the inspiration they have provided me
that led to the writing of this and other works.

And to the Monroe County Library,
without whose assistance this book
would never have been written.

TABLE OF CONTENTS

INTRODUCTION:
CUSTER AT FRONT ROYAL

War breeds atrocities. Civil wars breed more atrocities than any other kind of war. This was as true in the American Civil War as it was in any other civil war. One of the American Civil War's most celebrated atrocities occurred in the Shenandoah Valley town of Front Royal, Virginia, on September 23, 1864. It involved the execution of six men, guerrillas belonging to then Lt. Col. John S. Mosby's 43rd Virginia Battalion of Partisan Rangers, taken prisoner by Union cavalry who were supposedly under the command of Brig. Gen. George A. Custer. These Union troops then executed all six of the prisoners.

In about a month a seventh man, also one of Mosby's Rangers, was taken prisoner and executed by Union soldiers of the 2nd Cavalry Division, Department of West Virginia. The Union soldiers in both incidents were part of the Army of the Shenandoah, which was under the command of Maj. Gen. Philip H. Sheridan, one of the Union's primary and most ruthless advocates and practitioner of the new idea of total war, which by 1864 had become one of the strategic concepts guiding the Union's war effort.

Mosby's response to both of these incidents was to plan and put into effect a spectacular reprisal. His ultimate aim was to put an effective end to the practice of reprisal and counter reprisal. On November 7, 1864, about six weeks after the Front Royal incident, Mosby forced 27 Union prisoners of war to draw lots. Seven of them were marched off to a point near the camp of Custer's current command, the 3rd Division, Cavalry Corps, Army of the Potomac, serving with the Army of the Shenandoah. Three of them were hanged. Two others escaped and the final two were shot, and after being left for dead, also later escaped.

Mosby was convinced until the end of his days that Custer was personally responsible for the executions of his men at Front Royal. In *Gray*

Ghost: The Memoirs of Col. John S. Mosby, he repeated his accusation, bringing it to the general public's attention for the first time, although references to what happened in Front Royal do exist in official reports and correspondence of such Union officers as Maj. Gen. Alfred T.A. Torbert, Brig. Gen. Wesley Merritt, Col. Charles Russell Lowell, and among the Confederates, Lt. Col. Mosby and Gen. Robert E. Lee himself, which are included in the 128 volumes of *The War of Rebellion: A Compilation of Official Records of the Union and Confederate Armies,* and in other reports — citing various other witnesses — such as letters, journals and memoirs along with contemporary Northern and Southern newspaper accounts.

Because of Mosby's conviction that Custer and Custer alone was responsible for the Front Royal executions, and because Custer himself apparently never publicly said or wrote anything at all about the incident (something that Mosby used many years later as a justification for refusing to change his mind about Custer's guilt, even after considerable evidence for Custer's innocence had been presented to him after the war), many historians have assumed Mosby's accusation was true. Custer's later career as an Indian fighter on the frontier, in particular during the Battle of the Washita, has also led many students of his life and career to express little surprise that he would be accused of being the primary participant in an atrocity during the American Civil War and to use that as another justification of their condemnation of his actions while an officer in the Indian-fighting army.

However, Mosby's memoirs, which contained his first generally known public accusations of Custer's responsibility for the executions, were not published until 1917, a year after Mosby's death, 53 years after the event and 41 years after Custer himself had died at the Battle of the Little Bighorn.

I first became interested in the events of that September day in 1864 while reading a historical novel. It was set in 1866, a year after the end of the American Civil War, at the time of the Fetterman Massacre at Fort Phil Kearney. In this novel the reason for the main character's hatred of Custer was due to his witnessing the executions at Front Royal, which he recalled as being conducted by soldiers of the 2nd U.S. Cavalry at the command of Custer himself.

After I read this passage I realized that there was something terribly wrong with the entire scenario. At the time of the Front Royal incident

George Armstrong Custer did not have — and never did have — any command authority whatsoever over the solders in the 2nd U.S. Cavalry Regiment. At the time of the Front Royal incident, Custer commanded the Michigan Cavalry Brigade, which consisted of four Michigan regiments (the 1st, 5th, 6th and 7th Michigan Cavalry Regiments) and one New York regiment (the 25th New York Cavalry Regiment). The soldiers of the 2nd U.S. Cavalry Regiment were all members of the Reserve Cavalry Brigade under the command of Col. Charles Russell Lowell.

Lowell himself was not a regular officer, being a colonel in the volunteer army raised to fight the war, although most of his brigade consisted of regulars. His own regiment, the 2nd Massachusetts Volunteer Cavalry Regiment, had been assigned to the brigade in an effort to increase its numbers. He was in command of the brigade by virtue of being the senior officer present, although he was recognized by his superiors as a particularly effective officer.

Because Custer had no command authority over those men in the 2nd U.S. Cavalry, he could not have ordered them to execute anybody. Such orders could only have come from three men — Maj. Gen. Alfred T.A. Torbert, the commander of the Union forces in Front Royal that day, Brig. Gen. Wesley Merritt, the commander of Torbert's First Cavalry Division (to which Lowell's Reserve Cavalry Brigade and Custer's Michigan Cavalry Brigade both belonged), and Col. Lowell himself. All are documented as being present at Front Royal when the executions occurred. None of the eyewitnesses, Union or Confederate, ever mentioned seeing Custer at any of the executions or actually giving orders that anyone was to be executed.

For a moment let us take a look at the background of this George Armstrong Custer.

He was born in New Rumley, Ohio, on December 5, 1839. He was the third child of Emmanuel Henry and Mary Ward Kirkpatrick Custer. His father was a blacksmith and justice of the peace. Both of George Custer's parents had been widowed and the two previous children they had together had died. His father had two surviving sons from his first marriage and his mother had a son and a daughter from her first marriage. In 1849, when Custer was nine, his parents sent him to live with his half-sister, Lydia, who had married and was living in Monroe, Michigan, where he would go to school.

He returned to his parents' home in 1855 and taught school for a time. In 1857 he was appointed a cadet from Ohio and entered the U.S. Military Academy at West Point, N.Y. (His appointment as a cadet was somewhat unusual since he, following his father's lead, was a Democrat and the congressman representing their district was a Republican. According to one story the congressman was urged to make the appointment by a prominent farmer who wanted to break up a budding romance between Custer and his daughter.) An indifferent student, he managed to graduate from the academy in 1861, at the bottom of his class, and was assigned to the 2nd U.S. Cavalry Regiment (which was later re-designated the 5th U.S. Cavalry Regiment). He was cited in dispatches for his actions at the First Battle of Bull Run (or Manassas). Later Custer served on the staffs of Maj. Gen. Phil Kearney, Maj. Gen. George B. McClellan and Maj. Gen. Alfred Pleasonton, among others.

Physically he had grown to be a bit over six feet tall with a lanky and well-muscled frame. He had blue eyes and reddish blonde hair, habitually worn rather long. He later grew a long sweeping mustache and a goatee. His hands were large and heavily muscled, blacksmith's hands (his father was a blacksmith), capable of twisting a horseshoe out of shape with little or no effort. He also had a constitution of steel, able to function with only two hours or less of sleep a night. He had the knack of being able to catch a nap anywhere at any time. Anything he asked of his men he demanded of himself. The main drawback in all of this was that he was never able to recognize that common, ordinary mortals simply did not have his raw stamina and endurance.

In the summer of 1863, Custer was a brevet captain serving on Pleasonton's staff, which highlights the question of how a 23-year-old brevet captain on the staff of a corps commander becomes a brevet brigadier general of volunteers in command of a seasoned brigade of cavalry practically overnight. One possible answer of course is influence, either in the political or military hierarchy. Other possibilities cited by historians have included a freak accident (as cited in the movie *They Died with Their Boots On*) or just plain dumb luck.

In fact Custer owed his promotion to none of these things.

In Custer's case, to ascribe his promotion to undue influence is ridiculous because Custer had little or no influence in either the political or military sense. Influence in the military sense is usually inherited, in that different generations of the same family have a tradition of serving in the military. Although his father was an officer in the Ohio militia, Custer himself was the first member of his family to become a professional soldier.

That he used political influence is even more absurd. Custer, it must be reiterated, was a lifelong Democrat; he was at least lukewarm on the issue of slavery and in fact had many friends who were serving in the Confederate army, and was known to be a protégé of former Army of the Potomac commander George B. McClellan (whose name was anathema to the radical wing of Lincoln's Republican Party long before McClellan became the Democratic Party candidate for president in 1864), and he was not a native of Michigan.

Although Custer was mostly raised in Michigan (considering Monroe to be his home), he was born in Ohio and he was appointed to the U.S. Military Academy at West Point to fill an Ohio vacancy. In addition, by this time in the war any close associates of Gen. McClellan were going to be viewed with a great deal of suspicion and outright skepticism by Republican politicians. (Two general officers considered to be McClellan protégés had already been disgraced and in at least one case court-martialed and thrown out of the army.)

When the 7th Michigan Cavalry Regiment was formed, Custer made application to the Republican governor of Michigan to become its colonel. He, of course, cited his West Point credentials to plead his case. He was turned down, officially because he was too young. It was impossible that the Republican governor of Michigan was ever going to name a Democrat of such suspect affiliations to what at the time amounted to a major political plum. Under the Northern recruiting system the bulk of new recruits were organized into new regiments rather than being used to fill out the ranks of veteran units. This was due to the fact that most recruitment was in the hands of the states until the units were turned over to the federal government upon their being mustered into federal service. If these recruits were formed into new regiments, the governors of each state had a whole slate of political appointments to make in the selection of the unit's regimental officers.

Only the governors of a few western states, such as Wisconsin (and Michigan, in point of fact), were able to resist that temptation to a degree, since even in these western states new regiments were raised from time to time throughout the war. A Union commander was grateful indeed if his command included units from these states, as their numbers remained fairly constant and the veteran soldiers helped to teach the new recruits what they needed to know.

Accident and plain dumb luck had even less to do with Custer's promotion to brigadier general. The person who engineered it, one Alfred Pleasonton, knew exactly what he was doing. Pleasonton, although vain, boastful, and not particularly truthful, was one of the truly unsung Union heroes of the American Civil War. He was determined to change the Union cavalry from being the laughingstock of both armies, North and South, into actually being a major element in the North's eventual victory.

Pleasonton was the man who forged the Union Army of the Potomac's Cavalry Corps into the weapon Philip H. Sheridan would wield when he sought out, attacked and killed Confederate Army of Northern Virginia chief of cavalry Maj. Gen. James Ewell Brown (J.E.B.) Stuart on his first cavalry raid; when he denied the Confederacy the granary, which was the Shenandoah Valley; and trapped Lee's Army of Northern Virginia in the final campaign of the war in the east, thus forcing it to surrender at the sleepy town of Appomattox Court House.

Pleasonton was originally a divisional cavalry commander when Joseph Hooker first consolidated the cavalry and created the Cavalry Corps during his tenure in command of the Army of the Potomac, and eventually became the commander of the Cavalry Corps of the Army of the Potomac. Pleasonton realized that in order to reach his goal of reforming the Union cavalry, he needed bold, dynamic leaders for his brigades and divisions, finding many of them among his staff officers. Just prior to the Battle of Gettysburg he promoted three of them — Wesley Merritt, Elon J. Farnsworth and Custer — to the rank of brigadier general.

In Custer's personal case, his service on Pleasonton's staff gave the cavalry commander a chance to view Custer in action. It was not unusual at a critical point in a battle — if a regimental or even a brigade commander was killed or seriously wounded — for a Civil War general to order one of his aides, who may have only held the rank of lieutenant or captain, to take over, rather than follow the normal chain of command. A general would do this because at the critical moment he needed to know the officer who was in command so that he would know what to expect from that commander. Having to deal at such a moment with someone who was practically a total stranger was to be avoided at all costs.

This exact situation had occurred at the Battles of Brandy Station and Aldie, which opened the Gettysburg Campaign. At a critical moment in both battles Custer took charge of a faltering attack when the original commander had been killed or disabled, and he succeeded in carrying out the objectives ordered by Pleasonton. Therefore, Pleasonton, having tested Custer, found him capable of handling a brigade under the most trying of circumstances.

Pleasonton, having received permission to reorganize the cavalry corps to his satisfaction, then named Brig. Gen. Hugh Judson Kilpatrick to command his new 3rd Cavalry Division, which had joined the army from the garrison of Washington, D.C. Farnsworth and Custer were named to command the 1st and 2nd Brigades in Kilpatrick's division while Merritt received command of the Reserve Cavalry Brigade. (Merritt would eventually advance to command of the Cavalry Corps.)

During the battle of Gettysburg Farnsworth was killed while making a suicidal attack under the orders of Kilpatrick, while Custer and his brigade was instrumental in turning back an attempt by Confederate Maj. Gen. J.E.B. Stuart and his cavalry to turn the Union right flank at the same time that Maj. Gen. George Pickett was assaulting the Union center. Custer, supported by another cavalry division commander who needed Custer's brigade as reinforcements, did this in defiance of orders from Kilpatrick.[1]

Among other things, Custer was a "showman." He wore a unique and gaudy uniform. His critics claimed that he did it to show off. Custer himself said that he made his appearance conspicuous so that his men would be able to see him anywhere he might be upon the battlefield, for it was Custer's style to lead from the front, and the men he commanded during the American Civil War would have gladly followed behind him just about anywhere. At least one historian has wondered how Custer managed to so inspire his men battle after battle, despite large numbers of casualties[2]; one answer was through sheer leadership. Another was that under Custer, something was almost always actually accomplished in return for those casualty lists.

Custer had an instinctive understanding of what the mission of the cavalry was and how that mission could be accomplished. In defining that mission, three other American Civil War generals said it best:

- "The cavalry constitutes the eyes and ears of the army. The safety of the entire command depends upon their vigilance and the faithfulness of their reports."—Confederate Lt. Gen. Daniel Harvey Hill, February 26, 1863.

- "During the period of my immediate control of the Cavalry, I tried to carry into effect, as far as possible, the views I had advanced before and during the opening of the Wilderness Campaign, i.e., 'that our cavalry ought to fight the enemy's cavalry, and our infantry the enemy's infantry'; for there was great danger of breaking the spirit of the corps if it was to be pitted against the enemy's compact mass of foot-troops posted behind entrenchments, and unless there was some adequate tactical or strategic advantage to be gained, such a use of it would not be justified,"—Union Lt. Gen. Philip H. Sheridan, *Memoirs*, Vol. 1 (1888).

- "An attack of cavalry should be sudden, bold, vigorous. The cavalry which arrives noiselessly but steadily near the enemy, and then with one loud yell leaps upon him without a note of warning, and giving no time to form or consider anything but the immediate means of flight, pushing him vigorously every step with the confidence of victory achieved, is the true cavalry; while a body of men equally brave and patriotic, who halt at every picket and reconnoiter until the precious surprise is over, is not cavalry."—Confederate Maj. Gen. J.E.B. Stuart, General Order No. 26, Cavalry Tactics, July 20, 1863.[3]

George Armstrong Custer was one of the cavalry commanders who best embodied the sentiments stated above. In truth, Custer may have been one of the best brigade and divisional commanders in the Army of the Potomac. He certainly achieved results. Custer, like his eventual boss Phil Sheridan, was a battlefield commander. He was not a man to sit at a desk and devise plans and stratagems. He had an eye for terrain. He also had the capacity to make immediate decisions, more on an intuitive basis than an intellectual one. And he made his decisions rapidly. What he would do was to ride to the front, make a personal reconnaissance, look for and find any weaknesses in his enemy's position, and then once he had found that weakness, he made his decisions immediately and began barking out orders.

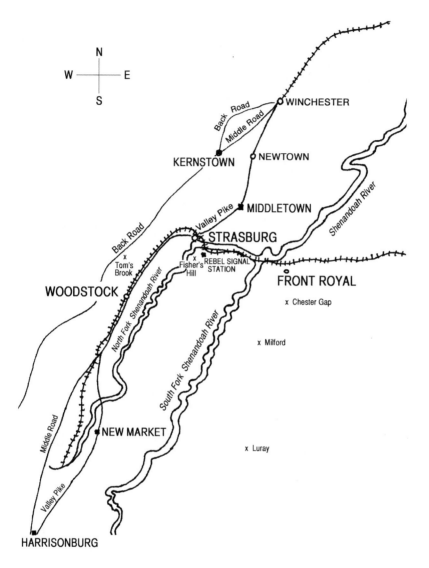

N
W — E
S

Back Road
Middle Road

WINCHESTER

KERNSTOWN

NEWTOWN

Valley Pike

MIDDLETOWN

Back Road

STRASBURG

x
Tom's
Brook

x
Fisher's
Hill

x REBEL SIGNAL
STATION

North Fork Shenandoah River

Shenandoah River

FRONT ROYAL

x Chester Gap

WOODSTOCK

South Fork Shenandoah River

x Milford

Middle Road

NEW MARKET

x Luray

Valley Pike

HARRISONBURG

On September 19, 1864, Jubal Early's army was driven from Winchester to Fisher's Hill; Sheridan, using a plan formulated by George C. Crook, drove the Confederates from Fisher's Hill on September 21. Meanwhile, A.T.A. Torbert, with four brigades of cavalry, was sent into Early's rear, where he allowed himself to be stopped by Williams C. Wickham and Thomas Munford at Milford. Their actions saved Early's army, which escaped from Sheridan through New Market Gap on September 25. It was during this period that the Front Royal atrocity occurred on September 23, 1864 (map prepared by Lynn Simson).

A perfect example of this occurred during the Battle of Tom's Brook in the Shenandoah Valley on October 9, 1864. Custer with two brigades was facing his old friend and former West Point roommate, Thomas Lafayette Rosser, with three brigades. In this situation, Custer knew just what to do. He had to tie down Rosser's resources — without hobbling his own — probe for a weak spot, find that weak spot, and then go for broke with all of his strength. When his two brigades were in position, Custer galloped far out in front of his line, stopping where every man on both sides could see him; then he raised his hand to his hat, swept it off his head and down to his knee in an extravagant salute. While he was doing this, he found the weak spot he had been looking for. After making his gesture, he then attacked with all of his strength the weak spot in Rosser's line and drove Rosser's division from its relatively strong position on the high ground, chasing it from the field for a good 10 to 12 miles.

Generally, he was acting while his opponents were still deciding.

In the fall of 1864 Custer was serving in Sheridan's Army of the Shenandoah when the Front Royal incident occurred. The incident has been used ever since to blot the military reputation that he had earned during the American Civil War. I intend to show — in this study of Front Royal incident, the background of events which led to it, and its aftermath — that while some of his soldiers may well have been peripherally involved in what happened Custer himself ordered no executions and chances are that he was not there when the executions occurred.

The evidence for this conclusion lies in his known position in the Union line of march as Merritt's 1st Cavalry Division approached the town of Front Royal, the examination of certain primary sources, even what was not said and likely reasons why so many people had nothing whatever to say about the Front Royal incident, and why Custer's character, as shown by his documented actions during his Civil War career, make it highly likely that Custer was no more than marginally involved in what happened at Front Royal.

1

INCIDENT AT FRONT ROYAL

On September 23, 1864, there occurred an incident near the town of Front Royal, Virginia, which in time to come would be seen as a major blot upon the Civil War career of then Brevet Brig. Gen. of Volunteers George Armstrong Custer. At the time of the incident Custer was in command of the 1st Brigade, 1st Division, Cavalry Corps, Army of the Potomac, serving with the Army of the Shenandoah, also known as the Michigan Cavalry Brigade or the Wolverine Brigade. His brigade consisted of five regiments, including the 1st Michigan Cavalry Regiment, 5th Michigan Cavalry Regiment, 6th Michigan Cavalry Regiment, and the 7th Michigan Cavalry Regiment, along with the 25th New York Cavalry Regiment.

A wagon train, whose escort was under the command of 1st Lt. Charles McMaster, 2nd U.S. Cavalry Regiment, part of the Reserve Brigade, First Division, Cavalry Corps, under the command of Col. Charles Russell Lowell, was proceeding in the direction of Front Royal. Following immediately behind the wagon train (which was transporting wounded soldiers along with the baggage and supplies of the 1st and 3rd Divisions of the Cavalry Corps) was the Reserve Cavalry Brigade, with Custer's Michigan Cavalry Brigade bringing up the rear. Both brigades were elements of the 1st Cavalry Division, under the command of Brig. General Wesley Merritt. Accompanying the division was Maj. Gen. Alfred T.A. Torbert, commander of the Cavalry Corps. At that time Lowell's brigade consisted of his own 2nd Massachusetts Cavalry Regiment, 1st U.S. Cavalry Regiment, 2nd U.S. Cavalry Regiment, 5th U.S. Cavalry Regiment and the 6th U.S. Cavalry Regiment. Aside from Russell's own regiment, the bulk of the brigade consisted of regulars, not volunteers.

Torbert had been involved with his 1st and 3rd Cavalry Divisions in an attempt to cut off Lt. Gen. Jubal Early's Confederate Valley Army in the Luray Valley just after the Battle of Fisher's Hill. Torbert had failed in his assigned task and was in the process of withdrawing with the intention of rejoining the main portion of the Army of the Shenandoah, which was under the command of Maj. Gen. Philip H. Sheridan. At the time the Front Royal Incident occurred, the two brigades of the 3rd Cavalry Division, under the command of Brig. Gen. James H. Wilson, were nearby at Buckton's Ford preparing to cross the North Fork of the Shenandoah River. Their job was to cover the retreating column's flank.

The wagon train was leading the column because Torbert believed that the front of his column was the safest possible place for the wagon train. He was concerned that his line of retreat might be threatened by the Confederate cavalry division in the Luray Valley, under the command of Brig. Gen. Williams C. Wickham. It was, after all, a confrontation with this division in the Luray Valley that was the cause of Torbert's current retreat. Therefore, the wagon train had been placed in the lead. To ensure the safety of the wagon train, Torbert had deployed his four cavalry brigades between it and the most likely enemy approaches. However, in the Shenandoah Valley in the fall of 1864 certain perceptions were rather blurred.

Union and Confederate forces had been moving back and forth across the valley since the beginning of the war, in part because strategically the Shenandoah Valley provided the Confederates with a major highway leading straight to the Union capital at Washington, D.C. The other end of the valley, however, did not lead to the Confederate capital at Richmond, Virginia, or anything else that was particularly important. It was not until the advent of Grant that the true strategic importance of the Shenandoah Valley under the concept of total war was realized by Union forces. This strategic importance lay in the fact that the Valley was also a major breadbasket for the rest of Virginia and from the beginning of the war it had been the chief source of rations and other supplies for Gen. Robert E. Lee's Army of Northern Virginia.

Maj. Gen. Sheridan, in command of the Army of the Shenandoah, had been given the job of clearing the Shenandoah Valley of the Confederate Valley District Army, under the command of Lt. Gen. Jubal Early. In addition to Early's army, there was also operating in the Shenandoah Valley area the 43rd Virginia Battalion of Partisan Rangers under the command of then Lt. Col. John S. Mosby. Mosby's Rangers, or guerrillas, were dedicated to making life hell for the Union soldiers in the Shenandoah Valley. Eventually Mosby and his Rangers controlled an area in and near the Shenandoah Valley, which became known as Mosby's Confederacy.

Mosby and his men then became such a thorn in the side of the Union forces operating there that eventually Lt. Gen. Ulysses S. Grant, as general-in-chief, after receiving what were admittedly conflicting reports from Sheridan, directed, in part, "Whenever any of Mosby's men are caught, hang them without trial."[1]

Sheridan took command in the Shenandoah Valley on August 7, 1864, and he was introduced to Mosby and his brand of operations nine days later on the morning of August 16, 1864. At that time Sheridan and his army were conducting their first advance within the Shenandoah Valley when Mosby and his Rangers waylaid a tardy supply train. The incident occurred outside of Berryville with Mosby's men burning most of the wagons, taking 200 prisoners and about 600 horses.[2] In effect, it was the beginning of what would become a dirty war within a war. Sheridan and his commanders considered Mosby and his Rangers to be nothing more than guerrillas and bushwhackers, not real soldiers at all. As such they were considered to be outside the bounds of formal warfare and thus subject to Grant's harsh directive.

After the war, when he had actually met Mosby, Grant moderated his opinion of the man. In his memoirs he commented about Mosby as follows: "Since the close of the war I have come to know Colonel Mosby personally, and somewhat intimately. He is a different man entirely from what I had supposed.... He is able, and thoroughly honest and truthful. There were probably but few men in the South who could have commanded successfully a detachment in the rear of an opposing army, and so near the border of hostilities, as long as he did without losing his entire command."[3]

The conflicting reports that Grant received were due mostly to Sheridan's own reaction to Mosby's activities, which had the tendency to be mixed; depending on Sheridan's audience and upon the purpose of his statements at the time that he was making them. Sheridan tended to dance along the very edge of insubordination, but Grant tolerated this since Sheridan was also one of the few believers in Grant's concept of total war, aside from William T. Sherman and Abraham Lincoln. After the war, Sheridan said that he considered Mosby and his men to be more of a benefit to him than a problem since they prevented straggling and kept his wagon trains well closed up.[4] Thus Mosby's Rangers were sometimes referred to — in jest — as Sheridan's provost guard. At other times when

Sheridan sought a justification for not doing something he did not want to do, he would claim, particularly to Gen. Grant, that Mosby and his Rangers were behind every bush and were responsible for every calamity suffered by his command.

The Rangers, for their part, considered the Union troops — due to the way they foraged (or looted) the countryside — to be little more than thieves. They would become even more enraged when Sheridan's troops started to burn out the Shenandoah Valley to deny Lee's army the provisions and other supplies that the Valley provided. But, the way "Sheridan's provost guard" sometimes operated would provide the grounds for a possible explanation for what happened at Front Royal.

For instance, several members of the 5th Michigan Cavalry Regiment were surprised by Mosby's men while foraging (the Union term) or looting (the Confederate term) a farmhouse and were shot or hanged. Hams had been tied to the victims' legs while a placard promised similar fates to other foragers. (This might explain the supposed part this regiment played at Front Royal as recorded by James Henry Avery, a soldier of the 5th Michigan Cavalry Regiment in his journal.[5]) On another occasion a straggler was killed while skinning a sheep. A hoof was jammed into the dead man's mouth, while a note left on the body stated: "I reckon you've got enough sheep now."

Thus until the Front Royal incident and its aftermath, Mosby's Rangers were to be subject when caught to being shot down or even hanged without trial or other military protocols.

On September 23, 1864, Capt. Samuel Chapman, with 120–125 of Mosby's Rangers from the 43rd Virginia's relatively newly formed E and F troops, had been given the mission to attack a picket post reportedly established by soldiers of the 6th New York Cavalry at Chester Gap, near Front Royal.[6] Chapman and his men were unable to locate the picket post and bivouacked. In Mosby's command it was not unusual for subordinate officers to conduct their own attacks upon Union troops. The next morning Chapman and about 12 men made their way to a shelf overlooking the valley and saw the wagon train, which preceded Torbert's column, approaching with an escort of about 200 men. Chapman divided his command in two, sending Capt. Walter E. Frankland with about 45 men to attack the train from the front while Chapman took the remaining 80 or so Rangers to attack the train from the rear. This was normal practice when attacking Union wagon trains. The problem was that Chapman had made a major blunder in not conducting a more thorough reconnaissance, and thus set up what would happen later at Front Royal.

Mosby himself was not available, since he was recovering from a bullet wound. He would not be fit to travel for several weeks. If Mosby had been present and in direct command at the time, then the blunder of an inadequate reconnaissance would not have been made. It is likely that if an adequate reconnaissance had been made, no attack upon the wagon train would have been made at all because two full brigades of Union cavalry were following the tempting wagon train. Due to Chapman's blunder, he was about to send his Rangers into an unintended trap.

In dividing his command into two parts and sending them to opposite ends of the train, the standard tactic for Mosby's Rangers, Chapman had compounded his original error, for the two components of his command were too far apart to provide any mutual support. Chapman took his contingent and had worked his way to the rear of what was actually the baggage train for the elements of two divisions of Union cavalry when he discovered his mistake. As he was leading his contingent of Rangers over a rise he suddenly ran into Col. Charles Russell Lowell and his Reserve Cavalry Brigade, which was following closely behind the baggage train. Only now realizing that he had ridden into this unintended trap, Chapman ordered the Rangers with him to make for Chester's Gap while he raced on his horse for the front of the train and tried desperately to warn Frankland. Apparently, the Rangers who had been delegated to attack the rear of the wagon train got away clean, but Chapman was too late to prevent Frankland from making his attack upon the head of the wagon train.

Frankland's attack and Chapman's arrival had actually coincided. Thus Chapman was forced to lead Frankland and his Rangers in what became a desperate attempt at a breakout, instead of what had started out as a seemingly easy raid, which had turned into a potential disaster. Lowell and his regulars stormed into Frankland's startled command, which scattered "like a flock a birds when a stone is cast into it," according to one of the Rangers.[7] Chapman and Frankland managed to rally their Rangers and proceeded to lead them to safety on the other side of Chester's Gap. According to the Rangers accompanying Chapman, they overran members of the wagon train's escort, killing about 15 or 20 of them.

As Chapman, Frankland and their Rangers made for Chester's Gap and their sole chance for escape, they were closely pursued by Lowell's regulars. Here and there a few of Mosby's Rangers turned and tried to fight against the overpowering odds. Much of the resulting running firefight swirled around Oak Hill Farm near the gap road. Here the two portions of the Rangers rejoined, the officer in charge of Chapman's detachment disobeying orders not to wait for his comrades. The fleeing Rangers bolted for the defile, only to run into more Union cavalry (possibly from Custer's 5th Michigan Cavalry Regiment or from a detachment of the 2nd U.S. Cavalry Regiment or both). These troops had circled east of Front Royal and attempted to cut off the Rangers' retreat through Chester's Gap.[8] The two sides blasted each other with pistols and carbines as the Rangers' momentum carried them through the Union force blocking their way. From there, the pursuit spilled into the mountain hollows and eventually the bulk of the Rangers managed to get away.

According to Confederate sources, Union 1st Lt. Charles McMaster of the 2nd U.S. Cavalry Regiment, the escort commander, was killed in the excitement of the fight by men who were seeking to escape from a superior force and were thus fleeing and fighting for their lives.[9] The Rangers ever afterwards contended that McMaster and the other casualties from the wagon train's escorting detachment simply got in their way and were run down and killed, and that they did not have time to take any prisoners.

There are various Union accounts, however, which suggest that McMaster survived the engagement and died later. The official report of Brig. Gen. Merritt, commander of the 1st Cavalry Division, states unequivocally that McMaster, who had been shot in the head and mortally wounded, had been shot and robbed after he had surrendered to the Confederates. According to some accounts, McMaster told Union troopers what had happened to him. At least one account even provides some documentary evidence that McMaster died about three weeks later from his head wound. Accounts of McMaster's statement that he had been robbed and shot after he had surrendered and had been taken prisoner exist only as hearsay. But, it must be noted that the robbing of prisoners and Union dead and wounded was a standard practice conducted by Mosby's Rangers. The reason for this practice is at least in part due to the fact the Mosby and his Rangers in many instances depended upon captured Union goods such as rations, guns and other equipment, and most especially horses, to supply their own needs.

It is certainly possible for McMaster to have been captured and robbed at the beginning of Frankland's attack upon the front of the wagon train.[10] Then when Lowell's troopers burst upon them, not knowing what else to do, McMaster's captors could have shot him before they took to their heels seeking to escape.

It is unknown how many Confederate casualties there were. At least one Union account, that of Capt. Robert A. Smith in a history of the 2nd U.S. Cavalry Regiment, from which Lt. McMaster and his escort detachment had been drawn, states that as many as 13 of Mosby's Rangers were taken prisoner. However, due to the accounts cited by most historians, it is generally accepted that at least six men were actually taken prisoner. Their names have been recorded as Thomas E. Anderson, a man named Carter (no first name was apparently recorded), William Thomas Overby, Lucien Love, Henry C. Rhodes and David L. Jones. The captives were then supposedly taken back to the town, which one Union soldier reported was in an "uproar." Jones and Love were reportedly grabbed and were taken behind the Methodist Church, where they were shot by a firing squad. Anderson was reportedly taken to Oak Hill Farm, where the main fighting had occurred, and was stood under an elm tree, where he was shot. Rhodes, a 17-year-old resident of Front Royal, was not a member of Mosby's 43rd Virginia Battalion of Partisan Rangers. In the excitement of the moment Rhodes had apparently joined Frankland's detachment of Rangers on a borrowed horse as they passed through the town to attack the wagon train. The borrowed horse had broken down during the pursuit and Rhodes was reportedly captured, dragged off and shot. Some reports by Confederate civilian eyewitnesses claim that this particular shooting occurred in the presence of his mother.[11]

Overby and Carter, when they refused to provide information about the whereabouts of Mosby's headquarters, were hanged. Upon each of the hanged men was reportedly pinned a placard. The exact wording of the placard pinned to Overby's body is uncertain. Some sources claim it said: "Such will be the fate of all Mosby's men." Other sources claim that it said: "Such is the Fate of All Mosby's Gang." The placard attached to Carter's body went directly to the main point: "Hung in Retaliation for the Death of Lieu. McMaster, 2nd U.S. Cav." There is no record whatsoever concerning what may have happened to the other seven Rangers who Smith reports were also taken prisoner.

Mosby, who was informed of the events at Front Royal on September 29, 1864, was outraged, particularly by the fact that two of his men had been hanged, without trial, like common criminals. Mosby was trained as a lawyer in civilian life, practicing law both before and after the war, and he thereupon launched an investigation into what had happened at Front Royal. It must be noted that Mosby in all likelihood did not conduct this investigation personally, since he was still recovering from a major gunshot wound. Therefore, he took his information from accounts printed in various newspapers (including the *Richmond Examiner*) and from men he had probably sent to question Front Royal residents. Thus he was receiving all of his information either second or even third hand. As a result Mosby, personally believed until the end of his days that his six men had all been executed by members of the Michigan Cavalry Brigade while acting under Custer's direct orders.

About six weeks later, after Mosby had recovered from his bullet wound, in the early morning hours of November 7, 1864, he would have his revenge or retaliation. But, first he informed his ultimate superior, Gen. Robert E. Lee, about what he intended to do, receiving Lee's full support. Mosby also received the endorsement of the Confederate Secretary of War, albeit after the fact, to whom Lee had reported what was about to take place. A total of 27 Union prisoners of war were forced to draw lots. Seven — one for each of the men who were executed in Front Royal — plus one for one of Mosby's Rangers who was later hanged by another Union cavalry commander in Rappahannock County, Virginia — were thereupon marched to a patch of woods near the location of the camp of Custer's new command, the 3rd Cavalry Division. Mosby's executions were botched. Two of the seven condemned men escaped outright. Two more were both reportedly shot in the head, feigned death and survived to escape by crawling away, while the other three, the only ones who were actually killed, were hanged. (This result speaks volumes about the reluctance of Mosby's men in killing these prisoners. After all, they had been taken performing their legitimate duties, not while foraging and looting. It is also a demonstration of their marksmanship, because in order to survive being shot in the head, they both must have been grazed by the bullets. It must be considered rather unlikely that both men survived by accident.)

Upon the corpse of one of the three Union soldiers who were hanged a placard was placed, which stated: "These men have been hung in retaliation for an equal number of Colonel Mosby's men hung by order of General Custer, at Front Royal. Measure for Measure."

Mosby thereupon wrote a letter to Sheridan, which the Union commander never admitted actually receiving, in which Mosby promised that unless his men were provided with the customary courtesies accorded to prisoners that there would be more retaliations, man for man. Grant's directive that Mosby's men were to be killed on sight was, thereafter, quietly disregarded.

Mosby did not seem to particularly care that he had managed to kill only three Union prisoners in exchange for the seven men he had lost. The important thing seemed to be that he had hanged three men in exchange for the fact that three of his own men had also been hanged.

Mosby forever afterwards justified his retaliations by proclaiming that this action, for which he had sought and received sanction by both Gen. Robert E. Lee and Confederate Secretary of War James Sedden, had put a final and complete stop to the killing of Confederate prisoners of war by Union troops.

In fact, Sheridan issued the following directive: "Leave Mosby's men alone, so long as they leave us alone. Live and let live. Besides they keep the coffee-boilers [stragglers] in line." Thus arose the standing joke that Mosby's Rangers had become nothing more than "Sheridan's Provost Guard."

2

The Battle of Fisher's Hill

The genesis of what happened at Front Royal on September 23, 1864, was a result of the Battle of Fisher's Hill, which Sheridan himself considered to be nothing more than an incident in the pursuit that followed the Third Battle of Winchester/Opequon Creek.

Grant had come east in the spring of 1864 determined to take the offensive and keep smashing at Lee. With him, he had brought Maj. Gen. Phil Sheridan to take command of his spearhead, the cavalry.[1] Between 1861 and 1863 the Confederate cavalry had run circles around their Union contemporaries. However, by 1863, the Union Army of the Potomac's cavalry under Maj. Gen. Alfred Pleasonton began to hold its own. But that changed during the winter with the death of Brig. Gen. John Buford, the exile of Brig. Gen. H. Judson Kilpatrick to the Western Theatre following his disastrous Richmond Raid, and the removal of Pleasonton himself in the aftermath of Kilpatrick's Raid due mostly to army politics.[2] Thus, the entire command structure of the Army of the Potomac's Cavalry had been disrupted and had to be completely put back together, practically from scratch.

Rather than going through the wholesale replacement of the Army of the Potomac's high command; Grant had brought only Sheridan and two other general officers with him when Grant had been summoned east. Upon the removal of Pleasonton, Grant named Sheridan his chief of cavalry, although Sheridan had little experience leading cavalry (early in the war Sheridan had command a Union cavalry regiment and later had commanded a small cavalry brigade of two regiments before being promoted to brigadier general and taking command of an infantry division) and none as a corps commander. In addition, an infantry officer (Alfred T.A. Torbert) was brought in to replace the dead Buford while one of the other two generals he had brought with him (who previously had distinguished himself as an engineer and who had never commanded troops in combat before), Brig. Gen. James H. Wilson, was named to replace Kilpatrick.[3]

All of this was part of the reorganization of the Army of the Potomac, which included the consolidation of both I Corps and III Corps into II Corps, V Corps and VI Corps, which were retained.

Sheridan had impressed Grant with his aggressiveness during the assault upon Missionary Ridge as part of the Battles of Chattanooga, which had driven the Confederate Army of Tennessee completely from the field. Sheridan retained his aggressiveness and in a raid aimed at eliminating Maj. Gen. J.E.B. Stuart, Sheridan managed to do just that at the

General Philip H. Sheridan was Custer's commander in the Shenandoah Valley (Library of Congress, Prints and Photographs Division).

Battle of Yellow Tavern. A member of Custer's Michigan Cavalry Brigade killed Stuart during the battle, in all probability.

By the fall of 1864 the American Civil War was at a stalemate. Lt. Gen. Ulysses S. Grant, general-in-chief of the Union armies, in a summer of one battle after another, had succeeded in pushing Gen. Robert E. Lee and his Army of Northern Virginia back to the final defenses of Richmond, the capital of the Confederate States of America, at the important railhead at Petersburg. It was here that the war settled into what was in effect a siege. It was a siege that resembled trench warfare, which would not be conducted again until half a century later during World War I.

Lee was just as happy that there was a stalemate since his strategy called for drawing out the war until after the November 8, 1864, general election. If by then there were no indications that the Union was about to win the war, there was the possibility that the Northern electorate would turn against the Republican administration of Abraham Lincoln and elect Democrat George McClellan, former general-in-chief and the first commander of the Army of the Potomac. If McClellan won the election it was believed by Lincoln himself and others that McClellan would be forced to enter negotiations with the Richmond government, which would result in a settlement (i.e., a peace of exhaustion), which in turn would allow the secession of the Southern states to stand, and would therefore permanently divide the United States into two nations.

In an attempt to repeat the success of Lt. Gen. Thomas J. (Stonewall) Jackson's 1862 Shenandoah Valley Campaign and further depress Union home front morale, Lee had sent Lt. Gen. Jubal Early and his II Corps to the Shenandoah Valley to reinforce Confederate troops already there under the command of Maj. Gen. John Breckenridge. Once Early joined Breckenridge, the reinforced Valley District Army, under Early's command, launched the last Southern invasion of the North in the Eastern Theatre, which was only turned back from the defenses of Washington, D.C., by the prompt intervention of VI Corps, sent by Grant, from the Army of the Potomac.

Another factor was probably the realization by Early that while he might capture Washington, D.C., he did not have the strength to hold it. Early's invasion of the North had been, in effect, a giant raid, and nothing more. Grant was determined to put an end to such excursions.

Early's raid had demonstrated once again the dual importance of the Shenandoah Valley. Grant realized that in order to close down the highway it provided, which led directly to Washington, D.C., Jubal Early's Valley District Army had to be either destroyed or dispersed. If Early's army could be eliminated, then holding the Valley and denying its fruits to the Confederacy — and most importantly to Lee's Army of Northern Virginia — would be relatively easy. However, eventually Grant would come to realize that if Early's army could not be eliminated, there actually was another way to keep the Valley away from Lee and his army.

Grant had gotten tired of the ongoing seesaw effort to control the Valley. For instance the Valley town of Winchester, Virginia, during the course of the war had changed hands 75 times. Grant finally realized that whoever has the power to destroy something ultimately controls it. If he could not physically control the Valley, Grant realized that Sheridan's Army of the Shenandoah could destroy what the Valley produced, and thus deny to Lee's Army of Northern Virginia the use of the Shenandoah Valley's breadbasket.

On August 6, 1864, Maj. Gen. Philip H. Sheridan, commander of the Army of the Potomac's Cavalry Corps, was given the job of clearing out the Valley. Sheridan was given the job because Grant realized that Sheridan had something that most other Union generals lacked: a killer's instinct. However, it was vital that Sheridan not suffer any defeat in the Valley due to the closeness of the election. Therefore, for the first month to six weeks, Sheridan was constrained by instructions from Gen. Henry W. Halleck, Army chief of staff in Washington, on how to conduct the campaign, and thus was unable to bring Early's army to battle. Finally, in the middle of September, in the course of a meeting with Grant, Sheridan was unleashed from these restrictions and the result was the rapid-fire battles at Winchester and Fisher's Hill.

To do the job, Sheridan was given those troops currently within the valley, the Army of West Virginia. This "army" consisted of two small divisions of infantry, under the command of Brig. Gen. George C. Crook, which were drawn from VIII Corps (the umbrella organization for all Union troops in the Washington, D.C., area) and two divisions of cavalry under the command of Brig. Gen. William W. Averell and Brig. Gen. Alfred Dufie. These troops had previously been under the command of Maj. Gen. David Hunter. In addition, Sheridan also had drawn from the Army of the Potomac the VI Corps and two divisions of cavalry (the 1st and 3rd Cavalry Divisions) taken from his own Cavalry Corps. The VI Corps was under the command of Maj. Gen. Horatio G. Wright. In command of all four cavalry divisions was Maj. Gen. Alfred T.A. Torbert, as chief of cavalry.

The final component in-

Bvt. Maj. Gen. William Woods Averell was guilty of failing Sheridan at the Battle of Fisher's Hill by preferring to secure booty rather than to pursue the fleeing Confederates (Library of Congress, Prints and Photographs Division).

cluded two more infantry divisions, which were taken from XIX Corps. These troops were under the command of Maj. Gen. William H. Emory. They had been serving in the Gulf of Mexico and had been recently transferred to the Eastern Theatre in Virginia to reinforce Grant and the Army of the Potomac. In the trenches at Petersburg, Grant retained II Corps, V Corps, IX Corps (which had been moved from Knoxville, Tenn.) and the 2nd Cavalry Division from the Cavalry Corps, under the command of Gen. David M. Gregg.

Fisher's Hill was the second pitched battle to be fought in Sheridan's 1864 Shenandoah Valley Campaign.[4] The first was the Third Battle of Winchester/Opequon Creek. That battle was fought on September 19, 1864, with Jubal Early's Confederate Valley District Army skillfully parrying Sheridan's attacks throughout the day. (Unfortunately, most of Sheridan's battles proved the adage that a general's battle plan usually does not survive the first contract with the enemy. Sheridan, however, was such a masterful battlefield commander that when his plans fell apart he could generally snatch a victory from the resulting chaos.) It was not until near evening, when Sheridan launched his cavalry in an assault upon Early's left using the divisions of Wesley Merritt and Averell (Custer's Michigan Cavalry Brigade spearheading Merritt's attack) that the Confederate line was broken and Early's army was driven into full retreat.

Sheridan was a master at combining old and new cavalry tactics, which turned his horsemen into a hard hitting mobile force, the like of which would not be seen on the battlefield again until World War II and the advent of blitzkrieg or armored, mechanized warfare.

The defeated Confederate army spent the night of September 19–20, 1864, withdrawing in disorder until they reached Fisher's Hill, with Early arriving there at about daybreak on September 20. Early in all probability would have been willing to fight Sheridan just about anywhere. However, he chose to make his new stand at Fisher's Hill. He informed Lee that in his judgment Fisher's Hill was "the only place that a stand could be made" with the "hope of arresting Sheridan's progress." According to Early's memoirs, his reasoning was as follows:

"To have retired beyond this point would have rendered it necessary for me to fall back to some of the gaps of the Blue Ridge, at the upper part of the Valley, and I determined therefore to make a show of a stand here, with the hopes that the enemy would be deterred from attacking me in this position, as it had been the case in August (during the period of Sheridan's enforced inaction)."

Fisher's Hill was a natural fortress which barred the entrance to the upper Shenandoah Valley. The terrain was a topographical anomaly. In fact, Fisher's Hill did not look like it actually belonged in the Shenandoah Valley at all. A Vermont soldier in Sheridan's army said it was formed so that it appeared to be a huge "billow of earth and rocks" which had rolled down the Valley until it was caught between two mountains and held still. The crest of the hill looked northward and frowned down upon Sheridan's approaching troops.

Fisher's Hill is positioned against Massanutten Mountain on the east and Little North Mountain on the west. The steep, rocky bluff extended nearly four miles and was cut by a number of ravines and included in 1864 several woodlots. Running along its base was Tumbling Run, which was referred to as a brawling brook, which ran into the North Fork of the Shenandoah River. Both sides considered it practically impregnable if its heights could be adequately manned. In August, Early had had the troops to adequately man the heights and Sheridan had declined to make any attack. But now, just past the middle of September, the situation had changed.

Following the casualties Early's Valley District Army had suffered just days before at the Third Battle of Winchester/Opequon Creek, Early no longer had the number of men required to adequately man the heights of Fisher's Hill.

With his victory at Winchester, Sheridan was no longer willing to be inhibited by the natural fortress at Fisher's Hill. Sheridan's Army of the Shenandoah's effective force still numbered, even after the battle at Winchester, some 35,000 men, while Early's effective force, following his defeat at Winchester, numbered less than 10,000 men. The position at Fisher's Hill, natural fortress that it was, was now simply too large for Early's small number of troops (particularly infantry) to effectively defend it.

Early completed his dispositions later in the day on September 20; his right flank was anchored where the bluff was at its steepest. In addition, the North Fork of the Shenandoah River served to confine the area of attack, making this point practically unassailable. Also in this area were located the "Three Sisters," a triple peak formation which rose to a total of 1,365 feet above the Valley floor, providing in effect a natural watchtower.

From this watchtower the movements of any Union troops preparing to make an attack upon this particular portion of Early's line would have been immediately visible.

From here Early positioned the remainder of his army along the heights. Dispatched to the far left end of his line was Lunsford Lomax's division of cavalry, minus one brigade, which was placed at the extreme right flank in the area of the Three Sisters. Lomax was filling in for W.H.F. (Rooney) Lee. Lomax's cavalry were deployed on low ground and along what was termed "a hog-backed ridge" which ran parallel to Fisher's Hill.[5] Sheridan's troops considered Fisher's Hill to be "one of the strongest positions ever seen." Others considered the hill to be unattackable, particularly if the Confederates had managed to "prolong their left sufficiently."

The cavalry, on both sides, was generally well equipped with revolvers. The main difference was in the quality of their shoulder arms, which were mainly used while they were dismounted. Sheridan's cavalry were armed with either single shot breech loading carbines or repeating rifles or carbines (by this time of the war most of Sheridan's cavalry were equipped with Spencer repeating rifles or carbines). The Confederate cavalry, while they had a few breech-loaders, were generally armed with muzzle loading carbines or cut down muzzle loading rifles.

A well-trained and experienced soldier with a muzzle-loader can fire up to three aimed shots in a minute. The same soldier armed with a breech-loader can fire up to 12 aimed shots in a minute. A soldier armed with a Spencer repeating rifle or carbine, carrying extra pre-loaded tube magazines, could fire as many as 21 or more aimed shots in a minute.

Sheridan conducted a personal reconnaissance as his troops moved into position and encamped on the Valley floor. There was no denying that the Confederate position was formidable. But, Sheridan intended to go ahead. The question was, how? On the evening of September 20 he called a council of war, which was attended by himself, Maj. Gen. Horatio Wright (commander of VI Corps), Maj. Gen. William H. Emory (commander of XIX Corps), and Brig. Gen. George Crook (commander of the VIII Corps troops in the Army of West Virginia).

It appears that any idea of a frontal attack was immediately rejected. Sheridan then proposed an assault upon Early's right flank, his strongest position. This idea too was rejected since it was immediately recognized that first it required that any attacking force be formed right under the noses of the Confederate lookouts posted on the Three Sisters. Second, such a force would then have to cross the North Folk of the Shenandoah River before making an attack, and third, they would then have to attack up a sheer bluff and from there go straight up a mountainside. This was also recognized as being impossible.

It was Crook, who had also conducted a personal reconnaissance of the Confederate positions, who came up with the solution. He suggested that a turning movement be made against Early's opposite flank, which was being held by Lomax and his dismounted cavalrymen. Gen. Wright and Gen. Emory were not in favor of this idea. However, Sheridan could see that Crook's idea had possibilities. In addition, Sheridan and Crook had known each other and had been friends since their days together at West Point. Although their friendship would eventually sour, at this point, Sheridan trusted Crook's judgment. Col. Joseph Thoburn and Col. Rutherford Hayes (who would eventually become the nineteenth President of the United States), the commanders of Crook's two infantry divisions, were then summoned to the council of war and asked their opinions (since they were the ones who would have to make the idea work). They supported Crook's proposal. From there the meeting turned to planning Crook's proposed turning movement.

The entire proposal depended on two elements: surprise and the ability to move Crook's men into position without their being noticed by Early's lookouts on the Three Sisters. Therefore, it was decided that Crook's men needed to be placed in position for their attack upon Lomax's dismounted cavalry at night. Sheridan also decided upon a secondary phase. He instructed his cavalry commander, Torbert, to take two brigades from Merritt's 1st Cavalry Division (Lowell's Reserve Cavalry Brigade and Custer's Michigan Cavalry Brigade) and join Brig. Gen. James H. Wilson's 3rd Cavalry Division (which also consisted of two brigades) at Front Royal, Virginia, sweep up the Luray Valley, cross the Massanutten Mountains at New Market Gap and form a barrier across the Valley, which Sheridan would use as an anvil with the rest of his army forming the hammer and thus destroy Early's Valley District Army once and for all. Crook was to make his attack on September 22 and if Torbert could get into position in time, it would be all over on September 23.

The plan was put into action at 5 A.M. on September 21 when Merritt moved out (with Torbert accompanying him) to join Wilson, leaving behind the brigade of Brig. Gen. Thomas Devin to protect the rear of Sheridan's army. Torbert found Wilson's division to be in possession of Front Royal. Wilson had spent the previous day skirmishing with two brigades of Confederate cavalry under the command of Brig. Gen. Williams C. Wickham between the towns of Front Royal and Cedarville. Wilson had been directed by Torbert on September 20 to find a "good position" between the two towns and had collided with Wickham on Crooked Run, which flows into the Shenandoah River, sometime after 12-noon that day. Wilson outnumbered Wickham and drove Wickham across the North Fork of the Shenandoah River. With that accomplished, Wilson had bivouacked for the remainder of the day.

At daybreak on September 21 Wilson attacked, hitting one Confederate brigade in front while sending two regiments around the flank. The Confederates held for a time, but when they were hit by the two detached Union regiments on the flank, the Confederate cavalry broke and then regrouped south of Front Royal. Wickham then retreated about four miles from the village, with Wilson in pursuit.

When Torbert and the troops of Merritt's 1st Cavalry Division arrived at Front Royal, Wilson had been stalled in his pursuit of Wickham at Gooney Run, about six miles south of the town. Wickham, learning of the arrival of Merritt's two brigades, then ordered a further withdrawal, waiting for nightfall, before pulling back to Milford. Torbert united his troops and then encamped north of Gooney Run.

Fisher's Hill itself on September 21 was mostly quiet. The men of VI Corps and XIX Corps rose at sunrise, cooked breakfast and relaxed. Crook's two divisions remained hidden north of Cedar Creek. Sheridan and Wright resumed their examinations of the Confederate positions on Fisher's Hill. At the same time, the Confederates strengthened their positions on Fisher's Hill by building entrenchments. Occasionally an artillery piece would fire. There was also some skirmishing. Then things began happening shortly before noon.

The men of VI Corps and XIX Corps formed marching columns with VI Corps swinging around the town of Strasburg. The movement was immediately detected from the Three Sisters, which brought fire from Confederate artillery and snipers. The movement of VI Corps continued until about 4 P.M., when the troops were halted west of the Manassas Gap

Railroad. These troops were headed south towards the heights of Fisher's Hill. The two infantry divisions of XIX Corps were then deployed to the left of VI Corps.

These Union troops came under artillery fire from Fisher's Hill. Sheridan therefore ordered them to seize a knoll known as Flint Hill, which would give Sheridan an unobstructed view of the Confederate lines on Fisher's Hill. It took three infantry assaults by the troops of VI Corps and XIX Corps to take Flint Hill. By that time it was past sundown and the Union line extended for two miles in front of the Confederate positions along Fisher's Hill.

The Union troops, during the night of September 21–22, were quite busy. The capture of Flint Hill caused the VI Corps troops to be shifted west, which due to broken ground and the various woodlots took most of the night to complete. This movement required a similar realignment by XIX Corps, which had been ordered for first light but which actually began at 4:30 A.M. It was also during the night that Crook's two small infantry divisions began moving and crossed Cedar Creek. They had spent the entire day hidden in the woods. They advanced shortly after dark into another woodlot north of Hupp's Hill, a mile from Strasburg, whereupon Crook's men rested.

Most of the Union troops' maneuvers had been completed by dawn. First light brought with it renewed skirmishing. The Confederates had spent the night sleeping on the ground they held between Sheridan's troops and Tumbling Run, taking full advantage of every terrain feature. As a diversion, Sheridan ordered VI Corps and XIX Corps to apply pressure to the main Confederate line while Crook marched his two small divisions to Little North Mountain, where the bulk of Lomax's dismounted cavalry troopers were positioned. The action against Early's primary position escalated about mid-day to spread the illusion that Sheridan was about to attempt a frontal attack.

Early watched the Union sorties from his headquarters on Fisher's Hill. He later told Lee and reported in his memoirs that he was convinced Sheridan might be preparing an assault. He therefore reported — after the fact — that he had issued orders for his troops to prepare to withdraw once it became dark. By this time Early was concerned that his lines on Fisher's Hill were very thin and could be outflanked. In his memoirs, Early stated that he knew that he did not have enough men to withstand a determined assault. As it was, Sheridan outnumbered Early three to one, which is considered to be the minimum odds necessary to assault and carry a well-defended position.

Although Early, apparently correctly, surmised Sheridan's intentions, he failed to calculate exactly when and exactly where the main attack would come.

By the time Early had issued his orders for the nighttime withdrawal (sometime between 2 and 3 P.M.), Crook's troops had reached the base of Little North Mountain, north of the Confederate left flank. Col. Hayes and Col. Thoburn had been marching their divisions since early morning, being led personally by Gen. Crook. His troops reached the Back Road at St. Stephen's Church, about a mile and a half from Lomax's position. William Averell and the two brigades of his 2nd Cavalry Division, Department of West Virginia, had formed a screen between the church and Lomax's men. Averell's division had been dueling with Lomax since early morning, thus holding Lomax's attention. Crook conferred with Averell and requested the support of one of Averell's brigades when Hayes and Thoburn's divisions made their attack. Averell's other brigade would protect the attackers from Confederate guerrillas and secure any Confederate troops and equipment captured during the assault. (This understanding may have been responsible for Averell concentrating on collecting booty rather than resolutely pursuing the Confederate troops once they had been forced off Fisher's Hill, as Sheridan expected him to do.)

Crook then had Hayes and Thoburn form their troops into two parallel columns, which were cleared for action. Then Crook continued his approach up and along the mountain. Their route passed through a clear area which exposed the advancing Union troops to the Confederate defenders. Confederate pickets and artillery fired on the two Union divisions; shortly thereafter Crook's advance troops stumbled into the Confederates' reserve picket post, which fled. However, the main body of the Confederate troops, if they suspected what was going on, made no adjustments to meet the threat posed by Crook's two divisions.

Crook halted his troops about 200 yards behind the picket post, faced them east and brought Thoburn's division into line on the left of Hayes' division. The two divisions included four brigades, about 5,500 men, as they deployed under Confederate artillery fire with their attack beginning at about 4 P.M.

Crook's two divisions in their attack swept down the eastern slope of Little North Mountain. Moving as fast as possible in the rough terrain, the individual units lost their cohesion and hit the Confederate line not in a compact mass but more like a swarm; however, their collision was solid enough to hit Lomax's dismounted cavalrymen with the force of a boulder rolled down a hill. Lomax's three brigades shattered upon impact, sprinting for their horses or disappearing into the wooded areas to the south. Although the Confederate 1st Maryland Cavalry Battalion launched a counter attack aimed at saving their comrades and the horses, they were easily brushed aside. The Confederate infantry division of Maj. Gen. Stephen Dodson Ramseur reacted swiftly. Ramseur pulled out his closest brigade to a ridge paralleling the Union advance. Confederate artillery also opened fire with canister, the result being a temporary slowing of the momentum of Crook's attacking troops. Ramsuer's defending Confederate infantry brigade was unable to dam the flood and was eventually forced from its position.

Ramseur pulled out another brigade and sent it toward the sound of the guns. However, it got lost and could do nothing except act as part of the rear guard as Early's army moved into full retreat. This allowed Hayes' division to enfilade the retiring Confederates from Ramseur's first brigade, which by this time had had enough and was scattering across the countryside with the Confederate artillery conducting a fighting retreat to cover the infantry. Crook's attacking troops then hit three regiments from North Carolina under Brig. Gen. Bryan Grimes. The North Carolinians momentarily stopped Crook's troops but to their right the rest of the Confederate line was collapsing under a frontal attack by VI Corps and XIX Corps.

Wright's troops and Emory's troops, along with Crook's troops, engulfed the Confederate position, which was reduced to complete and total confusion. As they retreated, the entire Confederate line west of the Valley Pike collapsed. Some Confederate units managed to maintain their organization as they were forced from their positions, but most of them ran from the field. Early's stampede continued for miles. A rear guard was patched together on a hill near Mount Prospect and the Confederate retreat continued through the night.

The Union troops had been almost as disorganized by their victory as the Confederates had been by their defeat. An organized pursuit took time to form due to jumbled units, impromptu celebrations, rain and simple darkness. When a pursuit was finally organized, Emory's XIX Corps led it. Wright's VI Corps followed while Crook's exhausted Army of West Virginia troops, having carried the brunt of the fighting, stayed behind guarding prisoners and bivouacking on the battlefield.

The vanguard of the pursuing Union army reached the town of Woodstock at 3:30 A.M. on September 23 with Sheridan and his staff arriving two hours later at 5:30 A.M. Once he arrived at Woodstock, Sheridan awaited anxiously for some word from Torbert and from Averell. When that word finally came it was not what Sheridan wanted, or expected, to hear.

3

WHAT SHERIDAN INTENDED

On the morning of September 23, 1864, Maj. Gen. Philip Henry Sheridan should have been quite satisfied. After a disappointing start, which had included over a month spent marching up and down the Shenandoah Valley, in less than a week his Army of the Shenandoah (a scratch force consisting of troops who had never operated together before) in something like 96 hours had defeated the Confederate Valley District Army in two pitched battles. Congratulations were flowing into his headquarters from President Abraham Lincoln, from Lt. Gen. Ulysses S. Grant, from Congress, from all points of the compass. In fact, to celebrate the twin victories, Grant ordered 100 gun salutes fired into the Confederate lines at Petersburg. But Sheridan, as he contemplated the actual results of his two victories, remained far from satisfied.

As far as he was concerned the job was only half done. It had never been his intention to simply defeat Confederate Lt. Gen. Jubal Early and his Valley District Army. He wanted to destroy them. If there was one thing that Sheridan had in abundance, it was determination. He also had a killer's instinct. It was his fighting style to go straight for the jugular. Sheridan — now that Grant had finally unleashed him and his army — had intended to search out, attack, and destroy Early's Valley District Army. Even with his eventual final crushing victory at Cedar Creek, fought in sight of Fisher's Hill on October 19, 1864, Sheridan would still fail to destroy the Valley District Army.

Nonetheless, at Cedar Creek he would accomplish something no other commander on either side during the war would do. He would take an army that had been completely defeated in his absence in the morning. On his way to the battlefield he would collect and reorganize that army from the mobs of defeated soldiers. And in the late afternoon he would take that defeated army, turn it around, counterattack, and win an almost complete and total victory.

At the end, the Valley District Army simply melted away after Lee was forced to recall the soldiers of his II Corps and his cavalry divisions back to the lines defending Petersburg, leaving Early in command of what was left over. (Basically this amounted to one tiny infantry division and some cavalry units.) This final remnant of the Valley District Army would eventually be dispersed and destroyed by George Armstrong Custer and his new command, the 3rd Cavalry Division, at the Battle of Waynesboro on March 2, 1865. But, in the meantime, Grant in the end would be quite happy with simply devastating the Valley.

Sheridan, however, would not be happy, with what he still considered to be only half measures. He wanted more. He wanted to eliminate all opposition. This was why, while with his main force Sheridan had been prying Early and his army out of the natural fortress at Fisher's Hill, Sheridan had detached Bvt. Maj. Gen. Alfred T.A. Torbert and elements of two divisions of cavalry, a total of four brigades, and had sent them on an end run. What he had intended for them to do was to block Early's escape route up the Luray Valley and hold the Valley District Army in place until his infantry from VI Corps and XIX Corps could arrive and hammer or otherwise force Early's entire enemy army to surrender. In effect, these were the same tactics that would be used between March 29 and April 9, 1865, that would lead to the surrender of Lee's Army of Northern Virginia at the village of Appomattox Courthouse.

In addition, Sheridan had also wanted his 2nd Cavalry Division, Department of West Virginia, under the command of Bvt. Maj. Gen. William W. Averell to directly pursue Early's retreating Valley District Army. However, Sheridan ended up having a problem communicating his wishes to Averell. Averell simply was not where Sheridan expected to find him, pressing the pursuit of the Confederate troops. Instead Averell was busy collecting what he thought were the spoils of the victory.

(What had happened pointed out the major flaw within the Army of the Potomac and its related commands within the Eastern Theatre of Operation — somewhere within the chain of command, someone was always screwing up. Either a commander did not fight with all of his strength, was too slow in his movements, arrived and conducted himself in some other way than he was supposed, ordered, or expected to do. This has been one of the unpublicized reasons for the reorganization of the Army of the Potomac in early 1864, to get rid of some of the army's deadwood by eliminating the commands of certain generals out from under them, rather than relieving them outright and leaving them with no readily apparent cause for complaint.)

Averell's big mistake had been in not understanding that Sheridan was not and had not ever been interested in the spoils of apparent victory. What Sheridan was after was the complete and total annihilation of the enemy. Sheridan's intentions are perhaps best expressed in his memoirs.[1] Like all memoirs written by the participants in the American Civil War, they sometimes have to be taken with a grain or two of salt. Sheridan's own memoirs were originally published in 1888, more than 20 years after the events they described. Sometimes such a gap can produce inaccuracies. Sometimes in an attempt to appear to be more on top of things than the writer actually was at the time, there can be some exaggerations. Unfortunately, Sheridan in his memoirs and even his official reports was not above letting a few inaccuracies escape or even making a few exaggerations.

For instance, Sheridan has been accused of taking credit for his friend George C. Crook's suggestions that led the victory at Fisher's Hill. Crook, in his own memoirs, which were not found and published until well after Crook's own death, took umbrage with his old friend. It seems that Sheridan in his official report on his 1864 Shenandoah Valley Campaign, which was filed with the War Department in 1866, wrote: "I resolved to use a turning column" when commenting on his plans for the Battle of Fisher's Hill. This statement skirted the truth. Did it mean that he took responsibility for the proposed movement around Early's left? If so, Sheridan was correct. But if he meant to convey that the turning movement had been his idea and that he was taking credit for it, then his friend Crook deserved better.

In the case of his intentions after the Battle of Fisher's Hill, it appears that Sheridan can be taken at his word, as indicated by his memoirs.

> Our success was very great, yet I had anticipated results still more pregnant. Indeed I had high hopes of capturing almost the whole of Early's army before it reached New Market, and with this object in view; during the maneuvers of the 21st (September 21, 1864) I had sent Torbert [who was serving as Sheridan's chief of cavalry] up the Luray Valley with Wilson's Division and two of Merritt's brigades [the Reserve Cavalry Brigade under the command of Col. Charles Russell Lowell and the Michigan Cavalry Brigade under the command of Brig. Gen. George A. Custer], in the expectation he would drive Wickham [and his Confederate cavalry division] up the Luray Pass by Early's right, and by crossing

Massanutten Mountain near New Market, gain his rear. Torbert started in good season, and after some slight skirmishing at Gooney Run, got as far as Milford, but failed to dislodge Wickham from his position, and with only a feeble effort withdrew. I heard nothing at all from Torbert during the 22nd [September 22, 1864], and supposing that everything was progressing favorably, I was astonished and chagrined on the morning of the 23rd, to receive intelligence that he had fallen back to Front Royal.

It appears that Alfred T.A. Torbert was not quite the commander that Sheridan had thought him to be when he named Torbert to be his chief of cavalry when the Army of the Shenandoah was created at the beginning of the campaign. Torbert had been an infantry commander until he was appointed commander of Sheridan's 1st Cavalry Division in April 1864. When Sheridan organized the available cavalry in his Army of the Shenandoah into a provisional cavalry corps of three or four divisions, Torbert was his choice for the chief of cavalry post even though Averell was his senior, and according to the U.S. Army's standard operating procedures, was therefore entitled to the command. Sheridan, however, had never served with Averell and had apparently disregarded Army procedures to give the command to Torbert without any apparent hesitation. Others had a different opinion of Torbert's ability.

One of these critics was Capt. George B. Sanford, who served on Torbert's staff as one of his aides. Sanford described Torbert as "a handsome, dashing fellow, at this time, a beautiful horseman, and as brave as a lion; but his abilities were hardly equaled to such large commands."

When Sheridan found out about Tobert's failure in the Luray Valley, he never forgave him. In both his official report upon the Shenandoah Valley Campaign of 1864 and in his memoirs, he noted his "extreme" disappointment with Torbert's lack of performance. In his official report, Sheridan stated: "Had General Torbert driven this defile and reached New Market, I have no doubt, but that we would have captured the entire rebel army." In his memoirs, Sheridan vented even more of his spleen at the failure to destroy Early's Valley District Army when he had it in his grasp, his chagrin having not dissipated even though the events in the Luray Valley had occurred over 20 years previously. While he admitted that the Confederate troops that day had held a formidable position, Sheridan still believed "Torbert ought to have made a fight." Finally, he exclaimed in his memoirs, "To this day, I have been unable to account satisfactorily for Torbert's failures."

Torbert, fortunately for him, was not the only cavalry general to have irritated Sheridan that day. In addition to sending Torbert with elements of two divisions to get around in front of Early's retreating army, Sheridan had also wanted Averell to move to the south with his division of cavalry in order to directly pursue Early's army. Instead of doing that, Averell came into Sheridan's camp at Woodstock from the north, not the south.[2] Possibly Averell had misunderstood Sheridan's intentions when he had taken it upon himself to gather the spoils, not to pursue Early's fleeing army, and to eventually bed down for the night on the battlefield, leaving the pursuit to Sheridan's slower moving infantry.[3] Torbert not being immediately available, Sheridan could only vent his anger and disappointment upon the hapless Averell.

When Sheridan first took command in the Shenandoah Valley, Averell was in command of the 2nd Cavalry Division, Department of West Virginia, which consisted of two brigades. Averell had been one of the first divisional cavalry commanders in the Army of the Potomac when Maj. Gen. George Hooker united the various cavalry units, which had until then been scattered among the various corps and divisions of the Army of the Potomac, and formed them into an autonomous corps under the command of Maj. Gen. George Stoneman. After their allegedly poor performance during the Chancellorsville Campaign, Hooker had sacked both Stoneman and Averell. Averell had been transferred from the Army of the Potomac to the Department of West Virginia, where he had taken what had been a badly led infantry brigade with extremely poor morale, mounted them, and turned them into an extremely competent and seasoned division of horse soldiers.

Sheridan could have had a number of reasons for passing over Averell in favor of Torbert for the post of chief of cavalry and commander of his provisional cavalry corps. As previously noted, Sheridan could have made this decision because he wanted his cavalry commander to be someone who had already served with him. There was another possibility; Sheridan may have been informed that Averell had not performed well at the Second Battle of Kernstown. This battle had occurred in the immediate aftermath of Early's raid upon the Washington, D.C., area, before Sheridan took command in the Shenandoah Valley. At the time, Early was withdrawing back into the Shenandoah Valley and was being pursued by VI Corps and Crook's Army of West Virginia's VIII Corps troops. Early had turned and counterattacked and it was said that it was Averell's refusal to commit his cavalry which had allowed the flank of Crook's corps to be turned, resulting in a sharp repulse of the Union pursuers. In his official report, Averell did not provide any explanation for what happened, but merely noted it in passing as if he had had little or nothing to do with the entire affair.

When Grant found out what had happened at Kernstown, he issued an optional order allowing for Averell's relief. For whatever reason, by the time Sheridan met with Averell at Woodstock, his temper was in complete and total control. Sheridan admitted in his memoirs that he and Averell had some "hot words." Sheridan had described the fleeing Confederate troops as a "perfect mob" that would have scattered under a forthright pursuit. Therefore, Sheridan wanted to know where Averell had been and why he had not pursued Early's fugitive army the previous night. Averell, on his part, claimed he could not possibly have pursued Early since he had received absolutely no information or any instructions whatsoever from Sheridan's headquarters. Averell understood his original instructions to have called for his cavalry division to stand by to collect Confederate prisoners and captured equipment in the aftermath of the battle. When Sheridan said he could not locate Averell, Averell on his part had rashly asked his infuriated superior if he had even tried.[4]

The big problem in the relationship between Sheridan and Averell was that Sheridan was a different commander from what Averell was used to. With Sheridan in command, simply beating the enemy was no longer enough. Collecting the spoils of victory was not enough. Throughout the entire campaign Sheridan aimed for the total annihilation of Early's Valley District Army. Therefore, Sheridan both demanded and expected, in particular, much more initiative from his subordinates than practically any other commander, and woe to the subordinate who failed (or who was perceived to have failed) to deliver.[5]

Sheridan in effect ordered Averell out of his sight and then sent him a direct order to take his division and find some Confederates to fight. Sheridan also sent a follow-up message calling "for actual fighting with necessary casualties." Averell joined Brig. Gen. Thomas Devin, commanding one of Merritt's brigades (which Sheridan had retained) in skirmishing with two Confederate infantry divisions, but neither he nor Devin pressed the attack. Sheridan was convinced that Averell had ignored both his direct order and his follow-up message. From that point on, as far as

Sheridan was concerned, Averell was through. When Sheridan found out that Averell, instead of attacking, had pulled back for the night, Averell was immediately relieved of his command and by midnight, Averell was sent packing, on his way to Wheeling, West Virginia, where he would be out of Sheridan's sight, out of Sheridan's army, and out of Sheridan's war.

According to Eric Wittenberg, the author of a number of works about cavalry actions in the Eastern Theatre during the later part of the Civil War, Averell's relief was unjust. With just his two brigades, even with the support of Devin's Brigade, he had no business trying to take on Early's entire army, which by this time was dug in on high ground, and Averell knew it. "He did the only thing that made sense — he broke off and withdrew," Wittenberg concluded.

As it was, Torbert may have owed Averell a certain amount of thanks. If Torbert had had the mischance of reporting to Sheridan, unsatiated, in his towering rage, then Torbert himself might have been sent packing from the army instead of Averell.

Even before the American Civil War, Sheridan's temper was legendary in the United States Army. While he was at West Point, Sheridan had been forced to repeat a full year at the military academy following an incident which occurred upon the parade ground. Sheridan had become enraged due to his mistaken perception about the way an order from an upperclassman from Virginia, William Terrill, had been given to him and he had actually attacked Terrill with his bayoneted rifle, stopping just short of impaling his fellow cadet upon his bayonet. At the beginning of the war Terrill remained within the Union Army and he and Sheridan became reconciled just before the Virginian's death in battle.

With the failure of what Sheridan had considered his great design at the Battle of Fisher's Hill — which he believed should have destroyed a third of Lee's infantry and which at a stroke would have brought the end of the war that much nearer — in his rage Sheridan was ready to start rolling heads. In part, Averell just happened to be handy, and so it was his head which was set rolling. If Torbert had also been handy it is certainly possible there would have been two heads rolling.

As for Torbert, Sheridan never forgot and never forgave him for his abject and inexplicable failure in the Luray Valley. Then, just weeks later there occurred another incident that most likely caused Sheridan to decide

General George A. Custer salutes Confederate General Thomas L. Rosser just prior to launching his attack upon Rosser at the Battle of Tom's Brook (sketch by Alfred R. Waud, Library of Congress, Prints and Photographs Division).

once and for all that Torbert would have to go. This time it was Torbert's lack of aggressiveness just prior to the Battle of Tom's Brook, which set Sheridan off. On October 6, 1864, Sheridan began withdrawing up the Valley while devastating it at the same time. By this time Custer's friend and former West Point roommate, Thomas Lafayette Rosser, had taken over command of Wickham's old division. Custer, who was now in command of the 3rd Cavalry Division, had been posted as the rear guard as Sheridan ordered his army to retreat while conducting what came to be called "The Burning." A good many of Rosser's men were from the Valley and they watched with impotent fury as Custer's troops put to the torch every barn, mill and haystack they passed. Seeking revenge for the destruction, Rosser's horsemen fell upon Custer's rear guard, the 1st Vermont Cavalry Regiment. The Vermonters held off two attacks but were finally driven back onto Custer's trailing brigade.

Custer wanted to turn around and smack Rosser down, but Torbert would not hear of it. In this case, Torbert was simply following what he perceived to be Sheridan's orders and intentions. After all, Sheridan had ordered the entire army to withdraw, not fight, and Torbert was not about to take it upon his own initiative to go against Sheridan's orders.

For three days, Rosser's jabs and attacks against Custer's division continued. The 18th Pennsylvania Cavalry Regiment was worn down to a frazzle trying to block Rosser's repeated jabs. Finally, the sound of the gunfire to the rear grew so intense that Sheridan decided to investigate. Custer has been described as being so angry at what he saw as Torbert's lack of aggressiveness that he was practically in tears. Earlier in the day Rosser's troopers had snatched up a wagon that had fallen behind, filled with runaway slaves and a blacksmith's forge with a broken wheel. To top it off one of Custer's aides blew up these incidents out of all proportion and had managed to give Sheridan the mistaken impression that Rosser had managed to capture an entire wagon train and a battery of artillery.

Again Sheridan lost his temper with Torbert. He cursed his way into a towering rage and went off in search of his chief of cavalry.[6] Torbert was unaware of the storm that was about to break over his head and was at his headquarters with his staff and was just about to finish devouring a turkey dinner when Sheridan arrived. He stormed into the room just as the last of the bones were being picked clean. Bursting through the dining room door, Sheridan must have been quite a sight.

Sheridan's short, livid figure, with blazing dark eyes accompanied by the ringing canastas of his spurs, stomped his way to Torbert's place at the head of the table. Then once he got there the dam holding his temper in check simply burst and he began thundering his wrath — the sound of his voice in his rage, according to some of the witnesses present, being enough all by itself to make the china rattle and the silverware jump.

"Well, I'll be damned! If you ain't sitting here stuffing yourselves, general, staff and all, while the Rebels are riding into our camp! Having a party, while Rosser is carrying off your guns! Got on your nice clothes and clean shirts! Torbert, mount quicker than hell will scorch a feather! I want you to go out there in the morning and whip that Rebel Cavalry or get whipped yourself!"[7]

The result, on October 9, 1864, was one of Custer's most complete and satisfying victories at the Battle of Tom's Brook.

Besides his towering temper, Sheridan's ability to nourish a grudge had also become legendary in the United States Army. Sheridan in carrying a grudge had the memory of an elephant and this was the second time that Torbert had managed to let him down. When Torbert failed once again in a raid aimed against the Virginia Central Railroad at Gordonsville, which occurred during one of the worst winters on record in the Shenandoah Valley, Sheridan had had his fill of Torbert. But, in Torbert's case, Sheridan bided his time until he could get rid of him with as little fuss as possible.

After going into winter quarters, Sheridan's command was reduced to the two cavalry divisions, which had been borrowed from the Army of the Potomac. Sheridan decided that he would begin operations well before spring actually arrived in the Shenandoah Valley. Concealing his plans for an early beginning of operations, Sheridan permitted Torbert to take a 20-day medical leave, which was extended to six weeks, and then made sure that no one sent Torbert a recall order as Sheridan's 1st and 3rd Cavalry Divisions were fitting out. Merritt became the new chief of cavalry while Devin was given command of the 1st Cavalry Division.

When Torbert arrived the next day he found that he had been kicked upstairs. Sheridan had left orders for him to take command of what little was left of the Union military forces remaining in the Shenandoah Valley.

Torbert had failed to realize one simple fact. While Sheridan would not forgive those officers who demonstrated they lacked initiative, he was, on the other hand quite willing to forgive a lot (up to an including direct disobedience of orders; if that was what was required) from those officers who demonstrated that they did have initiative and were willing to use it.

Both sides of this aspect of Sheridan's personality would be demonstrated at the Battle of Five Forks on April 1, 1865, which would result in the sacking of one Union general and the promotion of another. Both of them had made possible the kind of battle of annihilation that Sheridan had wanted to wage in the aftermath of the Battle of Fisher's Hill. The general who was sacked was Maj. Gen. Gouvernor K. Warren, who was perceived by Sheridan to have acted too slowly and demonstrated what Sheridan saw as apathy in his attitude, and the general who was promoted was Brig. Gen. Ranald S. Mackenzie, who did exactly what he was supposed to do.

During the Battle of Five Forks, Warren had apparently (to Sheridan) mishandled an attack by troops of his V Corps upon an entrenched position being held by Maj. Gen. George Pickett and his reinforced division of Confederate infantry. Pickett was also supported by what remained of Lee's cavalry. Merritt, with Devin and Custer plus their cavalry divisions, had been placed on the left flank and center, where their diversionary attacks were holding the attention of Pickett's troops. During the course of the attack by V Corps, one infantry division more or less attacked where it was supposed to while the other two got lost and almost marched off the battlefield. While Sheridan immediately moved to rally the division that was making the attack, Warren, his actions at the time being apparently unknown by Sheridan, had helped to redirect one of the other two divisions and was personally leading the third infantry divisions to support the attack at a critical moment.

This division had marched beyond the Confederate left flank and only needed to be turned in order to envelope that flank and trap all of Pickett's infantry in a pocket, where they were soon forced to surrender, in what was called the Confederacy's Waterloo.

Before the attack began Mackenzie and his small division of cavalry had already severed the only link between Pickett and rest of Lee's army, which was three miles away; from there Mackenzie had been ordered to cover the right flank of the Warren's attacking infantry.[8] After being unable to find Warren, Sheridan personally led a breakthrough by two of Warren's infantry divisions. Warren could not be found because he was busy redirecting his third division, which was still being screened by Mackenzie's cavalry against any interference from the Confederate cavalry, as it wheeled to the left and completed what would become Sheridan's single greatest and most complete victory of the entire war.

Seventeen years later — and three months after Warren's death — he was exonerated from the worst of Grant and Sheridan's charges against him by a court of inquiry. Mackenzie was promoted to brevet major general with his commission being backdated to March 31, 1865, the day before the victory at Five Forks, a victory that led directly to the fall of the Confederate capital at Richmond and the final surrender of Gen. Robert E. Lee's Army of Northern Virginia.

4

WITH TORBERT IN
THE LURAY VALLEY

Why did Alfred T.A. Torbert fail in the single most important mission of his entire military career?

That question, as can be seen from the previous chapter, was one that haunted his commander in the Shenandoah Valley, Philip H. Sheridan, for the rest of his career as a general in the American Civil War and even after the war when he commanded all U.S. Army forces upon the western frontier, as general-in-chief of the army and even after he retired, through the writing of his memoirs of the American Civil War and right up to the day of his death.

Remember that he was originally an infantry commander. Torbert had been appointed to command the 1st Division, Cavalry Corps, at about the same time that Sheridan had been named to command the corps. Although a reasonably competent commander, Torbert never had the flash or fire to match that of Sheridan, Merritt, Custer, or Mackenzie in the command structure of the Eastern Theater of Operations' cavalry. Remember, also, that although his bravery was never called into question, there were always those who wondered whether he was fully competent in the role of a cavalry corps commander.

He was thrust into the role of a corps commander when as the senior divisional commander he had taken command of the two cavalry divisions, which had been transferred to the Army of the Shenandoah from the Army of the Potomac when Sheridan had been advanced to army command. He was then named chief of cavalry for the new Middle Military Division formed from the unification of four departments in and around the Shenandoah Valley. Two other cavalry divisions from the Department of West Virginia, those of William W. Averell and Alfred Duffie along with other scattered units within the Middle Military Division, were also placed under Torbert's administrative command.

Torbert had started off on his mission well enough and Sheridan felt he had every reason to expect that Torbert's swing around Early's Valley District Army would ultimately be successful. The intended mission (as had been planned by Sheridan) to the Luray Valley called for Torbert, with his four brigades of cavalry, to form the hard place against which Sheridan, with the bulk of his infantry as his rock, intended to hammer Confederate Lt. Gen. Jubal Early's Valley District Army into complete and total surrender.

While Sheridan retained Averell and his division along with Devin's Brigade, Torbert had taken the Reserve and Michigan Cavalry Brigades of Merritt's 1st Cavalry Division to Front Royal to join Wilson's

Sheridan never understood why Bvt. Maj. Gen. A.T.A. Torbert, above, failed him in the Luray Valley and allowed Confederate Lt. Gen. Jubal Early and his entire army to escape from the trap Sheridan had prepared for him (Library of Congress, Prints and Photographs Division).

3rd Cavalry Division on September 21. Wilson had spent the past 24 hours sparring with Williams C. Wickham's Confederate cavalry division. Wilson had already driven Wickham across the North Fork of the Shenandoah River. At daybreak on the 21st, Wilson had again attacked, driving Wickham to Gooney Run. By the time Torbert and Merritt arrived at Front Royal, Wilson's continued advance had been stalled at Gooney Run about six miles south of the town. (It may well have been as part of this operation that the picket post had been established which Capt. Chapman with Troops E and F of Mosby's Rangers had been searching for near Front Royal on September 22 when he instead found the Cavalry Corps wagon train on September 23, not realizing that the picket post had in all likelihood been removed in the course of the movements of Torbert's two divisions of cavalry, which occurred on September 21 and 22.)

The action on the 21st had been limited to some artillery exchanges until Wickham learned about the presence of Torbert with Merritt's division at Front Royal. When he did learn about Merritt's approach, Wickham realized that he was now badly outnumbered, since he was facing the bulk of two divisions, four brigades, with his single division of only two brigades. Wickham decided that discretion was much the better part of valor and ordered an immediate withdrawal from his positions along Gooney Run. Wickham waited until nightfall and then moved south to Milford, about 12 miles from Luray, while the two Union cavalry divisions commanded by Torbert halted and camped north of Gooney Run.

Edward G. Longacre, in *Custer and His Wolverines: The Michigan Cavalry Brigade 1861–1865*, stated that every bridge for miles around had been destroyed, precluding a frontal attack upon Wickham's position along Gooney Run. In addition, the Luray Valley itself narrowed so as to seem to preclude the possibility of a flanking maneuver being initiated by Wilson. Torbert — not realizing that Wickham had already left the area, having used the darkness to mask his movements — decided, however, to go ahead and attempt a maneuver to turn Wickham's flank.

At midnight on September 22, Torbert directed Custer to take his brigade and march from Front Royal, following the South Fork of the Shenandoah River to McCoy's Ford. At that point, Custer, under Torbert's plan, was to move across the river to the west of Wickham's supposed position and then by a roundabout route place himself in Wickhamn's rear. If Wickham had not retreated on Milford it is likely that Torbert's maneuver would have succeeded and from there Torbert could have, upon eliminating Wickham, moved into position to be able to block Early's retreat and thus accomplish what Sheridan had intended when he had first sent Torbert and his cavalry around Early's army.

At first light Custer's brigade re-crossed the river. As part of his plan Wilson had been instructed by Torbert to take the two brigades of his division, which were lying north of Gooney Run, and attack the Confederates behind the stream when Custer appeared on their right flank. Custer arrived on schedule, but when Wilson moved out to make the attack, he discovered that Wickham and his Confederates had decamped during the night.

Torbert's entire force undertook a pursuit of Wickham and his division and found Wickham at about 7 A.M. on September 22 in a position behind Overall's Run at Milford. Wickham and his men had been constructing field fortifications all along their position from the moment they had arrived. Thus their new position was even more formidable than had been their positions from the previous day along Gooney Run. The Confederate dismounted cavalry was deployed on a bluff above the stream, giving themselves the advantage of holding the high ground. Their left flank was anchored on the South Fork of the Shenandoah River while their right flank was anchored on a spur of the Blue Ridge Mountains. One brigade was positioned along the edge of the river while the other brigade was positioned on ground between Milford and the mountain. The division's horse artillery was positioned on a knoll to the rear.

The entire position was truly strong and well chosen, as Sheridan himself was forced to admit in his memoirs. Ultimately, it provided a problem for which Torbert was simply unable to arrive at a solution. However, in the light of their service before and after this event, it leads one to wonder what Merritt, Custer or Lowell might have been able to accomplish if they had been left to their own devices.

Wilson's division made first contact by Torbert's troops with the Confederate position. Upon making contact Wilson brought forward his own horse artillery, opening the combat. Thus the battle began with artillery fire from both sides and then Wilson's dismounted skirmishers added their carbine fire to that of the artillery. The artillery and small arms fire continued for several hours since Torbert was reluctant to make a full out attack on what appeared to be such a strong position. Late that afternoon Torbert attempted a feint toward the Confederate brigade occupying the ground between Milford and the mountain spur, while at the same time attempting to outflank on the right the brigade positioned along the river.

Confederate Col. Thomas Munford, who commanded the brigade along the river, was also directing Wickham's entire division at this time, since Wickham had left the area to confer with Early. Munford countered Torbert's movement by sending a squadron to support the 2nd Virginia Cavalry Regiment, which was covering the flank. Munford also sent along three buglers and attempted a ruse. The buglers were positioned with enough space between them for a full regiment. At a given signal they blew the charge. Coupled with the fire they were receiving from the reinforced 2nd Virginia, Torbert's tentative move to turn the flank was itself turned back. For some totally inexplicable reason, whatever aggressiveness and initiative Torbert may have possessed suddenly deserted him.

Torbert thereupon disengaged retiring northward down the Luray Valley. In his official report Torbert attempted to explain his action: "Not knowing that the army had made an attack at Fisher's Hill, and thinking that the sacrifice would be too great to attack without that knowledge, I concluded to withdraw to a point opposite McCoy's Ferry." All in all, this was a rather lame excuse. Torbert certainly knew that his trip to the Luray Valley was intended to support an attack on Fisher's Hill. By this time Torbert should have known Sheridan well enough as a commander and as a particularly aggressive general not to be in any doubt whether or not he would actually attack Fisher's Hill.

Sheridan was disappointed to say the least, and it was not a good idea to disappoint Sheridan, as Averell would soon discover and as Torbert would eventually discover. Sheridan could never see any justification for Torbert's performance, or lack of it, and he never did quite understand exactly what in the expurgated hell had happened to spoil his plans.[1]

Sheridan was not the only one who could not understand what had happened to cause Torbert to simply give up when, by sweeping forward, he would have had delivered Early's entire army to Sheridan's tender mercies. Col. James H. Kidd, commander of Custer's 6th Michigan Cavalry Regiment, and also the man who succeeded Custer in command of the Michigan Cavalry Brigade, was one of those for whom Torbert's actions were incomprehensible.

Kidd left the following account:

> On the 22nd [of September], Torbert was sent to Milford in the Luray Valley, taking Wilson's and Merritt's divisions. His orders were to break through one of the passes in the Massanutten Mountains and come out in the rear of Early's army, where Crook's flanking maneuver on the other side would have driven him off Fisher's Hill. Crook's attack was completely successful and Early was "whirling up the Valley" again. Torbert made a fiasco of it.
>
> He allowed Wickham, who succeeded Fitzhugh Lee [who had been wounded at the Third Battle of Winchester/Opequon Creek], with at most two small brigades, to hold him at bay and withdrew without making any fight of it. I remember very well how the Michigan Brigade lay in a safe position at the rear of the line listening to the firing and was not ordered in at all. If Custer or Merritt had been in command it would have been different.[2]

This statement by Kidd shows that Custer and his brigade were totally uncommitted in the admittedly ineffective artillery and small arms skirmishing that had taken place on September 22. Apparently Torbert had decided to keep Custer in reserve. It seems odd that he did not utilize Custer as he had at Gooney Run on a wide end run to outflank Wickham's admittedly formidable position. Since Custer had been kept in reserve during the fighting, his troops were relatively fresh and well rested by the time Torbert began his retreat back to Front Royal. This fact becomes particularly important in piecing together what may have actually happened at Front Royal on September 23, particularly when it is added to what was not said or recorded by Kidd and others regarding the events at Front Royal and the part played in them (or not) by both Custer and his Michigan Cavalry Brigade.

By that time in the war Custer was considered to be one of the best brigade commanders in the entire Eastern Theater of Operations. After dismissing Averell, Sheridan would first make Custer his replacement. However, shortly thereafter Wilson would be transferred from command of the 3rd Cavalry Division and would be sent to the Western Theater of Operations. Once there, Wilson would raise a powerful force of cavalry, raid and destroy the Confederate armaments center at Selma, Ala., and be one of the few persons ever to defeat Confederate Lt. Gen. Nathan Bedford Forrest in open battle.

Before Wilson succeeded H. Judson Kilpatrick in command of the 3rd Cavalry Division, Custer had been one of Kilpatrick's brigade commanders. Custer had also been irked and greatly disappointed that he did not receive command of the 3rd Cavalry Division when Kilpatrick had been relieved. Although he never served under Wilson's command, and considerable steps had been taken to prevent that from happening, he had been one of Wilson's colleagues and most vocal critics, until the transfer. Custer had been thoroughly fed up with Kilpatrick's performance while he had served under his command, but he considered Wilson to be nothing more than a puffed up incompetent who should never had been given command of cavalry in the first place. Admittedly, Wilson did not exactly shine in a combat command until his raid upon Selma and his defeat of Forrest. (Sheridan's 1864 Shenandoah Valley Campaign, being the first time Wilson had ever commanded troops in the field, may have provided the experience that Wilson needed to become a truly effective troop commander.)

When Wilson's sudden transfer created the opening within the 3rd Cavalry Division, Sheridan gave the division to Custer and Kidd succeeded Custer in command of the Michigan Cavalry Brigade within days of the events at Front Royal. Sheridan probably decided to shift Custer over to the 3rd Cavalry Division rather than keep him in command of the 2nd Cavalry Division, Department of West Virginia (which Sheridan had done after Averell's relief), so that he could retain him once the 1st and 3rd Cavalry Divisions eventually returned to the Army of the Potomac. Col. William H. Powell succeeded first Averell and then Custer in command of the 2nd Cavalry Division, Department of West Virginia.

Torbert had resumed his retreat on the morning of September 23 when he pulled out of his camp at McCoy's Ford. Wilson's division crossed the South Fork of the Shenandoah River, at the ford proceeding to Buckton's Ford on the North Fork of the river. The wagon train and Merritt's division followed the Luray road to Front Royal. In order to protect it from the most likely danger, the wagon train was positioned first with Lowell's Brigade following it and with Custer's Brigade in the rear. Since he was following behind Lowell, Custer was therefore in the rear guard position as the column made its way to the atrocity waiting to happen at Front Royal.

This aftermath to the Battle of Fisher's Hill continued on September 24, 1864, before the final curtain fell. Kidd noted that Sheridan did not quite give up on his grand design when Torbert failed him on September 22 and 23. Sheridan tried one more time to trap Early's Valley District Army and bring the campaign to a triumphal closing. Success of a sort came when Torbert, due to Sheridan's pushing, finally did on September 24 what he probably could have and should have done on September 22.[3]

"Sheridan ordered Torbert to try again," Kidd recalled in his memoirs. "Custer, followed by Lowell, was sent to the front and in the forenoon of September 24, Wickham's troops were scattered in flight and the way opened for Torbert to carry out his instructions. Even then the march was leisurely and the two divisions arrived in New Market on September 25 only to find it was too late. Early had escaped again."

Once again what might have been is brought to mind. Merritt, or Custer, or Lowell would have pressed the advantage. The pace would have been forced and there would have been no leisurely advance. There would

50

have been no second disappointment and no second escape for Jubal Early and his Valley District Army.

Meanwhile, Sheridan had continued his pursuit of Early and his army. On September 23, George Crook's Army of West Virginia/VIII Corps troops, which had remained behind at Fisher's Hill, moved out to Woodstock. VI Corps and XIX Corps on September 24 pushed on for New Market Gap and what Sheridan had been hoping would become the ultimate battle of the campaign, being joined by Crook and his two small divisions.

Sheridan and his main army caught up with Early at Rude's Hill after they had cleared Mount Jackson. Sheridan probed the Confederate position with his artillery before sending Devin and his brigade of cavalry (still detached from Merritt's 1st Cavalry Division) along the river to turn the Confederate right flank. Col. William Powell (now acting commander of Averell's cavalry division) was sent to the west toward Timberville to envelop the Confederate left flank. Sheridan then sent forward infantry skirmishers to make contact with the Confederates on Rude Hill.

Rude Hill gave Early and his army an unobstructed view of the Union positions and they could see exactly what the Union troops were doing. Early's baggage train had already departed and he ordered his infantry and artillery to follow it. Half of the brigades in each of Early's divisions withdrew first, falling back about a mile up the turnpike and then redeploying. The remaining brigades released their hold on Rude's Hill, moved through the new line and redeployed themselves another two miles further back. Using this method, Early leapfrogged his army as it retreated with each new line providing cover for the troops on the move.

Early's army retreated through New Market before taking up a complete battle line position at Tenth Legion Church with Sheridan's troops dogging their footsteps every inch of the way. One witness labeled the entire procedure as one of the most magnificent sights of the entire war. Sheridan's troops and scouts from the tops of the hills overlooking the Valley could see Early's troops stretched in their lines of battle across the Valley floor as they moved away from their pursuers. Placed before the actual lines of battle were clouds of Confederate skirmishers seeking to delay the Union advance as the Confederate army leapfrogged its way to safety. The Confederate skirmishers were constantly under attack by Devin and Powell's cavalry. Behind the Union cavalry skirmishers came a line of Union infantry skirmishers. Whenever the cavalry skirmishers were checked, the infantry skirmishers thereupon reinforced them; meanwhile the Confederate troops kept moving back.

By 5 P.M. on September 24, Sheridan halted his pursuit for the night just south of New Market. Just before the halt, Sheridan made one more attempt to bring the Confederates to battle. He used Devin's cavalry to entice Early's infantry into making an attack. Early, however, wasn't biting and Sheridan knew that he could not force an engagement before dark. Sheridan was not about to try a night attack, which he knew would be almost impossible for him to control. (At the Battle of Chancellorsville in May 1863, such a night attack resulted in considerable confusion, which in turn had led to the wounding and eventual death of Lt. Gen. Thomas J. "Stonewall" Jackson. Robert E. Lee said after Jackson's arm had been amputated that while Jackson had lost his left arm, he, Lee, had lost his right).

In order for Early to extricate his army, Wickham's cavalry had to keep the New Market Gap open. This they did during the fighting with Torbert on September 24, mostly due to Torbert's excessive caution on that day. By nightfall, Wickham had managed to disengage his cavalry division and had moved south, camping for the night along the South Fork of the Shenandoah River. Torbert's troops, on the other hand, camped at the foot of New Market Gap. Thus Torbert failed to do what he was supposed to do once again.

That night Early's infantry and artillery were back on the road. They halted at midnight, slept for a few hours, and by daybreak were on the move by way of Port Republic. By sunset on September 25, Early's army was encamped at Brown's Gap of the Blue Ridge Mountains. Lomax and his cavalry were picketing the South Fork at Port Republic and Wickham and his cavalry rejoined the army during the night.

Jubal Early's Valley District Army was safe.[4]

Ironically, Early's army had been saved through the efforts of the cavalry division commanded by Williams C. Wickham. It is ironic because Early mistrusted his cavalry arm and did not expect much from it. Sheridan, on the other hand, was one of the few Union generals (particularly army commanders) who understood the potential of his cavalry and how best to use it. Sheridan used his mounted troops as a primary striking force much in the same way as 20th and 21st Century military commanders would use armored columns. But, in this instance, Sheridan was let down by his cavalry arm, or rather by the commander of that cavalry arm.

5

MOSBY'S STORY

Without Lt. Col. John S. Mosby the atrocity at Front Royal probably would have become nothing more than a rather obscure American Civil War incident. But Mosby was a natural leader and like any really good military leader he was concerned with the well-being of the men whom he led. Therefore, he was outraged that at least six of his men had apparently been killed, after being taken prisoner, for no better reason than that they were his men.

To a certain degree Mosby was as much a military character as Custer. However, he was not a professional soldier. Rather he was trained as an attorney and when the war came along he found his true niche, first as a cavalry scout for J.E.B. Stuart and then as Eastern Theater of Operations primary practitioner in the use of guerrilla forces and tactics.

In 1864 Mosby and his 43rd Virginia Battalion of Partisan Rangers operated in Loudon, Prince William, Fairfax and Farquier counties, located to the east of the Blue Ridge. From here he could strike east at the defenses of Washington, D.C., itself, north across the Potomac River into Maryland, and to the west he could move in and out of the Shenandoah Valley. Thus Mosby and his men were ideally positioned astride the lines of communications of any army invading Virginia as it advanced from Washington towards Richmond or attempted to penetrate the Shenandoah Valley.

Mosby was a man who defied almost all authority but his own for most of his life. Personally, Mosby had opposed the war, but when Virginia seceded he marched off to war with his militia company. He eventually joined the 1st Virginia Cavalry Regiment, at that time under the command of then Col. J.E.B. Stuart, and participated in the First Battle of Bull Run (or Manassas). From there he would become a scout and was detached to Stuart's staff. He and Stuart got to know each other quite well. They trusted each other explicitly and Mosby was able to persuade Stuart to detach his own self and 15 other soldiers from the 1st Virginia to operate behind Union lines. Mosby began his operations on January 24, 1863. From this beginning his guerrilla force grew and eventually became the 43rd Virginia Battalion of Partisan Rangers, which was officially formed in February 1863. Their mission was to serve behind the Union lines in northern Virginia and disrupt Union communications in their rear echelon areas. His first major success occurred on the night of March 8–9, 1863, when Mosby captured Brig. Gen. Edmond H. Stroughton in his headquarters at Fairfax, Virginia. With this success under his belt, Mosby went on to become the most successful, well known and feared commander of guerrilla raiders in the entire Confederacy.

But, there was one fish, Lt. Gen. Ulysses S. Grant, who got away.

Grant stated in his memoirs[1] that between March 26 and May 4, 1864, while his headquarters were at Culpeper, Virginia, he traveled to Washington, D.C., about once a week to confer with Secretary of War Edwin M. Stanton and President Abraham Lincoln. While returning from the last of these conferences before moving his headquarters, Grant narrowly missed being captured by Mosby. The story is as follows: "On my return to the field ... on this occasion as the train approached Warrenton Junction, a heavy cloud of dust was seen to the east of the road as if made by a body of cav-

Confederate Col. John S. Mosby, commander, 43rd Virginia Battalion of Partisan Rangers, remained convinced to the end of his days that Custer, and Custer alone, was responsible for the executions of his six captured rangers at Front Royal (Library of Congress, Prints and Photographs Division).

alry on a charge. Upon arriving at the junction the train was stopped and inquiries were made as to the cause of the dust. There was but one man at the station, and he informed us that Mosby had crossed a few minutes before at full speed in pursuit of Federal cavalry. Had he seen our train coming, no doubt he would have let his prisoners escape to capture the train. I was on a special train, if I remember correctly, without any guard."

In the summer and fall of 1864 Mosby was just 30 years old. In person, he was not an imposing man. He was about 5-foot-7 in height and weighed only about 128 pounds, being much like in character and appearance as his Revolutionary War predecessor in South Carolina, Francis Marion, who was known as the Swamp Fox. The men he chose for the 43rd Virginia were primarily young, courageous men who were superb horsemen.

Unlike other guerrilla units, the men of Mosby's 43rd Virginia normally wore Confederate uniforms, paroled or sent their captives south and in general, but not always, they operated according to the accepted rules of warfare. Aside from the 15 soldiers detached from the 1st Virginia, Mosby's men included discharged veterans, soldiers on furlough, convalescents, local farm boys from Virginia and Maryland, deserters and freebooters. In general they were drawn by the informal come-and-go nature, romance, and prospects of easy plunder. But, under Mosby's leadership this conglomeration was turned into a highly effective fighting force, although things could get out of hand if Mosby personally did not happen to be on the scene.

Mosby's command was basically a body of scouts whose aims, aside from making life as difficult as possible for Union troops, was to gather intelligence (which was forwarded directly to Gen. Lee), hamper Union plans in any way possible, and to harry Union outposts and supply lines.[2] Mosby, himself, had no supply lines or logistic concerns since he and his men lived off the countryside (with the enthusiastic compliance of the local population) and also helped themselves to whatever they captured from their enemies.

He had a number of advantages over the Union troops which were hunting him and which were attempting to destroy his command.[3] Aside from his lack of supply lines or logistic concerns, he also had no camp or fixed headquarters. Between raids the inhabitants of the area in which he operated sheltered him and his men. When a raid was planned, his men were summoned by word-of-mouth messages to a rendezvous. Since Mosby's Rangers functioned without much of the organized discipline of a regular military command, it was the personality of Mosby, not any particular discipline or other esprit de corps, which provided the glue that held them together.

Mosby himself explained his concept of guerrilla war this way: "A small force moving with celerity and threatening many points on a line can neutralize a hundred times its own number. The line must be stronger at every point than the attacking force, else it is broken. The military value of a partisan's work is not valued by the amount of property destroyed, or by the number of men killed or captured, but by the number he keeps watching."[4]

In response to Mosby's raids, he and his men were called "bushwhackers" by their Union opponents and were not considered to be legitimate soldiers, even though the 43rd Virginia Battalion of Partisan Rangers had officially been fully and completely inducted into Confederate service and was therefore considered to be a part like any other unit of the Provisional Army of the Confederate States. Therefore, in Mosby's view, his men were as much part of the Confederate Army as were the men of the 1st Virginia Cavalry Regiment, of which he had been a part prior to his detachment by Gen. Stuart. This in part explains his rage when some of his men were executed after being taken prisoner. In particular, he was incensed that at least three of his men had been hanged like common criminals. In his memoirs Mosby took considerable umbrage that he and his men were being called bushwhackers: "Now I never resented the epithet of 'bushwhacker'— although there was no soldier to whom it applied less — because bushwhacking is a legitimate form of war, and it is just as fair and equally heroic to fire at an enemy behind a bush or a breastwork or from the casemate of a fort."[5] This may have been a case of "methinks he dost protest too much."

Unfortunately for Mosby's men at Front Royal, the Union troops which were on the receiving end of his attacks and retaliations did not consider either Mosby or his troops as being covered by the laws of war due to what they considered to be Mosby's own flaunting of those laws. For instance, Mosby and his men did not stand and fight very often; they hit and then they ran and were highly successful. Mosby and his men were constantly present in the Valley and at times it seemed as if no wagon train or small detachment of Union troops were safe from the threat of sudden and vicious surprise attacks.

In addition, there were any number of atrocities against Union troops operating in the valley which were either the direct responsibility of Mosby's men or were blamed upon them, with or without any direct proof. The most noted of these included the death of 2nd Lt. John R. Meigs. About a week after Meigs was killed, Col. Cornelius Tolles, VI Corps quartermaster, and Dr. Emil Ohlenschlager, medical director for the Army of the Shenandoah, were both shot and killed within Union lines near Newtown, Virginia. Both deaths infuriated the entire Union Army of the Shenandoah.

Mosby received the gunshot wound that kept him from the field at the time of the Front Royal Incident on September 14, 1864, just five days before Sheridan began the offensive that eventually resulted in the incident. Mosby, in his memoirs, said that he was wounded after he and two of his men unexpectedly ran into five Union cavalry troopers at Fairfax, Virginia, with both sides opening fire at the same time. Two of the Union troopers' horses were killed and Mosby was wounded.

Mosby is on record as saying — regarding the Front Royal Incident — that his constant raids caused the enemy to retaliate by executing some of his men. In his memoirs, which were published over 50 years after the event, Mosby got the date wrong, apparently based upon one of the newspaper accounts upon which he also based, at least in part, his conclusion that Custer and his Michigan Cavalry Brigade were responsible for the executions (which may or may not say something about the general accuracy of his memoirs). The newspaper account stated that the Front Royal incident occurred on September 22, not September 23, the date upon which it actually did occur.

Mosby's memoirs make it quite clear that he heavily relied on the newspaper accounts, whose accuracy can be further questioned, particularly since it is also clear that their substance had been "enhanced" primarily for their primitive propaganda value. Most probably this was done to incite outrage among the Confederate civilian population at the activities of the Union soldiers in their midst.

The following account was from an "eyewitness" who was recorded in a Confederate newspaper, cited by Mosby's memoirs as follows:

The Yankee cavalry, under General Torbert, entered the town (Front Royal), and drove out the four Confederates on picket, who fell back to Milford. At this later point General Wickham met the Yankee force and repulsed it. A part of Mosby's men under Captain Chapman, annoyed the enemy very much upon their return to Front Royal, which with the mortification of their defeat by Wickham, excited them to such savage doings as to prompt them to murder six of our men who fell into their hands. Anderson, Overby, Love and Rhodes were shot and Carter and one other, whose name our informant did not recollect were hung to the limb of a tree at the entrance of the village.... Harry Rhodes was quite a youth, living with his widowed mother and supporting her by his labor. He did not belong to Mosby's command. His mother entreated them to spare the life of her son and treat him as a prisoner of war, but the demons answered by whetting their sabers on some stones and declaring they would cut his head off and hers too, if she came near. They ended by shooting him in her presence. The murders were committed on the 22nd day of September, Generals Torbert, Merritt and Custer being present. It is said that Torbert and Merritt turned the prisoners over to Custer for the purpose of their execution.

In point of fact, practically all other accounts of the Front Royal Incident agree that it was Overby and Carter who were hung, with the other four being shot. The newspaper account does not name the source of the claim that Torbert and Merritt had the prisoners turned over to Custer for the purpose of their being executed.

Rhodes, as has been noted, was not a member of Mosby's command. He was simply a boy, at age 17, who apparently had dreamed of becoming one of Mosby's Rangers and when the opportunity had presented itself had borrowed a horse and joined in the attack. At least one historian maintains that Rhodes was dazed and almost unconscious and that he was taken prisoner by troopers from Custer's 6th Michigan Cavalry Regiment under the command of Col. James H. Kidd, who threatened the boy's screaming mother, who had been told what was happening by certain other Front Royal residents.[7]

Front Royal resident Sue Richardson purportedly witnessed the execution of Rhodes.[8] In all likelihood she probably knew Rhodes, since they were of about the same age. Reportedly Union troopers — again supposedly from Custer's 6th Michigan Cavalry Regiment — led Rhodes (apparently with his screaming mother following close behind) to a field at the foot of Rose Hill, the name of Miss Richardson's home. She is supposed to have witnessed what happened next from a shuttered window. She reported how a Union soldier untied Rhodes, whose hands were tied behind his back, and he was then ordered to stand up. When Rhodes staggered to his feet another soldier emptied his revolver into the boy's body.

Her account is interesting in several ways. First, she personally does not identify the soldiers who executed Rhodes as being members of either the 6th Michigan Cavalry Regiment or even of being members of Custer's Michigan Cavalry Brigade. In addition, she makes absolutely no mention at all of seeing Custer at the scene of the execution. Custer's flamboyant uniform, in particular his bright red tie, ordinarily marked him out from a mile away on the most chaotic of battlefields. If Custer had been there at all for Rhodes' execution, it seems likely that Miss Richardson would most certainly have noticed him and if she had noticed him, it does seem rather odd on the face of it that she would neglect to mention him.

Mosby also quoted another newspaper account, this one being published by the *Richmond Examiner*, one of the major newspapers in the Confederate capital.[9] This newspaper account, which includes somewhat different details, is as follows:

> On Friday last Mosby's men attacked a wagon train, which was protected by a whole brigade, so that their charge was repelled with the loss of six prisoners. Two of their prisoners the Yankees immediately hung to a neighboring tree, placing around their necks placards bearing the inscription, "Hung in retaliation for the Union officer killed after he had surrendered — the fate of Mosby's men." The other four of our prisoners were tied to stakes and mercilessly shot through the skull, each one individually. One of those hung was a famous soldier named Overby, from Georgia. When the rope was placed around his neck by his inhuman captors, he told them that he was one of Mosby's men, and that he was proud to die as a Confederate soldier, and that his death was sweetened with the assurance that Colonel Mosby would swing in the wind ten Yankees for every man they murdered.

Again there are several interesting aspects to this report. In this newspaper account there is only one brigade of cavalry, which is mentioned as having been present at Front Royal that day; since Lowell's Reserve Cavalry Brigade was following immediately behind the wagon train, it is certain that the Union troops mentioned in the article refer only to Lowell's Reserve Cavalry Brigade and not to Custer's Michigan Cavalry Brigade. In addition, Custer's Michigan Cavalry Brigade and Custer himself are not even mentioned in the *Richmond Examiner* account. Finally, the newspaper account totally contradicts Miss Richardson's account when it states that all four of the victims who were shot were shot together and were first tied to stakes, and then each one received a single shot to the head.

Furthermore, while some accounts state that the executions took place over a number of hours, and that the hangings even included the playing of a band, the *Richmond Examiner* account indicates that the executions occurred almost immediately after the men had been taken prisoner. This particular possibility seems much more logically likely.

Overby and Carter, the two prisoners who were hanged, were reportedly taken to the local wagon yard, where they were interrogated in an attempt to find out where Mosby's headquarters was located. Since Mosby didn't have a headquarters, there was no way the two prisoners could reveal its location. In any event the two men reportedly refused and then soldiers from the troop of the 2nd U.S. Cavalry Regiment commanded by Lt. Charles H. McMaster led them to a large walnut tree north of town, where they were given one more chance to talk and save their lives. Both refused and were hanged. Overby was said to be defiant while Carter was said to have openly wept. (McMaster was the officer killed in the attack upon the wagon train. According to Mosby's men he was simply overrun and killed in the belated attack, while according to Union sources — including Merritt's official report and a report that noted he had actually died in a Union Army hospital at least three weeks after the Front Royal Incident — McMaster was captured, robbed, shot in the head and left for dead.)

The Confederate newspaper accounts cited by Mosby make absolutely no mention of at all of Lt. McMaster, either regarding his death or how he was killed. This could have been accidental, since their sources were probably mostly civilians who may or may not have seen the skirmish which preceded the executions. Or it may have been deliberately omitted in order to enhance the propaganda value of the two newspaper accounts.

Mosby himself, according to an official report on the matter to General Lee, did not learn about the executions until September 29, and while he did rely heavily on newspaper accounts for information, it is probable that these were not his only sources. There is no information concerning whether or not Mosby himself actually went to Front Royal to question any of the witnesses. Since he was recovering from a serious bullet wound, he may not have been physically able to go to Front Royal himself to find out what had happened. Therefore, aside from relying upon newspaper accounts, Mosby may well have dispatched subordinates to see to it that the dead were buried and to question the residents. However, many of the witnesses that were found were likely unable to provide any primary, first hand knowledge. Many of these witnesses could probably only offer second hand accounts of what other persons told them. In addition, being civilians, they were not knowledgeable about military ranks or the organization of Sheridan's army, particularly as to what officer was actually giving orders to whom. Thus, it is quite likely that it is upon these second and even third hand "eyewitness" and newspaper accounts that Mosby based his response.

Any person involved in law enforcement or who follows crime stories knows that eyewitness accounts must be taken with a grain of salt. People can be mistaken or they can be influenced by other people into believing they have seen something that in actuality, they have not.

Mosby, as a trained and experienced lawyer, should have been able to recognize this simple fact of life and should not have accepted such evidence of Custer's responsibility without more collaboration. But, it is apparent from his actions that he was not in a mood to be skeptical and that he accepted everything he was told — or what his subordinates were told — as the gospel truth. Most likely he believed what he was being told because he wanted to believe what he was being told.

The most important point to remember is that everybody on the Confederate side who were possible witnesses to what had happened at Front Royal on September 23, 1864, all knew who Custer was, at least by reputation, if they didn't know anybody else among the Union command structure.

Mosby, after hearing the reports from Front Royal, immediately fixed upon Custer as the Union officer most responsible for the atrocity, and therefore Mosby blamed Custer, and Custer alone, for what had happened to his men. He disregarded the fact that Custer was not in command on that particular day in Front Royal.

In any event, Mosby, in his memoirs, wrote that he swore to "demand and enforce every belligerent right to which soldiers of a great military power were entitled by the laws of war. But I resolved to do it in the most humane manner and in a calm judicial spirit." Mosby informed Gen. Lee that he intended "to hang an equal number of Custer's men whenever I capture them." Lee, after receiving Mosby's report on the Front Royal Incident, concurred with Mosby's conclusion and his planned reprisal, seeking and eventually receiving the endorsement of Confederate Secretary of War James A. Sedden, albeit after Mosby had already put his plans for the reprisal into action.

6

Where Was Custer?

At this point in the story of the Front Royal Incident there are two primary questions. First, where were Custer and his Michigan Cavalry Brigade? Second, what were they doing?

Torbert's marching order as he moved back to Front Royal indicates the answer to both of those questions. As he moved away from his defeat in the Luray Valley, Torbert had placed his wagon train in the front of the column, which he accompanied. Following the wagon train, he placed Lowell's Reserve Cavalry Brigade, which had been involved in the fighting against Wickham. These troops were positioned to provide immediate protection for the wagon train. Custer's Michigan Cavalry Brigade was positioned to bring up the rear. In addition, Torbert also sent Brig. Gen. James H. Wilson's two brigades of his 3rd Cavalry Division across the South Fork of the Shenandoah River at McCoy's Ford and had then ordered the division to proceed toward Buckton's Ford on the North Fork of the Shenandoah River.

This sparks another question; why had Torbert organized his marching order in this way?

The answer lies in the repulse Torbert had allowed himself to suffer in the Luray Valley. First, it must be remembered that Torbert was retreating. Detaching Wilson's 3rd Cavalry Division was probably done to protect the flank of his primary line of march, particularly since he had kept the wagon train with him and Merritt's 1st Cavalry Division. Since Torbert decided to accompany Merritt's Division as it fell back on Front Royal, the route followed by Merritt's Division should definitely be considered his primary line of march.

Since he was retreating, with Wickham's victorious Confederate cavalry division behind him, it is likely that Torbert placed his wagon train in what was the area he considered to be that of the least possible danger, the front of his primary line of march, since any threat from Wickham's cavalry was to the rear of his primary line of march. The next choice was which of the two brigades (Lowell's Reserve Cavalry Brigade and Custer's Michigan Cavalry Brigade) that were then with him would be positioned to directly follow the wagon train and protect it and which would be placed in the rear guard position, the area from which the threat of any Confederate attack was most likely to appear.

In the fighting against Wickham on September 22, 1864, Custer and his brigade were not committed. Against his own inclination and the inclination of his men, the Michigan Cavalry Brigade had been kept safely in reserve. Col. James H. Kidd's memoirs and letters make it crystal clear how much Custer must have chafed at the bit watching as Torbert mishandled Sheridan's plan to trap and permanently destroy Early's entire army.[1] Custer must have realized immediately what Sheridan had wanted Torbert's expedition to accomplish. Now, with Sheridan's plan in ruins, let us speculate for a moment and put ourselves in Torbert's shoes:

1. You have been checked by the enemy and have allowed yourself to be forced into a retreat.

2. You have at your immediate disposal two divisions of cavalry, each consisting of two brigades.

3. You have already detached one division of two brigades to protect your flank. Out of the two brigades remaining to you, which one do you place in the rear guard position?

For the rear guard position during the retreat from the Luray Valley back to Front Royal was the place that the greatest possible danger would most likely appear. If Wickham were to decide to follow up his success in the Luray Valley, he would certainly have attacked the rear guard.

Now let us examine the question much more closely; if you had allowed yourself to be placed in this position would you have selected as your rear guard a brigade that had been engaged in combat, was therefore fatigued, and which the enemy had already beaten? Or would you choose the freshest and most capable brigade under your command (which had not been committed to battle and which had not been defeated) and which also happened to be commanded by your best brigade commander? It seems elementary that in the situation that Torbert had allowed himself to be placed in, he would want Custer and his Michigan Cavalry Brigade to form his rear guard.

From there let us consider for a moment the implications of Torbert's line of march with Custer and his brigade serving as Torbert's rear guard as his troops approached Front Royal in their retreat from the Luray Valley on September 23, 1864. With Custer and his brigade forming the rear guard on the approach to Front Royal, they would have arrived last. Since they arrived last — at the end of a slow moving column burdened with a wagon train at its head — does that not make it possible that Custer and the bulk of his command likely arrived on the scene at Front Royal either after the executions had already been completed or possibly while they were already underway? If that is the way it happened, Custer and the bulk of his command would have had nothing whatsoever to do with what happened to the prisoners who were taken that day from Mosby's 43rd Virginia Battalion of Partisan Rangers.

Also consider that the timing of the events is rather unclear. To return to the various accounts, particularly those of the Confederate newspapers cited by Mosby, some of them seem to indicate that the executions occurred almost immediately after the skirmishing which resulted in the death of Lt. McMaster and in the capture of the six Rangers who were executed had ended. There are other accounts, however, which indicate that there was an interval of up to several hours between the captures and the executions. There is even a mention of a band being brought up to play the death march while Overby and Carter were being dragged to the tree where they were hanged.

Does it seem likely that there would have been such a long delay? After all, Torbert was retreating. He was in all likelihood still worried about the possibility that Wickham would follow up his success in the Luray Valley. (Or rather that of Col. Thomas Munford, since he was in tactical command of Wickham's Division, since Wickham was not present because he was conferring with Confederate Valley District Army commander Lt. Gen. Jubal Early.) If Torbert was concerned about the possibility of being attacked, would he have literally wasted hours while interrogating and executing a half dozen men, even bringing forward a brass band? Or if he had intended from the beginning to execute at least some of them, wouldn't he have it done immediately, without any delay?

After all, the attack on the wagon train in front of the column occurred as the wagons were approaching Front Royal with Torbert attempting to make the best possible time back to the safety of Sheridan's army. If there was no delay and if the executions occurred immediately, which seems rather more likely, then everything must have happened within a relatively short time frame. Therefore, the question to ask is, was it possible for Custer and his men to have arrived in time to participate in those executions?

Another factor to consider is what Custer's responsibilities were on that day. As commander of the rear guard brigade, he was responsible for protecting the rear of the marching column. A marching column, attacked from the rear or the flank, is in considerable danger of being overwhelmed before it can deploy effectively to resist such an attack. It was Custer's job as commander of the rear guard to prevent such a thing from happening. Custer certainly knew that if the column was placed under attack from the front, there were plenty of troops ahead of him to protect the wagon train. Also consider the difference between what Custer was accused of being and what he actually was. A common accusation against Custer has been that he was rash and reckless. There is no denying that Custer as a leader and commander of cavalry was bold and audacious. However, recklessness and boldness, although they have a tendency to look alike from a safe distance (in time and space), are not the same.

An examination of the careers of Hugh Judson Kilpatrick and George Armstrong Custer should demonstrate the difference between recklessness and boldness. In examining the record, it is quite clear that Kilpatrick was everything that Custer was ever accused of being and was not. Custer led from the front and accepted the same risks that he demanded from his men. Except for certain rare incidents, Kilpatrick commanded from the rear, with as little risk to his own life as possible.

It is quite likely that Custer's first instinct when he heard the firing in front of him caused by the Rangers' abortive attack against the wagon train at the head of the column was to "ride to the sound of the guns." However, it was his primary responsibility to protect the rear of the column and therefore he would not have blindly ordered the entire command forward. It is, however, quite possible that Custer would have detached his leading regiment, possibly sending it cross country around the town of Front Royal, to find out what was going on and to be in a position to offer any assistance that might be needed.

Custer had long demonstrated that he had an eye for terrain. A letter from Custer to his wife indicates that in August, Custer had fought some kind of minor action or heavy skirmish in the vicinity of Front Royal.[2] The action occurred on August 16, 1864, and in Merritt's report on the campaign, he noted that Custer's Michigan Cavalry Brigade was instrumental in stopping an attack by Confederate cavalry. Keeping Custer's eye for terrain in mind, isn't it likely that Custer remembered the lay of the ground around Front Royal? This may have been reinforced when the 1st Cavalry Division marched on Front Royal at the beginning of Torbert's Luray Valley expedition. Custer may well have noted the most likely escape route for any possible attackers and when the attack upon the wagon train came on September 23, with this knowledge in mind, he may well have sent his leading regiment forward with the intent to provide any assistance needed and to block such an escape. Custer certainly demonstrated in his Civil War career that he had the initiative to have taken such a step when the opportunity presented itself.

Testimony from Union sources who were present at Front Royal on that day and who did witness at least some of the executions indicate that that is exactly what Custer did, and that the unit he sent forward was most likely the 5th Michigan Cavalry Regiment.[3] (The 5th Michigan is the only unit mentioned by Union sources from Custer's Michigan Cavalry Brigade as being present in the vicinity of Front Royal when the attack upon the wagon train and the executions occurred. There is absolutely no mention by Union sources of any other units from the Michigan Cavalry Brigade being present, despite Confederate accounts that young Rhodes was executed and his mother was threatened by soldiers from Kidd's 6th Michigan Cavalry Regiment.)

As to why it was the 5th Michigan Cavalry to be dispatched on this mission and not, say, the 6th Michigan, it was likely due to the luck of the draw. It was common military practice to rotate the order of march on a daily basis. In all likelihood it was simply the 5th Michigan's turn to be located at the front of the brigade on that particular day.

James Henry Avery, a member of the 5th Michigan Cavalry Regiment — cited in *Under Custer's Command: The Civil War Journal by James Henry Avery,* edited by Eric Wittenberg — makes it clear that his regiment was present and was involved in the killings of at least two of Mosby's Rangers [4] (whether or not they were among the six men known to have been executed at Front Royal is at least open to question). His statement is as follows: "It was the 20th of September, the day following the Battle of Winchester, that I joined my company. We made a move up above Front Royal, capturing a few of Mosby's men at Front Royal. They were recognized as part of the band that had recently captured a lieutenant and some of our advance guard and murdered them, being caught and recognized by the lieutenant before he died, they were sentenced without court or jury and two of them were given over to our regiment."

There are a number of points which should be kept in mind while considering the information provided in his journal. First, his account makes no mention of who, if anyone, had actually turned these prisoners over to the 5th Michigan Cavalry. Second, it also does not state who actually took those two prisoners he mentions. The reference could simply mean that the soldiers of the 5th Michigan captured these two Rangers, an event which Capt. Theodore Bean's account — see below — indicates can be considered at least a possibility.[5] Third, it must also be remembered that soldiers of the 5th Michigan who were foraging had been killed in earlier incidents by Rangers from Mosby's command, which could explain why the summary executions Avery witnessed had occurred. The journal continues:

> Being brought in front of us, the colonel [Maj. Smith Hastings, at that time the senior officer present and acting commander of the regiment], said; "If any of the Fifth had a spite against Mosby's men to ride out." This was wrong, we all had a spite against them, but we did not feel like murdering them in cold blood. The only proper way, would have been to detail a firing party, under orders. Only two men rode out; one was a man who just had a brother killed by them at Berryville; the other was a bugler of the regiment who had nothing but his own spleen to vent.
> The boys, one about sixteen, the other about eighteen years old, were to be shot. They begged of the chaplain a chance to run for their lives, but no such boon was allowed them, they were placed a short distance away and the two men began firing at them. The first shot killed the younger, but the other received two or three balls before he fell. I pronounced this barbarous, and some of the boys muttered at me, but I did not care, why should we be obliged to see those boys shot down like dogs, right at their doors in this savage style? Two others [referring to Overby and Carter] were led along to a piece of wood and hung to a tree. This was a terrible warning to bushwhackers, and this kind of work was carried out until Mosby was obliged to quit.

Avery's account, however, appears to be in conflict with many of the other accounts of what happened that day in September of 1864, particularly those provided by the various Confederate witnesses. At least two of the victims, Henry Rhodes and Lucien Love, were teenagers, both being 17 years old, and the mechanics of the execution of Rhodes seems to fit Avery's account. However, practically all Confederate accounts agree that Rhodes was killed alone while Jones and Love, of those who were shot, were killed together.[6] In addition, if Rhodes was one of the two boys killed by the soldiers of the 5th Michigan in Avery's account, where was the boy's mother, which all of the Confederate accounts agree, was present at her son's execution (or as the Confederate sources termed it, murder)? If the mother had been present, wouldn't Avery have mentioned that fact, disgusted as he was with the executions in general?

Although Confederate accounts state that Jones and Love were shot together, there is no mention of Jones' age. Although he might have been a teenager, the various accounts seem to agree that the only teenagers executed were Rhodes and Love. Age aside, Avery's account still seems to come closest to matching the accounts of the deaths of Jones and Love, since they were the only ones of those who were shot who were killed together. However, Avery's account reads as if the two were killed in front of the whole 5th Michigan Cavalry Regiment. Purportedly they were killed in a town lot located behind the Front Royal Methodist Church.[7] Thus the next question is, would the lot have been big enough to allow the shootings to be conducted in front of the entire 5th Michigan?

In addition, Avery's account, although it does not state where the two were killed, does refer to only two men of the 5th Michigan as being the killers while other Union witnesses stated: "The squad of executioners then turned and walked away." [8] Thus it appears as if there were more than two soldiers involved in these killings and that the killings were conducted with more deliberation and organization than the killings described by Avery. Finally, Avery's account only mentions four men being killed at Front Royal, not six; which is the generally accepted number.

Another Union witness to the entire affair was Capt. Theodore Walter Bean, provost marshal (or chief military policeman) for the 1st Cavalry Division (which included Lowell's Reserve Cavalry Brigade and Custer's Michigan Cavalry Brigade). He reported — during the skirmishing with Mosby's Rangers — seeing in the distance what he believed to have been Custer's 5th Michigan overrunning some of the fleeing raiders. This report seems to be confirmed by accounts which state that as Capt. Chapman and Capt. Frankland were attempting to lead their Rangers in a break out, they had to fight their way through some Union troops who had circled the town and were blocking their escape route through the Chester Gap. Could these troops have been the 5th Michigan Cavalry Regiment? Capt. Bean also reported that Lt. Charles McMaster was definitely captured and shot during the attack upon the wagon train. There is also a theory that in its pursuit of Mosby's Rangers, the 2nd U.S. Cavalry split into two parts; one directly pursued the raiders and the other was the force that circled the town in an attempt to cut off the rangers. Although this is a definite possibility, no primary documentation for this to have happened has been discovered.

Could the two Rangers who were killed in Avery's account have been in addition to the six men who are recorded as having been executed in and around Front Royal that day? Could the 5th Michigan not even have been in the vicinity of the four locations where the other executions occurred?

From what Avery does not seem to know, it could very well be that the 5th Michigan Cavalry Regiment never entered the town of Front Royal at all except possibly to march through it with the rest of the Michigan Cavalry Brigade with Custer at its head, as has been described by Dr. R.C. Buck in his testimony.[9] Dr. Buck is important because he was apparently the only witness, Union or Confederate, to the events in Front Royal who actually describes having seen Custer in Front Royal at all on that day.

Gen. Merritt, in his official report for the period between August 9, 1864, and October 20, 1864, states as follows: "...The command on the following day [September 23, 1864], returned to Front Royal. Near this town, the advance of the Reserve Brigade encountered a body of guerillas, under a Capt. Chapman, who were in the act of capturing an ambulance train of our wounded. The gang was quickly dispersed with a loss of 18 killed. [Merritt does not clearly state whether the 18 killed were Union or Confederate soldiers, or both.] Lt. McMaster of the 2nd U.S. Cavalry was mortally wounded in this affair being shot after he was taken prisoner and robbed...." In their official reports, neither Torbert, Merritt, nor Lowell makes any mention of having executed Confederate prisoners of war. Custer, in his report, makes no mention at all of his men being involved in anything that occurred in Front Royal on that day.

Capt. Robert S. Smith, 2nd U.S. Cavalry Regiment, in a history of the regiment, also stated that McMaster surrendered to Mosby's attacking

70

Rangers and was then robbed and shot by them, mortally wounding him. He also reported that a total of 13 prisoners were taken. (Perhaps the two boys — who according to Avery were shot by the soldiers of the 5th Michigan — were among the additional prisoners who have literally disappeared from the accounts of the Front Royal Incident, or perhaps they all were among the 18 reported killed by Gen. Merritt and that the 5th Michigan rather than shooting prisoners simply was not taking any.)

In addition, there are records which indicate that McMaster actually died in a Union military hospital on October 15, 1864, three weeks after the incident at Front Royal. This, in the face of the fact that all of the accounts of the incident written by Mosby's men or quoting Confederate sources state that McMaster was killed instantly in the attack and that he was killed in the line of duty, not after he had surrendered. This discrepancy alone indicates that all of the accounts provided by Mosby and his Rangers about what happened at Front Royal should be considered at least suspect and therefore should be taken with a grain of salt.

The discrepancy concerning the actual number of prisoners taken at Front Royal has never been explained. All other accounts, Union and Confederate, appear to agree that only six of Mosby's men were taken prisoner and that those six were executed, four by being shot to death and the other two by being hanged. No explanation has ever been given about what happened to the other seven prisoners. If they actually existed at all, the simplest explanation is also the most likely — they were turned over to the proper authorities and they were eventually incarcerated in a prisoner of war camp. In addition, there appears to be only one mention of other casualties (aside from Merritt's official report), Union or Confederate. According to this report, Union casualties were estimated at about 20 for the entire affair. This includes the attack upon the wagon train, the skirmish with Mosby's Rangers who were fleeing from the wagon train, and the pursuit, which had resulted in the taking of the Confederate prisoners. No one appears to have been keeping a real record of the haul of prisoners, whether there were six of them, as most accounts record, or whether there were 13 of them, as stated by Capt. Smith in his history of the 2nd U.S. Cavalry Regiment.

Only Merritt's report officially mentions any other possible casualties, dead or wounded, suffered on either side in the original attack upon the wagon train, or in the subsequent skirmish as the Rangers fled through the barrier created by the Union troops (whether or not this was the 5th Michigan Cavalry Regiment) who purportedly maneuvered around Front Royal and into a blocking position, or in the final pursuit of the fleeing Rangers by the Union cavalry. The only primary source whose testimony indicates who those blocking troops may have been, specifically Capt. Bean's, seems to support the possibility that Custer had dispatched one of his five regiments, specifically the 5th Michigan Cavalry Regiment, to the assistance of Lowell's Reserve Cavalry Brigade, and that this regiment may have indeed attempted to cut off the retreat of Mosby's men.

Since Mosby supported his account of what happened at Front Royal with Southern newspapers, it is at least fair to wonder what Northern newspapers had to say if anything at all about the incident. The Northern newspapers' reports concerning what happened at Front Royal were contradictory. The *New York Herald* reported on October 5, 1864, in a dispatch from Front Royal dated October 1, 1864 (one week after the Front Royal Incident), that troops under Merritt's command shot or hanged 12 of Mosby's men for wantonly killing an officer and two soldiers. In this first report there was no mention at all of Custer's involvement. It is likely that the sources of this dispatch were Union troops who were on the scene, particularly Capt. Smith, who claimed that 13 prisoners were taken. A month later the *Herald* printed a second dispatch, this one stating that Custer was responsible for the executions at Front Royal. It is likely that the sources of this dispatch were the residents of Front Royal or the reports of the incident that were carried in Confederate newspapers.

It is also possible that the writing and the publishing of the second dispatch was sparked by the letter to Sheridan (which Sheridan never acknowledged receiving), which Mosby wrote after he had conducted his reprisal for the executions of his Rangers at Front Royal and a later incident which occurred in Rappahannock County involving Sheridan's 2nd Cavalry Division, Department of West Virginia, which was then under the command of Col. William Powell. Until the publication of Mosby's memoirs in 1917, the second dispatch in the *New York Herald* appears to have been the first public accusation in the North that Custer was responsible for the executions at Front Royal. Thus it is likely that whoever wrote the second dispatch received his information either from Confederate sources or at some point that he had, or was given, access to Mosby's letter.

One of those sources could have been Dr. Buck of Front Royal; he reported that on the day of the Front Royal Incident, he saw Custer riding through the village at the head of his men. However, his statement has a number of inconsistencies:

1. He implied that Custer was in command of the troops in Front Royal, which he was not.

2. He stated that Custer commanded a division, which he did not. (At the time of the Front Royal Incident Custer's command was only the Michigan Cavalry Brigade. Within days after the incident Custer was named, very briefly, to command the 2nd Cavalry Division, Department of West Virginia, but within days of that announcement Custer was named to command the 3rd Cavalry Division when James Wilson was reassigned.)

3. Dr. Buck claimed to have recognized Custer, but makes no mention at all of Torbert, Merritt or Lowell, who are all documented to have definitely been on the scene in Front Royal at the time of the executions.

4. Dr. Buck's statement also said that Mosby's men were ambushed in the fighting, which had resulted in their captures. If there was an ambush, it was the federal troops escorting the wagon train at the head of Torbert's column that were ambushed, and both sides ended up sharing the surprise.

5. Finally, Dr. Buck did not state that he had actually personally witnessed any of the executions.

7

WHO GAVE THE ORDERS?

By the autumn of 1864 the American Civil War had changed from a limited war being fought for limited objectives to a total war waged for total objectives. There were only two options, either the Confederate States of America would win their independence or they would be forced to return to the Union. As part of that transformation had come another truth. If the Union won, it was clear that the Southern way of life — epitomized by the "peculiar institution" of slavery — would be utterly destroyed.

From the very beginning the Southern states had been on the short end of the stick by almost any measure of comparison with the North. They could not match the North in population, industrial output, railroad mileage, or mechanization. (The McCormick reapers and threshing machines became Lincoln's secret weapons because they allowed Northern agriculture, in the Midwest especially, to maintain its output despite the shortage of farm labor that resulted from the large numbers of men from that region who entered the army, as noted by James Bissland in his *Blood, Tears, & Glory: How Ohioans Won the Civil War.*) In its desperation, the South soon turned to such strategic alternative efforts as guerrilla warfare.

In turning to guerrilla war in areas such as Missouri in the west and in the Shenandoah Valley in Virginia, Union political and military officials became convinced that the Confederacy was moving beyond the pale. Union soldiers were being killed in any number of incidents where they could have been taken prisoner, and earlier in the war probably would have been taken prisoner.

When it came to Mosby and his Rangers, Maj. Gen. Philip Henry Sheridan, commander of the Army of the Shenandoah, was somewhat two-faced. Depending on the impression that he wished to convey and, most particularly, on the audience that he was conveying that impression to, Mosby and his Rangers tended to be either a nuisance which one good

General Phil Sheridan confers with his primary subordinates. Seated, left to right, are Wesley Merritt, George Crook, and George A. Custer. Standing are Sheridan, left, and James William Forsyth (woodcut taken from a photograph, Library of Congress, Prints and Photographs Division).

regiment could clear out at any time or they were a looming threat to his entire army that not even a full corps of infantry could or would be able to eradicate properly.

For instance, Sheridan maintained at times that Mosby and his 43rd Virginia Battalion of Partisan Rangers acted more as his "provost guard," since just the threat that they might be in the area was enough to cause his soldiers to reduce their tendency to straggle as they moved up and down the Shenandoah Valley either in pursuit of or retreat from Lt. Gen. Jubal Early and his Valley District Army. In general Union and Confederate army officers found that it was practically impossible to keep their soldiers from straggling while they were on the march, i.e. falling out whenever a whim or a need took them and then catching up to their unit later.

On the other hand, Sheridan was also writing to Lt. Gen. Ulysses S. Grant, general-in-chief of all the Union armies, stating, "Every train, every small party, and every straggler has been bushwhacked," making it appear that Mosby was everywhere. It seems that Sheridan was gearing his messages (at least to Grant) about Mosby to the level of compliance he was prepared to give each particular directive received from Grant concerning the movements of Sheridan's own army. If he was prepared to comply with a particular directive, Mosby was not a particular problem. If he was not, then Mosby was such a serious problem that Sheridan found himself unable to comply, particularly if it involved movements that he did not want to make.

The situation at Harpers Ferry offers a prime example. At one point, during Sheridan's Shenandoah Valley Campaign, the commander of the Union garrison at Harpers Ferry, West Virginia, wanted some help from Sheridan in defending the politically and militarily sensitive railroad against repeated Confederate incursions, for some of which Mosby and his Rangers were directly responsible. (It must be noted that Mosby's Rangers was not the only guerrilla force operating in the Shenandoah Valley, although it was the most prominent.) Sheridan, however, did not want the strength of his army frittered away by bits and pieces in chasing the "Gray Ghost." He was somewhat unsympathetic and responded as follows: "If the 12th Pennsylvania Cavalry cannot keep that country clear of guerrillas, I will take the shoulder straps off of every officer belonging to it and dismount the regiment in disgrace."

However, the best evidence of Mosby's effectiveness can be found in a directive drafted by Gen. Grant on August 16, 1864, just as Sheridan's Shenandoah Valley Campaign was beginning and just nine days after Sheridan officially took command of the Middle Military Division, which had been newly created by Grant, and it's Army of the Shenandoah: "The families of most of Mosby's men are known, and can be collected, I think they should be taken and kept at Fort McHenry (located within the harbor of Baltimore, Md.), or some other secure place, as hostages for the good conduct of Mosby and his men. Where any of Mosby's men are caught, hang them without trial."

The first portion of this directive would have established what would have amounted to the first concentration camp in history. In point of fact, it was never actually carried out. The last sentence of Grant's directive, however, in effect declared that it was now open season on any of Mosby's men. It was this part of Grant's directive that provided the justification of the executions at Front Royal.

Grant also directed that an entire division of cavalry be utilized to remove Mosby. Sheridan was not about to lose the services of an entire cavalry division just to chase down a few hundred guerrillas. That part of Grant's intentions Sheridan ignored, or when pressed went back to playing down the success of Mosby's raids. However, Sheridan eventually did go as far as to instruct all of his commanders to arrest able-bodied male citizens under the age of 50 who were suspected of aiding or assisting or belonging to Mosby's command or other guerrilla bands.

Such precautions (including those in Grant's directive) are not recommended against the ineffective.

There was no denying that Philip Sheridan himself was an exceedingly hard man and within days of the Front Royal Incident an event would occur that would demonstrate that it was not a good idea to provoke Sheridan. As for Custer, he would prove to be prepared to carry out any orders issued by Sheridan.

It was within this period, shortly after the Front Royal Incident, that Custer himself would be promoted from brigade to divisional command, eventually taking command of the 3rd Cavalry Division. Sheridan may have been secretly pleased when James H. Wilson was unexpectedly named chief of cavalry for the Military Division of the Mississippi, providing the vacancy for Custer's promotion. Wilson's tenure as commander of the 3rd Cavalry Division had been less than brilliant, despite what Wilson's memoirs and his admirers had to say. Not only had he proved somewhat slack in executing Sheridan's orders, but he also had demonstrated a tendency of leading his division into tight spots, at least once being extricated by Custer and his Michigan Cavalry Brigade, instead of victories. On the very day (September 30, 1864, just one week after the Front Royal Incident) that Sheridan was informed of Wilson's transfer, he named Custer as Wilson's permanent replacement.

Just days later on October 3, 1864, Sheridan's chief engineer, 2nd Lt. John R. Meigs, in the company of two orderlies was on his way to a celebratory party being held at Custer's headquarters. Near the village of Dayton, about a mile and a half inside Union lines, Meigs and the two orderlies, were accosted by another trio, all six of the men wearing waterproof ponchos against the drizzling rain. The ponchos made it impossible for the men in either party to immediately distinguish whether or not their opposite numbers were wearing Union or Confederate uniforms (although it was later claimed that the Confederates were in fact wearing

Union uniforms). Meigs and the two orderlies only realized that the other three were Confederates after it was too late to avoid a confrontation. Both sides shouted for the others to surrender and shots rang out. After it was all over Meigs lay on the ground, dead, having been killed instantly.[1]

One of the two orderlies escaped, rode back to Sheridan's headquarters, and reported that Lt. Meigs had been shot down in cold blood "without even the chance to give himself up." Sheridan was enraged at the death of the popular young officer, who had helped Sheridan plan his entire campaign. Meigs was a topographical engineer and cartographer who had just graduated from West Point. He had made the maps of the Shenandoah Valley which Sheridan had used to familiarize himself with the general terrain of the Valley. Sheridan immediately blamed Mosby and his Rangers for the outrage.

Some years later the three Confederates involved in the confrontation gave a different story. They were not members of Mosby's 43rd Virginia. They were members of Brig. Gen. Thomas Lafayette Rosser's Laurel Brigade, many of whose soldiers (like Mosby's men) were natives of the Valley and who had newly arrived as reinforcements to Early's Valley District Army. The three Confederates were on a scouting mission and according to them, Meigs had fired the first shot, severely wounding one of the Confederates, whose own pistol had misfired. The other two returned Meigs' fire, killing him. The wounded Confederate, George W. Martin, whose pistol had misfired and who therefore had had nothing to do with the death of young Meigs, was forced into hiding for a number of years after Meigs' father, Montgomery C. Meigs, the Union quartermaster general, placed a $1,000 bounty on his head under the mistaken belief that Martin had murdered his son.

First thing the next morning Sheridan sent an aide to Custer's headquarters summoning him for an immediate meeting.[2] Artist James Taylor happened to be at Sheridan's headquarters that morning, and he described what happened next:

> I happened to be at headquarters, professionally, in connection with the dead engineer, while Custer was closeted with his chief receiving his orders — and saw them appear. Never shall I forget the dramatic episode of Custer, while his chief stood by reiterating his stern edict — vaulting into the saddle and exclaiming as he dashed away — "Look out for smoke!"
> News spread rapidly, and soon the hill was alive with blue coats awaiting the outcome. Ever quick to obey orders like a true soldier, however,

disagreeable the task, "Yellow Hair" [indicating that this popular *nom de guerre* predated Custer's service upon the frontier] was prompt on the spot with his command when we were treated to a sight which must have appeased the ghost of him (Lt. Meigs) to whom the holocaust was offered (and spread above like a funeral pall)....

The prescribed area included the hamlet of Dayton, but when a few houses in the immediate neighborhood of the scene of the tragedy had been fired, Sheridan relented and sent orders to Custer to cease his devastating work, but to fetch away all of the able-bodied males as prisoners.

It soon became apparent after this incident that Sheridan was determined to deal with any possible threat posed by Mosby and his command. While he did not dispatch a full cavalry division to deal with Mosby, Sheridan did create what would today be called a special operations unit, one whose primary mission was the destruction of Mosby and his 43rd Virginia.

Sheridan created the Independent Scouts and placed them under the command of Maj. Richard Blazer from West Virginia. Blazer and his men were equipped with the best weapons available, Spencer repeating rifles, and were turned lose. Blazer adopted the hit-and-run tactics of Mosby, acting upon information supplied by spies or Union sympathizers. The unit came to an end after it had annoyed Mosby enough that he sent his Rangers, under one of his two sub-commanders, Maj. A.E. Richards, looking for Blazer's Scouts. In a running fight Mosby's Rangers triumphed and captured Blazer and all but 29 of his men; Blazer was sent to Libby Prison in Richmond and was one of the few adversaries that Mosby respected.

These and other incidents, egged on by Grant's directive that whenever any of Mosby's Rangers were captured they were to be summarily executed, created the atmosphere that resulted in the executions at Front Royal and in Rappahannock County. It was a situation that as commander of the 43rd Virginia Mosby found to be intolerable and which he was determined to bring to an end.

While John S. Mosby to the end of his life believed that George A. Custer had ordered and participated in the execution of his six men at Front Royal, it is of considerable importance to note who most likely actually ordered those executions and who actually carried them out.

The first and most important evidence about who ordered the executions is included in a letter by Col. Charles Russell Lowell, commander of the Reserve Cavalry Brigade, to his wife, Josephine Shaw Lowell, the sister of Col. Robert Gould Shaw, the commander of the American Civil War's most famous colored unit — the 54th Massachusetts Volunteer Infantry Regiment. The letter was dated October 5, 1864, just 12 days after the incident at Front Royal.[3]

Lowell himself was something of a renaissance man. He was a consummate scholar, a skilled bookkeeper, a mechanic, a railroad treasurer, an iron-master, and he became a superb cavalry commander. He was born in Boston on January 2, 1835. He graduated from Harvard at the age of 19 and was his class valedictorian. From there he gained experience as a bookkeeper and as a common laborer, even though his family was numbered among the Boston elite. Due to poor health he spent two years touring the Southern states and Europe.

At the start of the Civil War he was given a captaincy in the 6th U.S. Cavalry Regiment — quite an achievement for a man straight from civilian life with no formal military training. Following McClellan's Peninsular Campaign, Lowell joined McClellan's staff as an aide-de-camp, where he served during the Battle of Antietam. (This is when Lowell first met Custer, who was also serving as one of McClellan's aides.) After the battle Lowell was named colonel of the brand new 2nd Massachusetts Cavalry Regiment.

He was first advanced to brigade command in the summer and autumn of 1863. In July of 1864, his regiment formed the basis of a provisional brigade. In September he was given command of the Reserve Brigade, and his regiment was duly transferred to that unit. Lowell was killed in action on October 19, 1864, during the Battle of Cedar Creek (just two weeks after that letter to his wife). His commission as a brevet brigadier general of volunteers arrived at Sheridan's headquarters on the evening of his death.

The pertinent portions of Lowell's October 5, 1864, letter to his wife are as follows: "I was sorry enough the other day that my brigade should have had a part in the hanging and shooting of some of Mosby's men who were taken — I believe that some punishment was deserved — but I hardly think we were within the laws of war, and any violation of them opens the door to all sorts of barbarity — it was all by order of the division commander, however...."

The 2nd U.S. Cavalry Regiment was part of the Lowell's Reserve Cavalry Brigade and soldiers from that regiment (according to most accounts) apparently conducted several of the executions, in particular the hangings of two of Mosby's men. According to various testimonies by Union soldiers at the scene of the executions Lowell, Wesley Merritt (his divisional commander) and Alfred T.A. Torbert (the commander of all of the soldiers involved in the Luray Valley expedition) were all present at Front Royal and were involved in the execution. There is no statement by any of these witnesses, however, that Custer himself was actually present, although that simple fact has not kept historians from speculating that he was.

It must be reiterated that the only person who actually claimed to see Custer at Front Royal was Dr. R.C. Buck, a Front Royal resident, whose testimony has already been reviewed. It must be remembered that Dr. Buck was a civilian. He had no knowledge about the organization and command of the Union forces, occupying his town. Although his statement implies that Custer was in command, he most definitely was not. However, Custer was simply the most well known of the Union officers at Front Royal that day.

It must again be remembered that Dr. Buck's statement boils down to one simple fact: he saw Custer riding at the head of his brigade (which Dr. Buck thought was a division) through the streets of Front Royal and he most likely saw this happen after the executions had already occurred, since the column was apparently on its way out of town. Dr. Buck never claimed in his statement that at any time he personally saw or heard Custer giving any orders for the execution of anyone on that day.

But, if Custer did not give the orders, then who did?

Modern historians seem to be divided upon the subject. Jeffry D. Wert, in his books *Custer: The Controversial Life of George Armstrong Custer* and *Mosby Rangers,* states flatly that Custer was there, but apparently had no hand in the execution of the prisoners. Wert also maintains that at least two of the men were killed by members of the 6th Michigan Cavalry Regiment, which was of course part of Custer's Michigan Cavalry Brigade, even though the only account by a member of the Michigan Cavalry Brigade which describes any executions, that of James Henry Avery, states that it was the 5th Michigan Cavalry that was involved and that it was involved only upon the orders of the senior officer present and its acting regimental commander, Maj. Smith Hastings, and not Custer. There is no mention of any orders being received from Custer, nor is there any mention of Custer being present. Wert, however, does agree that the actual orders were in all likelihood issued by Torbert, or Merritt, who were acting under what they understood to be Sheridan's intentions.

Lowell's letter makes it clear that soldiers from his brigade conducted at least some if not all of the executions, since he mentions both the shootings and the hangings in reference to his men's actions. There are versions of this tale in which Lowell's men are acknowledged to have taken part in the hangings, with soldiers from Custer's brigade, in particular those of the 6th Michigan Cavalry Regiment, being involved in at least the shooting death of Henry Rhodes. Wert accepts this version. In his letter, however, Lowell accepts the responsibility for both, making it clear, however, he had grave objections to the entire affair. He made no mention of Custer at all or of the participation in the executions by any troops belonging to any other command but his own. It was Lowell apparently — and not Custer — who was directed to carry out the executions.

Let's take another look at Lowell's October 5 letter to his wife. He said that the executions were conducted at the orders of his divisional commander. That divisional commander was Wesley Merritt, and his 1st Cavalry Division included both Lowell's Reserve Cavalry Brigade and Custer's Michigan Cavalry Brigade. But, there is another question — was Merritt acting on his own or was he simply passing along the orders of his immediate superior, Bvt. Maj. Gen. Alfred T.A. Torbert? Everyone agrees that Torbert was there. At least one officer on Merritt's staff, Capt. Theodore Walter Bean, Merritt's provost marshal, stated for a fact that the two hangings, at least, were conducted under Torbert's direct orders.[4] Even without that statement, it does not seem likely that Merritt would have taken it upon himself to issue such an order, particularly if his direct superior was on hand. Therefore, there can be no other conclusion than that the orders for the executions were either issued at the instigation of Torbert or with his full and complete approval.

Torbert would have definitely known about Grant's directive of August 16, 1864. He knew, or thought he knew, just what Grant and Sheridan wanted. Torbert himself certainly knew about Sheridan's volcanic temper and he may even have feared what Sheridan's reaction would be when he discovered how badly Torbert had stumbled in his failure to execute Sheridan's grand design for the complete destruction of Early's army. He may have therefore sought to use the capture and execution of Mosby's

Rangers at Front Royal as something of a consolation prize, particularly if he could have persuaded some of his prisoners to betray the location of Mosby's headquarters and thus eliminate what was (either a major or minor) thorn from Sheridan's side.

The testimony about what happened at Front Royal came from soldiers from the 1st Rhode Island Cavalry Regiment who were serving as the escort for Torbert's headquarters and staff.[5] Frederic Denison, chaplain of the 1st Rhode Island Cavalry, stated simply that the six prisoners were executed upon orders from Torbert himself. Sgt. Samuel Willis, also of the 1st Rhode Island, provided more information. He said that Torbert gave two of the prisoners (believed to have been Overby and Carter, although they are not identified) the choice of providing information or of being hung. According to Sgt. Willis, they both defied Torbert and were therefore hung. In addition, Sgt. Willis said that Torbert also ordered the executions of the other four prisoners, who were shot to death.

The hangings reportedly were witnessed by soldiers of the 2nd U.S. Cavalry Regiment — members of which may have carried them out — along with soldiers of the 17th Pennsylvania Cavalry Regiment, which belonged to the Brigade of Thomas Devin, which had remained with Sheridan's main force. It is likely that these particular soldiers of the 17th Pennsylvania had been detailed as orderlies and were with the Luray Valley expedition, most likely while serving as part of Torbert's staff.

Robert Craig Wallace, an officer of the 5th Michigan Cavalry Regiment who was attached to Torbert's staff and who also witnessed the executions, supports the basic testimony provided by Denison and Sgt. Willis. In addition, after the war he specifically exonerated Custer from any personal involvement in the executions. In a letter to Edward W. Whitaker, Custer's first biographer, he stated; "I never heard that Custer ordered it done, nor did I see him during the affair."

Another person who exonerated Custer was his West Point roommate, friend, and American Civil War opponent Thomas L. Rosser. Rosser participated in a post war newspaper debate stating that in 1873, when he and Custer renewed their friendship, Custer had told him that he (Custer) was not involved in any way with the executions that had occurred in Front Royal. Furthermore, Wallace was also among those who apparently believed that what sparked the executions was the reported death of Lt. Charles McMaster, after his surrender during the original attack on the wagon train by Mosby's Rangers. Like Capt. Bean, he believed that McMaster had died shortly after being shot and that what McMaster said was in effect a deathbed statement. It is likely he believed that McMaster was dead since he had been shot in the head, and such a wound is almost always immediately or quite soon thereafter fatal. However, both Wallace and Bean seem to have been wrong about McMaster dying shortly after he was shot, since McMaster is recorded as having actually died in a Union military hospital on October 15, 1864, about three weeks after the incident.

Wallace's account of the executions also differs from that given by Sgt. Willis. In his account Sgt. Willis stated that Torbert ordered the shootings, as well as the hangings. Wallace in his account, however, suggests that the shootings were more of a spontaneous reaction to the death of Lt. McMaster — and the reports that he had been robbed and shot after he had surrendered — rather than being deliberately ordered by Torbert, Merritt or Lowell.

First, it should be remembered that the six executions actually occurred in four separate locations using two different forms of execution. If the intention was to execute all six of the prisoners, wouldn't it have been easier to have gathered all six in one location? And why use two different methods of execution, hanging two and shooting four?

Looking at accounts of the executions themselves, it appears that the individual executions of Rhodes and Anderson may well have been spontaneous. These shootings actually occurred away from the town and do not appear to have been particularly well organized. The shootings of Love and Jones, however, did occur within the town of Front Royal and appear to have been better organized with indications that some kind of a firing squad actually conducted these two executions, thus appearing to support Lowell's contention that his men did conduct the hangings and at least two of the shootings.

Secondly, if Custer had himself ordered soldiers of the 2nd U.S. Cavalry Regiment to conduct the executions, he would have been giving what would have amounted to illegal orders, since he would have been acting outside of the chain of command. The soldiers could have quite properly refused to carry out such orders since Custer was not part of their chain of command.

Thus, it appears clear that Torbert must bear the direct responsibility at least for the deaths of the two Rangers who were hanged, since it appears that these deaths were due to his direct orders. Although at least one source indicates that the four who were shot were also killed on Torbert's orders, other accounts make it appear that there is enough reasonable doubt as to whether Torbert gave any orders for the shooting deaths of at least two of the other four who were executed. It appears to be at least possible that those deaths may have been more the case of the individual soldiers deciding not to take any prisoners (including the incident described by Avery of the 5th Michigan Cavalry) rather than there being any orders actually issued to shoot those particular prisoners.

8

MOSBY'S REVENGE

John S. Mosby wanted revenge for his seven men at Front Royal who were executed without cause, as he saw it, or even a semblance of a trial. But, his determination to retaliate had become even more pronounced when a seventh soldier of his 43rd Virginia was executed. This time, however, it was clear that Custer had not been involved.

Col. William Powell, then in command of Sheridan's 2nd Cavalry Division, Department of West Virginia, had caught one of Mosby's men, Absalom Willis, on October 13, 1864, in Rappahannock County. In this case the execution was somewhat spectacular. Powell's men had first tied the rope they used to hang Willis with to the top of a young sapling, which was then bent nearly double. When it was released it shot Willis skyward in an abrupt, strangled flight. Powell was jubilant about the execution he had ordered. Powell stated in his report: "I wish it distinctly understood by the Rebel authorities that if two to one is not sufficient I will increase it to 22 to one, and leave the consequences in the hands of my Government."[1]

From Powell's report it is clear that this particular execution was in retaliation for such incidents as the deaths of Lt. John R. Meigs, Col. Cornelius Tolles, Dr. Emil Ohlenschlager and others (mainly stragglers or foragers caught by Mosby's Rangers and summarily dealt with). Although Mosby's Rangers usually adhered to the normal laws of war regarding prisoners who were taken in battle, if they caught Union soldiers red handed forging (or stealing) from residents of the areas they were operating in, they often took drastic measures.

Mosby probably did not see the jeering statements made in Powell's report concerning the execution of Willis. However, considering the amount of espionage under way by both sides and the fact that it was extremely difficult to keep any kind of a secret during the American Civil War, it is quite possible that Mosby knew at least the gist of what Powell had written in his report. If Mosby had known, it would have been Powell's attitude which would have put Powell and any of his men beyond the pale along with Custer and his men.

By this time Mosby was sufficiently recovered from his bullet wound to take personal action. However, Mosby was trained as a lawyer and he had decided to seek the backing of a higher authority before he took his vengeance and moved forward with his planned reprisal. That higher authority was Gen. Robert E. Lee, the commander of the Army of Northern Virginia. As such Mosby reported directly to Lee (and was one of Lee's primary sources of intelligence in Mosby's area of operations within the Shenandoah Valley and beyond, since he also operated within the vicinity of Washington, D.C., and even the state of Maryland) and apparently was not under the authority of Lt. Gen. Jubal Early, commander of the Valley District Army.

Mosby therefore dispatched to Lee the following official communication:

> Near Middleburg,
> October 29, 1864

Gen. R.E. Lee
Commanding Army of Northern Virginia
General:

I do desire to bring through you to the notice of the government the brutal conduct of the enemy toward citizens of this district since their occupation of the Manassas Road. When they first adventured upon the road we smashed one of their trains, killing and wounding a large number. In retaliation they arrested a large number of civilians living along the line, and have been in the habit of sending an installment of them on each train. As my command has done nothing in contrary to the usages of war it seems to be that some attempt at least ought to be made to prevent a repetition of such barbarities. During my absence from my command the enemy captured six of my men, near Front Royal; these were immediately hung by order and in the presence of General Custer. They also hung another lately in Rappahannock. It is my purpose to hang an equal number of Custer's men whenever I capture them. There was passed by the last U.S. Congress a bill of pains and penalties against guerillas and as they profess to consider my men within the definition of the term, I think it would be well to come to some understanding with the enemy with reference to them. The bearer of this, my adjutant, will give you all the information you desire concerning the enemy in this country. Of course, I did not allow the conduct of the enemy toward citizens to deter me from the use of any legitimate weapon against them, but after throwing off the train, they guarded the road so heavily that no opportunities were offered for striking any successful blow, and I thought that I would be more usefully employed in annoying Sheridan's communications. I received the list of deserters you sent me. I will do what I can toward arresting them, but none are with my command.

John S. Mosby
Lieutenant Colonel

Upon receipt of this message from Mosby, Gen. Lee immediately decided to seek an endorsement for Mosby's intended reprisal from his civilian superior, Confederate Secretary of War James Sedden. He therefore forwarded Mosby's letter to Richmond with the following endorsement:

Headquarters,
November 3, 1864

Respectfully referred to the honorable Secretary of War
for his information:

I do not know how we can prevent the cruel conduct of the enemy toward our citizens. I have directed Colonel Mosby, through his adjutant, to hang an equal number of Custer's men in retaliation for those executed by him.

R.E. Lee
General

H.L. Clay, assistant adjutant general, affixed a second endorsement to the message as follows:

Adjutant and Inspector General's Office
November 11, 1864

Respectfully submitted to the Secretary of War.

H.L. Clay
Assistant adjutant general

Eventually, three days later (and 11 days after Lee sought Sedden's endorsement) word of Mosby's intentions were finally kicked all the way up the Confederate War Department's chain of command to Confederate Secretary of War James Sedden, who appended his endorsement (a week after Mosby had actually committed his reprisal) as follows:

November 14, 1864

Adjutant General:

General Lee's instructions are cordially approved. In addition, if our citizens are found exposed on any captured train signal vengeance should be taken on all conductors and officers found on it, and every male passenger of the enemy's country should be treated as prisoners.

J.A. Sedden
Secretary

Having received permission from General Lee, Mosby wasted no time waiting for further possible agreement from any higher authorities. Within a week Mosby acted upon Lee's verbal permission, which was given to his adjutant. Receiving an endorsement by the secretary of war was not worth any delay in Mosby's eyes.

Mosby conducted his reprisal on November 7, 1864.[2] The preparations began innocently enough on a quiet Sunday morning (November 6, 1864) when 27 Union prisoners of war were ushered with no explanation about what was happening out of a brick storehouse located in Rectortown, Virginia. Mosby had been stockpiling Union prisoners of war ever since he had been informed on September 29, 1864, of the executions at Front Royal. It has generally been supposed (and Mosby never did anything to dispel the notion) that these men were drawn particularly from among those prisoners, which had been taken from Custer's former Michigan Cavalry Brigade command and his current 3rd Cavalry Division command for the sole purpose of the retaliation Mosby had in mind. However, Mosby did not limit the stockpiling of prisoners from either Custer's present or his former command, including infantrymen and artillerymen who had never been under Custer's direct command. (It is possible that his Rangers simply did not capture enough prisoners from either the Michigan Cavalry Brigade or from the 3rd Cavalry Division to supply the seven men necessary for the man-for-man reprisal that Mosby had in mind.)

The 27 prisoners, upon being gathered together, were then marched to the banks of Goose Creek, about half a mile away. Some, but definitely not all, of this specially selected pool of 27 prisoners belonged to Custer's commands, both past and present, and it is not known if there were any men from Powell's 2nd Cavalry Division, Department of West Virginia, which was responsible for the execution of Absalom Willis. However, when considering Mosby's retaliation, it is interesting to consider the actual composition of this group.

At the time of the Front Royal incident, the 3rd Cavalry Division had been commanded by Brig. Gen. James H. Wilson and had been dispatched to cover the flank of Torbert's retreat from the Luray Valley after Confederate Brig. Gen. Williams C. Wickham and his division of Confederate cavalry had bested him. Mosby, in his memoirs, his letter to Lee and a letter to Sheridan explaining his actions (see below), made it appear that he intended to confine his reprisal only to those responsible for the execution of his Rangers. The fact that he included soldiers from the 3rd Cavalry Division and other units (infantry and artillery) — which held no responsibility for the executions — demonstrated that Mosby lied when he claimed he was only retaliating against Custer and Powell and those soldiers whom they commanded when his Rangers were executed at Front Royal and in Rappahannock County. In truth, of the seven men eventually selected to die on Mosby's orders, only two were actually members of the Michigan Cavalry Brigade.

All 27 of the prisoners were lined up along Goose Creek and then made to draw slips of paper from a hat. Twenty of those slips of paper which were part of the macabre lottery were simply that, blank pieces of paper. The other seven — one each for each of Mosby's men executed at Front Royal and in Rappahannock County — were marked with a number. Mosby intended to have executed each and every one of those seven men in retaliation for the men who had been executed (he thought) by Custer and Powell.

Of the men who were forced to draw those slips of paper, some of them simply stared into space. Others, once they understood what was happening, prayed. There were a few of them who simply broke down.

Among the prisoners was a young drummer boy, who couldn't possibly have been part of either Custer's or Powell's commands, since they were cavalry and did not use drums or drummer boys, who broke down completely, sobbing. "Oh, God, spare me!" he was said to have cried.[3] When it was his turn to draw his slip of paper he prayed. "Precious Jesus, pity me." He drew a blank slip and immediately proclaimed; "Damn it, ain't I lucky!" When a second drummer boy was found to be unlucky enough to have drawn one of the marked slips of paper, upon the request of the men who had been spared, Mosby personally ordered the boy to be released from the seven condemned prisoners and the 18 remaining prisoners (excluding the first drummer boy) drew from the slips of paper for a second time.

Mosby assigned Lt. Ed Thompson to command the execution detail, which rode off with the seven condemned men in tow. These seven, including an officer, Lt. Israel Disoway, 5th New York Heavy Artillery Regiment (who again was not and could not possibly have been part of either Custer's or Powell's commands), were led down the Winchester Turnpike toward Berryville. Mosby's purpose was to conduct the executions as close to the camp of Custer's 3rd Cavalry Division as possible. While en route to the execution site the Rangers detailed for this dismal duty met a second group of Rangers who were returning from a raid. This group was led by Capt. Richard Montjoy, who wore a Masonic pin in his lapel. Lt. Disoway, who also happened to be a Mason, flashed to Montjoy the lodge's distress signal. Realizing the appeal was from a fellow Mason, Capt. Montjoy persuaded Disoway's guards to exchange the lieutenant for one of the prisoners he had just captured from Custer's 3rd Cavalry Division. The swap was quickly made, but when Mosby heard about it, Montjoy received a tongue lashing from his chief. "This [the 43rd Virginia Battalion of Partisan Rangers] is not a Masonic Lodge," Mosby angrily told his subordinate (thus once again showing that Mosby, despite his protestations, in fact did not particularly care where the men for his reprisal same from. Particularly since Disoway, who as a member of a heavy artillery regiment could not possibly have participated in either of the executions of Mosby's men, and had in fact been exchanged for a soldier from Custer's 3rd Cavalry Division, who, if he also could not have been involved in the Front Royal executions, at least had the merit of now being one of the men under Custer's command).

At 4 A.M. on Monday, November 7, 1864 (the day before the national election which would give Abraham Lincoln his second term in the White House and would therefore become the signature on the death warrant of the Confederacy), the Rangers and their prisoners reached the execution site in Beemer's Woods, a mile west of Berryville, and the executions were carried forward. However, everything did not go exactly according to plan.

In the pre-dawn darkness and confusion (either through carelessness or lack of caring for their orders, since none of the prisoners had actually been involved in depredations against Confederate civilians) the Rangers allowed two of the seven prisoners (one of whom, G.H. Soule, 5th Michigan Cavalry Regiment, punched out a guard) to escape outright. Two other prisoners were apparently shot in the head, but surviving, having only been grazed, also escaped since they pretended, and were apparently believed, to be dead. The remaining three prisoners were hanged. The identities and whether or not these three prisoners were members of either Custer or Powell's commands are unknown. Lt. Thompson, in accordance with his orders, attached a placard to one of the hanged men (just as similar placards had been attached to the bodies of all three of Mosby's hanged men). Mosby's placard read: "These men have been hung in retaliation for an equal number of Colonel Mosby's men hung by order of General Custer at Front Royal. Measure for Measure."

Once the executions forming his reprisal had been completed, Mosby then wrote his personal letter to Gen. Sheridan as follows:

November 11, 1864

Major General P.H. Sheridan
Commanding U.S. forces in the Valley
General:

Sometime in the month of September, during my absence from my command, six of my men who had been captured by your forces, were hung and shot in the streets of Front Royal, by order and in the immediate presence of Brigadier-General Custer. Since then another (captured by Colonel Powell in a plundering expedition into Rappahannock) shared a similar fate. A label affixed to the coat of one of the murdered men declared, "That this would be the fate of Mosby and all his men."

Since the murder of my men, not less than seven hundred prisoners, including many officers of high rank, captured from your army by this command have been forwarded to Richmond; but the execution of my purpose of retaliation had been deferred, in order as far as possible, to confine its operation to the men of Custer and Powell. Accordingly on the 6th instant, seven of your men, were by my order, executed on the Valley Pike — your highway of travel.

Hereafter, any prisoners falling into my hands will be treated with the kindness due to their condition, unless some new act of barbarity shall compel me, reluctantly, to adopt a line of policy repugnant to humanity.

Very respectfully,
Your obedient servant,
John S. Mosby
Lieut. Colonel

In his memoirs, Sheridan neglected to mention a number of things which may have been embarrassing. In this instance they included the executions at Front Royal and in Rappahannock County, Mosby's reprisals for those executions, and Mosby's personal letter to Sheridan protesting the executions and implicitly promising more reprisals against Union soldiers under Sheridan's command if anything like the original executions were ever contemplated again. Somewhat surprisingly, Mosby's letter had the desired effect.

There were in fact no Union retaliations at all for these executions, or for any later actions by Mosby's Rangers. This appears to indicate that Sheridan took Mosby's message and threats to heart. Sheridan was both a professional soldier and a realist, regardless of any statements he may have made. Sheridan's actions imply that he decided that one thing he was not going to do was to trade Mosby reprisal for reprisal. He either found it to be wrong (a somewhat unlikely supposition), or he had decided further reprisals would simply be stupid and useless. And whatever faults Sheridan may have had, stupidity was not to be counted among them.

Whatever the reason, when Sheridan turned Merritt and his 1st Cavalry Division loose on raids into Mosby's Confederacy on November 17, 1864, he was careful to give him specific instructions about the treatment of civilians. "No dwellings are to be burned and ... no personal violence will be offered to the citizens." Sheridan had in the interim received orders to break up Mosby's band of "outlaws." These orders made clear that whatever conclusions Sheridan had reached concerning the legitimacy of Mosby's command, the official line in Washington, D.C., was that they remained "bushwhackers" and "outlaws."

Therefore, Sheridan's orders to Merritt also called for him to "consume and destroy all forage and subsistence, burn all barns and mills ... and drive off all stock in the region." Although Merrit was ordered to respect their homes and their persons, Sheridan had decided that since the populace had allowed Mosby and his men to live in their midst that the residents of Mosby's Confederacy had therefore forfeited their property rights (it did not matter if said populace included pacifist Quakers or even Union sympathizers) and "the responsibility of it must rest upon the authorities at Richmond, who have acknowledged the legitimacy of guerilla bands." This acknowledgement was in the form of the Partisan Ranger Act approved by the Confederate Congress, which provided for the organization and official recognition of guerrilla units. Although the act was later repealed, Mosby's 43rd Virginia was one of only two guerrilla units specifically exempted from the repeal of the Partisan Ranger Act.

In addition, Sheridan had other things to worry about just now than whether or not to continue a reprisal contest with Mosby. For one thing, it was getting very late in the campaign season and the weather had turned bad and would result in the worst winter to hit the Shenandoah Valley in years. Aside from that, Sheridan now had to make any number of decisions about what would be the next move by his Army of the Shenandoah, since in the interim he had already won the Battle of Cedar Creek and had smashed Early's Valley District Army once again. Soon Lee would decide that he needed the infantry from his II Corps and cavalry back, and what Confederate strength remained in the Valley would mostly evaporate.

Sheridan's apparent decision to stop the retaliations, however, ensured that there would be no more incidents like those at Front Royal, Rappahannock County, or Beemer's Woods. All three incidents together provided one of the ugliest series of events to occur during the entire American Civil War and serve to prove that neither side could claim to be fully justified in their actions.

On the one hand, Sheridan had a tendency to conveniently forget embarrassing, unpleasant, and unpalatable truths. (Even Ulysses S. Grant — who published one of the best and most honest memoirs to come out of the American Civil War — was not above leaving out the embarrassing parts. Things he did not want to talk about, including his directive for the execution of any members of Mosby's Rangers if they were caught, were not included.) And Mosby himself was no paragon of virtue, falsely claiming after the fact that he had retaliated only against members of Custer's Michigan Brigade, which had been at Front Royal, where six out of the seven original executions had occurred, and Powell's 2nd Cavalry Division, Department of West Virginia, which was responsible for the execution in Rappahannock County. Therefore, it is clear that Mosby, in this case, was telling a bald faced lie. In addition, drummer boys (two of whom participated in Mosby's death lottery) could also be considered at least semi-noncombatants since they and other musicians, particularly underage musicians, were normally delegated to be stretcher-bearers when actual combat happened to occur.

It must also be remembered that of the seven prisoners chosen for execution by Mosby, only two appear to have been soldiers from Custer's former command, the Michigan Cavalry Brigade, one of whom actually escaped completely unscathed.

These facts thus eliminate Mosby's argument that in conducting his reprisal he was only seeking justice and not vengeance, since it showed that he was not all that interested in limiting his punishment to the guilty parties involved. An atrocity remains an atrocity whether it was committed by Union soldiers such as Alfred T.A. Torbert, Wesley Merritt, Charles R. Lowell, and Col. William Powell (but not George Armstrong Custer) or by a Confederate guerrilla chieftain such as John Singleton Mosby.

9

How Did Mosby
Get It Wrong?

From the day that six of John S. Mosby's soldiers from the 43rd Virginia Battalion of Partisan Rangers were shot or hung in and around the little village of Front Royal, Virginia, on September 23, 1864, to the day he died on May 16, 1916, prior to the publication of his memoirs in 1917, he blamed those executions upon George Armstrong Custer and his Michigan Cavalry Brigade.

But he was wrong. How did that happen?

Here's how the situation likely existed on September 29, 1864, when Mosby was first informed about what had happened in Front Royal almost a week earlier.

The only persons who were directly involved in the Front Royal Incident whom it is practically certain he would have talked to would have been the two officers in command of the force which had attacked the Union baggage and supply train that day, Capt. Samuel Chapman, commander of E Troop, and Capt. Walter E. Frankland, commander of F Troop. Due to a faulty reconnaissance, they were unaware that two full brigades of Union cavalry happened to be following on the heels of this particular wagon train.

However, while they could have reported directly to Mosby about what had happened to their commands when they had attacked the wagon train, they could not have provided any first hand information as to what happened to the six prisoners they left behind after Union Col. Charles R. Lowell's troopers (from the Reserve Cavalry Brigade) — who were following immediately behind the wagon train — counterattacked and had driven them off.

Chapman, for instance, as soon as he realized that a full brigade of enemy cavalry was following behind the wagon train, had immediately attempted to abort the attack and extricate his Rangers. He had no trouble at all calling off the attack by the 80 Rangers who were under his immediate command, since they were attempting to attack the rear of the wagon train when Lowell and his troopers appeared, since his Rangers had not made direct contact with them. Once Chapman had called off the attack of the Rangers with him, he had ridden for the opposite end of the wagon train in a vain attempt to call off Capt. Frankland, who was busy attacking the head of the wagon train with about 45 Rangers. Chapman was too late — Frankland was already engaged when he arrived.

But, he did manage to extricate most of Frankland's men before they were overrun by Lowell's command and possibly the 5th Michigan Cavalry Regiment — which, as we have seen, Custer likely dispatched from his Michigan Cavalry Brigade cross-country to circle around Front Royal from his rear guard position in an attempt to cut off the Rangers' escape.

One thing that Mosby may have asked Chapman and Frankland about was the fate of Lt. Charles McMaster, whose death was apparently the excuse for at least some of the executions of the six rangers who had been taken prisoner during the fighting in and around the wagon train. It is likely that Chapman and Frankland told Mosby what became the standard Confederate story about McMaster; he was overrun and killed by the Rangers either in the original attack upon the front of the wagon train or as they were attempting to flee the scene. This totally contradicted the claims by Union troopers (and the official report of McMaster's divisional commander, Brig. Gen. Wesley Merritt, which was dated October 5, 1864) that McMaster had surrendered, was robbed, and was then shot in the head, living long enough to tell Union soldiers what had happened to him. McMaster's death is documented as having occurred about three weeks later in a Union military hospital.

The fact that McMaster's death occurred well after the Front Royal Incident puts the standard Confederate story about his death into question — whether or not he was actually robbed or had been shot after he surrendered — and supports the contention that he was in effect deliberately killed by the Rangers in cold blood. (Like at least some of the executions at Front Royal, this in fact may have been more of a matter of not taking prisoners than a matter of executing prisoners. But, whatever the circumstances, McMaster was still dead.)

There can also be no doubt that Mosby dispatched some of his men to investigate what had happened to his six captured rangers at Front Royal. Thus, at best, as has been previously noted, he most likely received any accounts second hand or even third hand, elicited by persons who, however trustworthy, were likely without his legal training and expertise, and who thus may have been all too willing to accept the various accounts they heard of the executions at face value.

In addition, Mosby, in his outrage, may not have been all that interested in ferreting out and hearing the exact truth. Mosby's memoirs make it quite clear he accepted at face value newspaper accounts, which also blamed the executions upon Custer personally and upon the soldiers under Custer's command. However, any unbiased reading of those two newspaper accounts furthermore makes it abundantly clear that the articles in question were little more than war time propaganda, and any reasonably intelligent person knows that such propaganda can very often have only a passing relationship to the truth.

The most glaring example of the lack of reliability of propaganda in American history is the story of the Boston Massacre. What actually happened at the Boston Massacre was that British soldiers had opened fire upon a threatening mob. The event was a riot, not a massacre in any true sense of the word. Revolutionary propagandist Samuel Adams took the event and blew it entirely out of proportion for purely political ends.

The two newspaper accounts reprinted in Mosby's memoirs did exactly the same thing for exactly the same reasons. For instance, consider the language in the first newspaper account (the name of the newspaper is not mentioned) quoted by Mosby: "A part of Mosby's men, under Captain Chapman, annoyed the enemy very much on their return to Front Royal, which with the mortification of their defeat by Wickham, excited them to such savage doings as to prompt them *to murder* six of our men who fell into their hands." Mosby's memoirs as previously recorded also quoted a report in the *Richmond Examiner*, which stated, in part: "The other four of our prisoners were tied to stakes and mercilessly shot through the skull, each one individually." Unbiased reports, these are not.

In addition, accounts of the execution make it clear that two of the victims were killed by a firing squad and no account, even that of those of the killing of Henry Rhodes, notes that anyone was tied to a stake and was then shot point blank directly through the head. This particular newspaper account deliberately contained the most gruesome imagery that the writer could concoct and was not attempting to accurately state what actually happened.

For another thing, there is absolutely no mention at all in either of these accounts of Lt. McMaster and his fate, whether or not he was killed instantly in the attack (the version put forward by Mosby and his Rangers) or whether he was captured, robbed and shot, dying about three weeks later (the version put forward by Gen. Merritt and which was supported by Union records, at least concerning the date of McMaster's death).

Beyond doubt, it is these reports, received by Mosby at either second or even third hand, which were what he based his "opinion" that Custer and his Michigan Cavalry Brigade were the villains of the piece and were solely responsible for the executions. There is no hint that the actions of his own men could have possibly had anything whatsoever to do with the admittedly intemperate Union response when they managed to capture a few of his rangers during the actual commission of one of their raids.

It is clear that biased newspaper accounts and at least questionable if not actually unreliable personal accounts were the foundations upon which Mosby based his subsequent actions. Let us return for a moment to the only known Confederate eyewitness account that actually mentions seeing Custer in Front Royal at all on that day, provided by Dr. R.C. Buck. Although Dr. Buck does state that he believed that Custer ordered the executions, the only thing that he could testify to actually having seen with his own eyes — and not relying upon what someone else told him — was his view of Custer riding through the town at the head of his troops, which occurred when they were leaving Front Royal, after the executions.

Although Torbert, Merritt and Lowell were all there in Front Royal on September 23, the emphasis from the Confederate side is entirely upon Custer. The article from the *Richmond Examiner* cited by Mosby does state that Custer, Merritt and Torbert were all there in Front Royal when the executions occurred. But, it does not make any mention of the source of this particular tidbit of information. In addition, neither article makes any mention of what Lowell's soldiers did or did not do, while Lowell, in his letter to his wife, admits that soldiers under his command had participated in the executions. The report from the unnamed Confederate newspaper cited by Mosby does state (and is likely the original source of the claim) that Torbert and Merritt turned all of the prisoners over to Custer for the executions, which on the face of it makes no particular, logical, or even military sense.

If the prisoners were taken by Lowell's Reserve Cavalry Brigade, then the responsibility for their final disposition rested with Lowell's Reserve Cavalry Brigade, and if executions were to be ordered, then it only makes sense that the troopers who took the prisoners would be the ones who were ordered to execute those prisoners. From the previous analysis of Avery's journal, his 5th Michigan Cavalry Regiment did not enter the town of Front Royal itself, at least until after the executions, since Avery only heard about and did not witness the hangings, and knew nothing about the Confederate prisoners who were shot, since according to his account only four persons appear to have been executed. It is also likely that the 5th Michigan only arrived at Front Royal in time to participate in Custer's parade through the town as his brigade was leaving the area, as recorded by Dr. Buck.

Part of the reason that so much Confederate attention was focused on Custer was that he had a definite tendency to stick out from the crowd. Perhaps it is a good idea to examine whether some of those Confederate civilian "eyewitnesses" may have made a very simple mistake, which may have had more to do with Custer's sense of showmanship than it had to do with anything he may or may not have actually done at Front Royal.

When Custer became a brigadier general on June 25, 1863, just prior to the Battle of Gettysburg, he created his own uniform, which caused at least one staff officer to remark that Custer looked "like a circus rider gone mad." Originally the uniform was of black velveteen, not Union blue. The jacket bore the insignia of his rank: a double row of gilt buttons set in twos, and five rows of gold braid arranged in five loops on each sleeve (a decoration normally used in the Confederate and not in the Union army). His shoulder straps each bore a single star. The lapels, collar and bottom of the jacket were also trimmed in gold. His black riding breeches bore two narrow gold stripes running down the outside seams. Worn under the jacket was a blue flannel sailor's shirt whose broad collar was laid over it. The collar was piped in white with a white star sewn into each corner.

The crowning touch was a bright red tie, which ensured that Custer could be seen and identified by his troops (which Custer claimed was the entire point of the exercise) from a mile away or more. The entire ensemble was topped off by a black slouch hat punctuated by a rosette in the crown.[1]

By wearing such an outlandish uniform, Custer made himself conspicuous. The reason may have had something to do with publicity. But, it also had everything to do with the style of leadership demanded by the rank and file, and which was a very close fit to Custer's own flamboyant personality. The only officers who succeeded in winning the respect of their men (such as Custer, from all accounts of the ordinary soldiers who served under him during the Civil War) were those who led from the front, rather than commanding from the rear. He made himself conspicuous in appearance and battlefield behavior on purpose. He deliberately demonstrated his courage and courted danger to allay his own soldiers' natural fear. He wore an outlandish uniform to ensure that they would always know exactly where he was in the thick of any fight.

However, during Sheridan's 1864 Shenandoah Valley Campaign, by which time Custer had been a brigadier general and commander of the Michigan Cavalry Brigade for over a year, he rather significantly toned down his uniform (although he could and did drag out the splashy version for special occasions, such as at the Battle of Tom's Brook on October 9, 1864, a little more than two weeks after the Front Royal Incident).

He kept the black riding breeches with their two narrow stripes down the outside seams and he also kept the sailor shirt, the slouch hat and the bright red tie. What he put aside was the rather elaborate jacket of black velveteen with the rather excessive gold braid loops on each sleeve.

The uniform issue brings to mind the possibility that at least some of the witnesses questioned may have actually gotten Custer confused with Torbert (who definitely was there at Front Royal and in all probability actually gave the order for the executions). Various Civil War photographs of Sheridan and his officers offer a clue about how this may have happened. In at least one widely published photograph Torbert can be seen wearing a uniform which includes a similar sailor shirt to the one worn by Custer, with a wide collar featuring white stars which have been embroidered upon each of the collar tips.

Confederate civilians who witnessed the executions would have known all about Custer's uniform, since it was part of the image he deliberately cultivated. It is possible that they might not have been able to tell Torbert from Custer since neither of them had served in the Shenandoah Valley prior to Sheridan's 1864 campaign. Seeing the officer who was issuing the orders for the executions of Mosby's Rangers wearing a uniform which was in some ways was similar to Custer's trademark, people who may have never seen either one of them before could have understandably confused Torbert with Custer. And although Custer's letters to his wife Libby and Torbert and Merritt's reports for the year 1864 make it clear that he had fought a skirmish in the vicinity of Front Royal in August 1864, there is no evidence that he had actually been inside the town prior to September 22 and 23, 1864.[2]

Another possible area of confusion may also have been due to Custer's elevation to divisional command, which occurred within days of the Front Royal incident. Sheridan, after naming Custer to succeed Gen. W.W. Averell in command of the 2nd Cavalry Division, Department of West Virginia, days later transferred him (even before he was able to assume command of that division) to command of the 3rd Cavalry Division in place of Gen. James H. Wilson.

Getting back to Dr. Buck's statement, he noted that he had seen Custer riding through Front Royal at the head of his "division." The actual divisional commander that day was Gen. Wesley Merritt, but Custer's promotion may have also caused him to be confused with Merritt by Dr. Buck. This is important since Lowell said in his letter to his wife that he had received orders for his soldiers to conduct the executions from his "divisional commander," — who was Wesley Merritt, but whom Southern witnesses, due to confusion over the timing of Custer's promotion, may have thought was actually Custer.

Aside from the mistakes Mosby may have made in reaching his conclusions a modern reader needs to be aware of a reason why many modern historians have accepted the accusation against Custer for his alleged involvement in this atrocity without at least some questioning of its basic likelihood.

George Armstrong Custer has always been a controversial figure. But, as long as the men who had actually followed Custer in the American Civil War lived (and particularly as long as his wife, Elizabeth Bacon Custer, lived) it was impossible for the Custerphobes to effectively efface Custer's image as a bold and capable leader.[3] Custer excelled at leading volunteers, willing and motivated soldiers, during the American Civil War. But when the war ended, the U.S. Army returned to normalcy — the historic peacetime normalcy, which called for the U.S. Army to return to being something small, weak and politically inoffensive. The enlisted men were no longer motivated volunteers but were instead isolated time-serving regulars who were not attracted to Custer's brand of leadership. Custer's biggest problem after the war was that his only experience was in the wartime army, and he had absolutely no experience at all with the realities of the peacetime army.

While Custer was growing up in Monroe, Mich., he certainly knew who Elizabeth "Libbie" Clift Bacon, the daughter of the socially prominent Judge Daniel Bacon, was. They probably actually met at a Thanksgiving party in 1862. The families would not have known each other since they were of different social strata, based upon religious denomination, the Custers being Methodists and the Bacons being Presbyterians. But that did not stop Custer, who managed to create something of a friendship with her father while their courtship continued quietly and somewhat secretly for over a year. They were eventually married on February 9, 1864, and from the beginning of their life together Libbie embodied the spirit of Ruth in the bible when she told her mother-in-law, Naomi: "Do not ask me to abandon or forsake you! For wherever you go I will go, wherever you lodge I will lodge, your people shall be my people, and your God my God. Wherever you die I will die, and there be buried. May the Lord do so and so to me, and more besides, if aught but death separates me from you."

Only actual campaigning or combat would separate Libbie from her "Autie," a childhood nickname of Custer's. When Custer was killed at the Battle of the Little Big Horn in 1876, it was Libbie who was the person most responsible for the creation of the Custer myth and legend through her books and the lectures she gave about his career for the next 57 years. Libbie died on April 2, 1933, just six days prior to her 91st birthday. It was actually on that day that she was laid to rest at West Point, beside her "own bright star."

The process of diminishing Custer's reputation began when a novelist by the name of Frederick F. Van de Water published what one historian has called his most enduring work of fiction, *Glory Hunter: A Life General Custer,* under the guise of historical biography.[4] Van de Water dispensed with documentation, twisted the facts and even added rhetorical embellishments in order to misinterpret everything that Custer ever said and did. Van de Water depicted Custer as an egomaniac, bully, braggart and unrepentant social climber, in effect a fabricated hero. The year that

Van de Water's "masterpiece" was published was also of considerable importance. The year of publication was 1934, the year after Libbie, Custer's widow and most vociferous defender, had died. Van de Water's muddying of the waters where Custer's reputation was concerned has over the years helped to create an atmosphere which has tended to make Mosby's accusations sound eminently reasonable.

Many Custerphobes (including most particularly those who ascribe to the modern absurdity known as "political correctness") have also maintained that it does not matter whether Custer was or was not there at Front Royal, or whether or not he did or did not give the order to execute those prisoners at Front Royal. Their argument runs that since he most likely agreed with it; he should share the guilt for it.

In the words of Hamilton Burger (who regularly confronted Perry Mason in novels, movies and television), such a position is "irrelevant, incompetent and immaterial!" If he was not there on the scene (or did not arrive until the executions were actually under way), he could not possibly have given the orders. Since Torbert was in command and Custer was subordinate to both him and Wesley Merritt (who most definitely were there), then he could not have given the orders. If he did not give the orders — no matter what his personal opinion may have been (and there is no way in God's green earth of knowing exactly what his personal opinion might have been) — Custer bears absolutely no responsibility for the executions at Front Royal whatsoever.

10

Why They Never Said a Word

One of the most enduring mysteries which arose from the Front Royal Incident is why so many of the people who were involved, or were supposed to be involved, apparently never said or wrote a single word about it. (Or if they did say or write anything about it, they said or wrote very little.) These include such persons as Custer himself; James H. Kidd of the 6th Michigan Cavalry Regiment; Asa B. Isham, the author of the regimental history of the 7th Michigan Cavalry Regiment; various other officers in the 1st, 6th and 7th Michigan Cavalry Regiments and the 25th New York Cavalry Regiment (including commanding officers); and even to a degree Custer's wife, Libbie.

Kidd, himself, was one of Custer's most loyal and trusted subordinates during the American Civil War and most particularly during the period from the end of June 1863 to the end of September 1864, during which Custer commanded the Michigan Cavalry Brigade. Kidd eventually became the colonel of the 6th Michigan Cavalry Regiment and, as senior officer present, assumed command of the Michigan Cavalry Brigade after Custer was named to take command of the 3rd Cavalry Division.

Custer was most particularly welcomed to the 3rdCavalry Division by the officers and men of the 1st Vermont Cavalry Regiment. After the Battle of Gettysburg the 1st Vermont Cavalry had been transferred to the Michigan Cavalry Brigade, for a time, to make up for casualties suffered during the Gettysburg Campaign and to bring the brigade back up to strength. The men of this regiment were overjoyed to be back under the command of Custer after suffering through the periods when they were under the divisional command of such leaders as Brig. Gen. H. Judson Kilpatrick (known as Kill-Cavalry for the wasteful attacks he ordered and declined to lead) and Brig. Gen. James H. Wilson, the protégé of Lt. Gen. Ulysses S. Grant, the Union general-in-chief, whose tenure in command of the 3rd Cavalry Division, from April to September 1864 during the Overland and Shenandoah campaigns, had tended to be lackluster.

While under Custer's command, the 3rd Cavalry Division (like Custer's previous command, the Michigan Cavalry Brigade) would suffer casualties in plenty, but there would be no sense that those casualties had been suffered in vain, as there had been under Kilpatrick. In addition, while under Custer's command, the lackluster period of Wilson's tenure had come to a definite end.

In fact, Custer, Col. Kidd and the other members of the Michigan Cavalry Brigade had high hopes that eventually they would also be transferred back to the 3rd Cavalry Division in order to be under Custer's command once again. However, that transfer never came and they finished out the war as part of Wesley Merritt's 1st Cavalry Division. The supposition is that it was personally extremely difficult for Merritt to voluntarily part with what was recognized as probably the best brigade of cavalry, or the best brigade period, in the entire Army of the Potomac.

At the beginning of the American Civil War, Kidd was an untested 22-year-old college student. After Kidd had completed his sophomore year at the University of Michigan, he recruited enough men to form a company of cavalry which was inducted into federal service in October 1862 as E Troop, 6th Michigan Cavalry Regiment. Before the Battle of Gettysburg, which saw George Armstrong Custer take command of the Michigan Cavalry Brigade, of which the 6th Michigan formed a part, Kidd had advanced to the rank of major, and a year later he was advanced to the rank of colonel and received command of the 6th Michigan. When he succeeded Custer in command of the Michigan Cavalry Brigade, it insured that he would end the war with the rank of brevet brigadier general of volunteers. After the war, Kidd became a newspaper publisher and eventually published his memoirs, the first edition of which appeared in 1908.

Historian and Custer biographer Robert M. Utley stated in his introduction to the 1991 edition of Kidd's memoirs (*A Cavalryman with Custer*) that Kidd well told a good story.[1] During the war he wrote a number of graphic letters home, which served to refresh his memory about events that (by the time he wrote and published his memoirs) had occurred 40 years previously. Utley also praised Kidd's memoirs for going beyond simply naming names, but also giving voice to the people behind those names and showing their distinctive appearances, personalities and military proficiencies (or lack thereof).[2]

There were those outside of the Michigan Cavalry Brigade who wrote

Custer off as a reckless wild man with an insatiable passion for glory, but James H. Kidd was never one of them.[3] Kidd knew — from his own experience — that there was a critical, vast and important difference between the audacity, which was part and parcel of the character of George Armstrong Custer, and rash recklessness, which was demonstrated by the career of officers the like of H. Judson Kilpatrick.

It would have been difficult to have found a man in the Michigan Cavalry Brigade, at this time, who did not venerate Custer. Kidd was only among the most vociferous. He praised Custer as a tactician who instinctively was able to choose exactly the right moment when to charge, when to retreat, and when to hold his ground. In his view, Custer was a man who boldly acted on his instincts without the kind of hesitation which so often resulted in wasted lives. Throughout the letters he wrote during the war and the memoirs he published well after the war, Kidd lauded Custer's generalship to the skies. Not only that, he backed up his praise and his judgment of Custer's qualities as a commander by citing in particular the many instances when he most demonstrated those qualities.

At the time of the events which occurred before and during the Front Royal Incident, Kidd was ill with jaundice. This did not keep him from participating in the Third Battle of Winchester (or the Battle of Opequon Creek, as it was also called). Since he felt better after the battle, although he had been considering taking a medical leave, he had decided to remain with the army. In any event he was definitely there when Torbert took elements from the 1st and 3rd Cavalry Divisions and moved up the Luray Valley in accordance with Maj. Gen. Philip H. Sheridan's grand design for the aftermath of the Battle of Fisher's Hill to cut off Early's retreat and to trap and destroy his Valley District Army.

In the study of the American Civil War, what is said is sometimes not quite as important as what is not said. For instance, there is no mention at all in Kidd's report for the year of 1864 about what happened at Front Royal on September 23, 1864. There is only the mention of the attack upon Wickham, which Torbert was directly ordered by Sheridan to make on September 24. Kidd's letters and his memoirs both discuss all of the events which led up to the Front Royal Incident in the days immediately following the Battle of Fisher's Hill, and all of the events which immediately followed the Front Royal Incident itself. Kidd's personal disgust with Torbert's timidity during the skirmishing in the Luray Valley and his failure to fulfill Sheridan's expectations there is quite evident in both his words and his tone. But, the single missing item in his narration of these events, is any mention whatsoever of the Front Royal Incident itself; it is as if it never happened, as far as Kidd and his 6th Michigan Cavalry Regiment were concerned.

Kidd's apparent silence over the Front Royal Incident is more than a little odd when his reaction to "The Burning" is examined.[4] Within days of the Front Royal Incident, Sheridan ordered what became known in the Shenandoah Valley as "The Burning." In ordering The Burning, Sheridan was acting under the direct orders of General-in-Chief Ulysses S. Grant, who wanted to deny Lee's Army of Northern Virginia the fruits of the huge granary which was the Shenandoah Valley. What Grant wanted, and what Sheridan specifically promised him, was to ensure that any crows crossing the Shenandoah Valley would be forced to carry their own rations.

The Burning was the complete destruction, by fire, of all of the crops standing in the fields along the Army of the Shenandoah's line of march as well as the contents of the Shenandoah Valley residents' well-filled barns. Kidd, who by this time was in command of the Michigan Cavalry Brigade after Custer's promotion to divisional command, wrote in his memoirs how he was personally reprimanded, by Gen. Merritt, for not destroying some gristmills in a timely manner. Kidd had been using those gristmills to grind wheat into flour so that his men could bake their own bread. Once the wheat had been ground into flour those particular gristmills were immediately put to the torch. Kidd wrote:

> It was a disagreeable business and — we can be frank now — I did not relish it. One incident made a lasting impression on the mind of every man there. The mill in the little hamlet of Port Republic contained the means of livelihood — the food of the women and children whom the exigencies of war had left bereft of their natural providers, and when it was found that it was the intention to destroy that upon which their very existence seemed to depend, their appeals to be permitted to have some of the flour before the mill was burned were heartrending. Worse than all else, in spite of the most urgent precautions, enjoined upon the officers in charge, the flames extended. The mill stood in the midst of a group of wooden houses and some of them took fire. Seeing the danger, I rode across and ordered every man to fall in and assist in preventing the spread of the flames, an effort that was happily successful. [Kidd also demonstrates by this account that wanton burning of civilian homes, something that Mosby routinely accused Sheridan's troops of, was not a matter of settled policy of Sheridan's army.] What I saw there is burned into my

memory. Women with children in their arms stood in the street and gazed frantically upon the threatened ruin of their homes, while tears rained down their cheeks. The anguish pictured in their faces would have melted any heart not seared by the horrors and 'necessities' of war. It was too much for me [and] at the first moment that duty would permit I hurried away from the scene. General Merritt did not see these things, nor did General Sheridan, much less General Grant.

Kidd's description of The Burning makes it surprising that he had nothing whatsoever to say about the Front Royal Incident. Kidd was one of Custer's favorites. If Custer had been present and had witnessed the executions at Front Royal, it is almost certain that Colonel Kidd and his 6th Michigan Cavalry Regiment would have also been present. Yet Kidd never wrote a word about those executions. But, only a few days later he witnesses The Burning, an event whose memory compelled him to record his uneasiness about the whole business. Wouldn't you also have expected someone like Kidd to be as upset, if he was there, about the executions at Front Royal, as Col. Charles Russell Lowell obviously was when he wrote about them in that letter to his wife? Perhaps the operative words lie in the question, if he was there?

Would the possibility that Kidd, his 6th Michigan Cavalry Regiment, the Michigan Cavalry Brigade as a whole (with the previously noted possible exception of a single unit, the 5th Michigan Cavalry Regiment), and Custer himself were not there at Front Royal when the executions were occurring explain this seeming paradox?

Consider the implications of the fact that Custer and his brigade were serving as Torbert's rear guard as his troops approached Front Royal in their retreat from the Luray Valley on September 23, 1864; if Custer and his brigade had formed the rear guard, then they would have arrived at Front Royal last. If they arrived last — at the end of a long slow moving column burdened with a wagon train at its head — does that not make it likely that they arrived either after the executions had been completed or possibly while they were already under way?

After all, the attack on the wagon train, which was in front of the column, occurred as it was arriving at Front Royal. According to many accounts, Union and Confederate (which have already been cited), the executions had most likely occurred immediately after Mosby's Rangers had been dispersed and the six unfortunate men had been taken prisoner. This offers a possible explanation why Custer and Kidd seemingly never made any public mention whatsoever of the Front Royal Incident. By the time they had arrived on the scene in Front Royal, it was all over, but for the shouting, with Mosby doing most of the shouting himself.

There is the possibility, of course, that the Front Royal Incident was so personally disturbing that Kidd deliberately omitted it. However, Kidd made no attempt to conceal his own personal involvement and that of the soldiers under his command in The Burning. It seems odd that Kidd would be perfectly willing to include a description of The Burning in his memoirs — which he noted he found to be personally "distasteful" — and that he would omit any mention of the executions at Front Royal.

Now, consider the possibility that they were serving as part of the rear guard and were thus last to arrive at Front Royal, that Kidd and his 6th Michigan missed the executions. If they were not there, they were not involved, and if they were not involved, Kidd may not, therefore, have considered the incident relevant or worth mentioning in his reports, letters, and memoirs. Again it must also be emphasized that Kidd was one of Custer's favorite officers and his memoirs make it clear that while Custer was in command of the Michigan Cavalry Brigade, anywhere that Custer was, the 6th Michigan was somewhere close.

The likelihood that most of the rest of the Michigan Cavalry Brigade was not there can also be borne out by Asa B. Isham and his regimental history of the 7th Michigan Cavalry Regiment, *The Seventh Michigan Cavalry of Custer's Wolverine Brigade*. Like Kidd, Isham also does not mention what happened at Front Royal.[5] His account of the 7th Michigan's activities during that period in September of 1864 is as follows:

> Before day on the morning of the 20th [September 20, 1864] we were following Early toward Strasburg, by way of the Valley Pike, and found him in a strong position at Fisher's Hill, from which he was scared by Sheridan's maneuvering. After this we were actively engaged beating up the country, here, there, and everywhere, without meeting with anything noteworthy except an engagement at Luray on September 24.

This statement in Isham's History of the 7th Michigan Cavalry Regiment is echoed in the official reports and communications of various other officers (including the commanding officers) in the 1st, the 6th and the 7th Michigan Cavalry Regiments, as well as the 25th New York Cavalry Regiment. They all indicate that nothing noteworthy regarding their units or commands occurred on September 23, 1864. It does seem hard to believe that if the men of the 1st, 6th and 7th Michigan Cavalry Regiments and the 25th New York Cavalry Regiment had actually been present at the execution of six of Mosby's Rangers, it would have been considered noteworthy and worth mentioning.

Therefore, like Kidd and the historian of the 7th Michigan Cavalry Regiment, Custer himself may not have mentioned the Front Royal Incident due to the simple fact that he was not there and since he was not there did not consider the incident to have been particularly personally relevant. In his letters to his wife, Libbie, Custer makes only two mentions of Front Royal at all.[6] The first mention is in an August 21, 1864, letter from Berryville, Virginia, in which he mentions a successful skirmish having been fought near Front Royal. The second occurs in an October 1864 letter to Libbie in which he mentions being congratulated by the Cavalry Corps surgeon, a Dr. Ruliston, for a successful fight at Front Royal. It is not known if this is reference to the incident mentioned in the August 21 letter or if it refers to the fighting against Wickham in September 1864 which led to the Front Royal Incident. The October letter offers no other details.

Libbie, in her later books and lectures, appears to have made no direct reference to the Front Royal Incident, although it seems likely that she knew about it. After all, she cooperated wholeheartedly with Edward W. Whittaker in his writing of the first biography of George Armstrong Custer.[7] During the course of writing his book, Whittaker had obtained the statement of Robert Craig Wallace, a member of the 5th Michigan Cavalry Regiment who was detached to Torbert's staff and was among those present at the executions. Wallace stated that Custer did not give any orders for any executions, nor did he see him at any time while the executions were being conducted.

However, what happened at Front Royal did bear a considerable bit of personal relevance to George Armstrong Custer. After all, he was being blamed — officially by the Confederate Army, in the guise of Lt. Col. John S. Mosby and Gen. Robert E. Lee himself, and the Confederate government, due to Confederate Secretary of War James Sedden's endorsement of Lee's communication of October 29, 1864, concerning Mosby's report of the executions and his planned response to those executions — for an atrocity that could certainly be considered a violation of the laws of war. In effect Custer was accused of being a war criminal. And the *New York Herald* article seemed to confirm those accusations.

Why was Custer silent? If he did not have anything to do with the executions, why did he decline to say so? There are any numbers of historians who have interpreted his silence on this issue as being a tantamount to a confession of guilt. In the 140 plus years since the Front Royal Incident itself, this appears to have been one of its greatest mysteries. However, there are a number of possible explanations.

First of all, simple ignorance must be discounted out of hand. It is extremely unlikely that Custer was simply ignorant of the fact that he was being blamed for the executions at Front Royal. Since it is at least possible that Custer was not even there at Front Royal (and no witness, either Union or Confederate, explicitly states that Custer was present when the executions occurred), he may have originally felt much like Kidd and the soldiers of the 1st, 6th and 7th Michigan Cavalry Regiments and the rest of his brigade (with the exception of the 5th Michigan Cavalry Regiment) that since they were not present and were therefore not involved in any executions, whatever happened in Front Royal on September 23, 1864, did not involve them and was not relevant and therefore did not require any kind of a statement.

In addition, there is Mosby's letter to Sheridan, which was sent following Mosby's reprisal for the executions at Front Royal and in Rappahannock County. Although Sheridan made no mention of the letter in his memoirs, there still remains the plausible possibility that he at least showed it to the officers most closely involved: Lowell, Custer, Merritt and Torbert.

They say that ignorance is bliss, but in Custer's case it is impossible that he remained ignorant of the implications of what happened at Front Royal and his rumored involvement there, whether the rumor had any amount of truth to it or not.

A second possibility is simple pride. Custer may have simply felt that it was beneath his dignity to make any kind of answer to the charges being made against him by the enemy. He may also have felt that a public denial of his involvement in the executions would have looked cowardly and self-serving. No one who knows anything at all about Custer's personality can possibly deny that Custer had a healthy ego, which leaves open another possibility: that Custer declined to make any denial because the accusations themselves may have added a furious machismo to his reputation. There were times during Custer's American Civil War career that he was

111

accused of being soft on the Rebels, in particular because he had many friends from his West Point days among the Confederate officer corps, most especially his former roommate Thomas Lafayette Rosser, whom Custer faced more than once across a Shenandoah Valley battlefield.

Another possibility is that Custer may have felt sympathy for the person who was actually responsible for the executions, Maj. Gen. Alfred T.A. Torbert. Custer, if he were to defend himself from the accusations, would have been forced to point the finger of blame at Torbert. There is no question whatsoever that Torbert was there at Front Royal when the executions occurred. In addition, specific testimony from eyewitnesses — the 1st Cavalry Division's provost marshal, Capt. Theodore Walter Bean; Robert Craig Wallace, who was a member of Torbert's staff; the Frederic Denison, chaplain of the 1st Rhode Island Cavalry Regiment, which comprised Torbert's escort; and Sgt. Samuel Willis, 1st Rhode Island Cavalry — all agree that Torbert issued the orders for at least some, if not all, of the executions. True, some of the statements claim that Torbert only issued orders for the hangings, and Bean's statement suggests that the shootings were a spontaneous reaction of the soldiers to the original attack on the wagon train and the shooting of Lt. McMaster. Custer was always someone who showed loyalty to his friends and he considered Torbert to have been "an old and intimate friend." He may have simply considered it unworthy to implicate Torbert.

He may also have kept quiet in order to protect Torbert from any retaliation or reprisals by Mosby and his rangers. There is no evidence that Mosby and his men ever realized that it was Torbert and not Custer who was their villain by ordering the execution of those six men in Front Royal. Mosby had already amply demonstrated his ability for personal revenge in this regard by capturing at least one Union general, out of bed, practically nude, from his own headquarters — which were under heavy military guard at the time. George C. Crook and Alfred Duffie were two other Union generals who were captured by Confederate guerrillas.

Another motive for Custer may have been simple indifference, that he may not have particularly cared what people said about him.

Then again, Custer may have simply run out of time. Veterans, particularly officers, and most especially general officers, of the Civil War tended to save their attacks upon the reputations of others or the defense of their own reputations for their personal memoirs. Most of these memoirs were not published — like those of Jubal Early and Philip H. Sheridan and others — until well after the events they described. Or such as those by George Crook, John Pemberton (who surrendered the fortified city of Vicksburg, Mississippi, to Ulysses S. Grant on July 4, 1863), and even John S. Mosby, which were not published until after their authors' deaths (sometimes well after their deaths). As a matter of fact, Custer demonstrated in a series of articles published by *Galaxy* magazine and later collected into a book under the title *My Life on the Plains* that he was a quite good writer.

He was also a voluminous letter writer, as demonstrated by his letters to Libbie. It was not unusual for him to write nightly letters to his wife of 20 or more pages whenever they were apart. Custer had in fact started writing his own Civil War memoirs, and who knows what he might have or might not have said about the Front Royal Incident. However, he had only completed the first six chapters when he was killed at the Battle of Little Big Horn on July 25, 1876.

But, what he declined to say in public he might still have revealed in private. Let us return to the fact that Thomas Lafayette Rosser was probably among the best, if not the best friend, Custer ever had.

Rosser was a native Virginian who had grown up in Texas. At West Point he had been Custer's roommate, and while there the two had shared a friendly rivalry which had continued after their graduation. Rosser had become a protégé of Maj. Gen. James Ewell Brown (J.E.B.) Stuart, Lee's chief of cavalry. It was at Stuart's instigation that Rosser had become a colonel and had been named commander of the 5th Virginia Cavalry Regiment, eventually was promoted to brigadier general, and was given command of the Laurel Brigade, which included the 7th, 11th and 12th Virginia Cavalry Regiments along with the 35th Virginia Cavalry Battalion.

When Williams C. Wickham resigned his commission as a brigadier general — and command of what had been Fitzhugh Lee's cavalry division — for a seat in the Confederate Congress, Rosser was given command of Wickham's division by General Early. Although Confederate Col. Thomas Munford, one of Rosser's brigade commanders, hated the ersatz Texan with a passion, he did concede that Rosser fought gallantly in combat but that he lacked "other qualities." Munford's sour grapes may have in part resulted from Rosser's rapid promotions under Stuart's prodding.

Munford himself, despite his obvious abilities, would never be promoted to brigadier general and ended the war as a simple colonel.

While in the valley Custer and Rosser continued their basically friendly rivalry. They raided each other's headquarters upon occasion, and Custer, with the 3rd Cavalry Division, shattered Rosser's own division at the Battle of Tom's Brook. Still, despite the war and everything which had happened since their graduation from West Point, the two men remained friends. After the war Rosser became a railroad engineer surveying possible transcontinental railroad routes through various western territories (every West Point cadet was, among other things, a trained civil engineer).

It was during one of these survey expeditions that Custer and Rosser met once again. At that particular time Custer's post-war command, the 7th U.S. Cavalry Regiment, had formed the escort for a railroad survey party under Rosser's direction, and the two men had a thunderous reunion in 1873, about nine years after Sheridan's Shenandoah Valley Campaign. After Custer's own death in 1876, Rosser reported on several occasions that during their reunion in 1873 Custer had denied to him any personal involvement whatsoever in the Front Royal Incident.

11

A QUESTION OF CHARACTER

In looking at whether or not George Armstrong Custer had anything to do with the executions that occurred at Front Royal, Virginia, on September 23, 1864, the question of character must be examined. Such an examination of character boils down to one simple question: was Custer capable of ordering or participating in the executions at Front Royal?

One facet of his character was the fact that family was very important to him. He could be quite the practical joker and had no objections to being on the receiving end. In addition, Custer was not noted for holding grudges. After he and the former Elizabeth "Libbie" Bacon were married, that became her department. Furthermore, he personally sympathized both with his Confederate opponents during the war and with his Indian opponents after the war. His personal letters to Libbie and to others, the various magazine articles he authored, and certain other writings and statements of his make this absolutely clear.

It was Josephine Tey, a British mystery writer, in her novel *The Daughter of Time,* who outlined the importance of character in such a question. After all it was her novel which convinced many of her readers, including a number of historians, that there was a possibility that English King Richard III might have been innocent of the murder of his two nephews in the Tower of London, despite the accusations of certain Tudor historians, Shakespeare, and even Sir Thomas More, who traditionally had been considered an eyewitness to the events surrounding the disappearance and presumed deaths of the two "Princes of the Tower," which he described in a certain book, but who was actually all of five years old at the time. (This particular book was actually authored by one of Richard's enemies and was found in manuscript form in More's handwriting after his own execution at the command of King Henry VIII).

In *The Daughter of Time,* Tey's detective while conducting an academic investigation into the case of Richard III and the disappearance of the Princes in the Tower notes: "He [Richard III] is the author of the most revolting crime in history, and he has the face of a great judge; a great administrator. Moreover, he was by all accounts an abnormally civilized and well-living creature. He actually was a good administrator, by the way. He governed the North of England and did it excellently. He was a good staff officer and a good soldier. And nothing is known against his private life.... One could not say: Because Richard possessed this quality and that; therefore he was incapable of murder. But one could say: Because Richard possessed these qualities, therefore he is incapable of this murder."

Can the same thing be said of George Armstrong Custer? The problem is how to get at the character of Custer in regards to the Front Royal incident.

He never completed his Civil War memoirs and his letters to his wife make no mention of what happened at Front Royal. However, something of his character can be deduced from his actions, particularly if we compare his actions and career to those of the man who was his antithesis, Bvt. Maj. Gen. Hugh Judson Kilpatrick.[1] Both men were thought to be bold. Both men were accused of being reckless. By looking at the careers of Custer and Kilpatrick — side by side — the differences in the characters of these two men, between the reckless and the bold, soon becomes readily apparent. It must also be said that throwing the word "reckless" around is an extremely easy accusation to make, especially for someone who was not, has not, and never will be within the cauldron of war.

Both Custer and Kilpatrick were graduates of West Point. Although they both graduated in the same year, 1861, they were not classmates. At the beginning of the American Civil War the U.S. Military Academy at West Point had a five-year course of study. With the start of the war upon the United States Army it was a definite fact that well-trained junior officers were at a premium, so the course of study was immediately cut back to four years.

Therefore, there were two graduating classes in 1861. The first had been originally scheduled to graduate in 1861 and included Kilpatrick. The second class of 1861 became eligible for graduation when the course of study was reduced to four years and it was this class that included Custer.

Upon graduation, Custer was assigned as a brevet second lieutenant with the 2nd U.S. Cavalry Regiment (later redesignated the 5th U.S. Cavalry Regiment) and distinguished himself (being mentioned in dispatches) during the First Battle of Bull Run (or Manassas, if you prefer). His command, G Troop, was the last organized body of Union soldiers to leave the battlefield. Custer, even though he was only a brevet second lieutenant, was in command of the troop since the other officers had been killed, wounded or reassigned during the course of the battle. The rank of brevet second lieutenant was reserved for recent graduates of West Point; they would remain as brevet second lieutenants until a vacancy among the actual second lieutenants in the regiment occurred.

Kilpatrick got himself commissioned as a captain in a volunteer regiment, the 5th New York (Zouaves) Volunteer Infantry Regiment. He was the first regular officer to be wounded in battle, at the Battle of Big Bethel, albeit in the buttocks. Kilpatrick also began at this time his practice of inflating his own accomplishments.

In the interim between the First Battle of Bull Run and the Gettysburg Campaign, Custer became a staff officer. He served on the staffs of, among others, Philip Kearney, George B. McClellan and Alfred Pleasonton. Kilpatrick remained a line officer, transferring from the 5th New York Volunteer Infantry Regiment, to the 2nd New York Volunteer Cavalry Regiment where he obtained the political promotion to the rank of lieutenant colonel of volunteers. It was during this time that Kilpatrick stumbled upon his particular niche as a raider, since he was able to operate on his own and thus usually no one was in a position to contradict his glowing reports of his own achievements. Kilpatrick also used his position for his own personal gain. This resulted in him being charged with a number of crimes, including taking bribes, stealing (and then selling) horses and tobacco, and with impropriety in borrowing money, which resulted in Kilpatrick being incarcerated for a time in Washington's Old Capitol Prison.

However, since Kilpatrick was perceived to be an effective cavalry officer, a commodity of which there was an acute shortage in the Union Army, the investigation into his alleged criminal activities was soon dropped, he was released from prison, and given a promotion to full colonel and command of the 2nd New York Cavalry Regiment. Later, as senior officer, Kilpatrick assumed command of a cavalry brigade. When the Gettysburg Campaign began he was promoted to the rank of brigadier general of volunteers and was given command of the Army of the Potomac's new 3rd Cavalry Division.

No such offenses have ever been attributed to Custer. It is true he enjoyed gambling and at the time of his death he was $100,000 in debt, mostly due to poor business investments as well as gambling debts. In addition, just prior to the Little Big Horn Campaign, he was removed from command of the entire Montana column and almost lost tactical command of his own 7th U.S. Cavalry Regiment when he tried to expose corruption in the Grant administration involving the Indian Ring and the awarding of military post trader ships. Custer pointed the finger at Grant's secretary of war for the corruption and at Grant's own brother for serving as the bagman or collector for the entire operation. While most historians do not doubt the accuracy of these charges, Custer's own testimony at a Congressional hearing was dismissed as hearsay.

While Kilpatrick was having his troubles, Custer was busy impressing the commander of the Cavalry Corps of the Army of the Potomac, Maj. Gen. Alfred Pleasonton, on whose staff he was then serving. Having demonstrated what he could do, particularly at the First Battle of Brandy Station and the Battle of Aldie, which opened the Gettysburg campaign, Pleasonton selected Custer along with fellow aides Elon J. Farnsworth and Wesley Merritt for promotion to brigadier general and brigade command. Custer and Farnsworth commanded the brigades in Kilpatrick's 3rd Cavalry Division while Merritt was given the regulars of the Reserve Cavalry Brigade.

At the Battle of Hanover, Custer and Farnsworth distinguished themselves in a confrontation with Robert E. Lee's chief of cavalry, Maj. Gen. J.E.B. Stuart, and in effect won the battle before Kilpatrick could arrive on the scene, although Kilpatrick did manage to kill his own horse in a desperate attempt to arrive in time to have some influence on the course of the battle. The importance of this engagement, which was fought on July 1, 1863, was that it kept Stuart from joining Lee at Gettysburg for at least another full day.

On July 2, 1863, Custer and Stuart again collided, this time at the Battle of Hunterstown. Instructed to protect the right flank of the Army of the Potomac, the 3rd Cavalry Division with Custer's Michigan Cavalry Brigade in the lead collided with Confederate skirmishers. Custer then took what some have described as the single most reckless act of his entire career. The standard evaluation of Custer's actions at Hunterstown is as follows.

Thinking that there were only a few skirmishers needing to be dispersed,

Custer deployed the rest of his brigade into supporting positions while taking only one company of the 6th Michigan Volunteer Cavalry Regiment and charged the enemy.[2] What they were attacking turned out to be the entire brigade of Brig. Gen. Wade Hampton, consisting of three cavalry regiments and the mounted contingents of three legions drawn from North Carolina, South Carolina and Georgia. Custer's single company was smashed like a snowball hurled into a brick wall. Custer, himself, lost his horse and was almost captured, although he was rescued by a bugler who had joined the charge from the 1st Michigan Cavalry Regiment. The survivors were driven back to where Custer had deployed his brigade, which then drove off Hampton's counterattack.

However, there is another interpretation.[3] Under this interpretation what Custer was actually trying to do was to persuade the Confederates to pursue a decoy party into a trap. The only reckless portion of the entire affair was Custer's decision to join and personally lead the decoy party. Custer was successful in that his brigade decimated Cobb's Legion, the unit that pursued the fleeing decoy party, which among its heavy casualties lost almost all of its officers as dead, wounded, or missing.

Custer, perhaps recognizing that he had acted more like a wild staff officer, and not like a responsible brigade commander, never repeated this performance.

Returning to the Battle of Gettysburg itself, Custer gained fame by disobeying Kilpatrick's verbal orders when the 3rd Cavalry Division was ordered to be moved from protecting the right flank of the Army of the Potomac to protecting its left flank. Custer would help to stop Stuart in his tracks when he attempted to turn the right flank of the Army of the Potomac. Custer was asked to remain by General David M. Gregg, who commanded the 2nd Cavalry Division.

Gregg has been considered to have demonstrated a certain initiative and audacity by doing so. However, at least one historian has stated that audacity and initiative had little to do with Gregg's motives, while shielding his own reputation and obtaining a handy scapegoat, if one were to be needed, had a great deal more to do with it.[4] Some revisionist historians also maintain that once the smoke cleared, Gregg attempted to claim all the credit for turning back Stuart when Custer and his brigade did all the real work, which is obvious to anyone looking at the official casualty figures for the engagement.

Kilpatrick during Gettysburg would cause the death of Farnsworth by first ordering and then shaming him into leading what was in effect a suicidal mounted attack launched upon entrenched Confederate infantry and over terrain that was completely unsuited to cavalry.

By this time the two very different command styles of Custer and Kilpatrick were readily apparent. Custer led from the front. He took the same risks as his men. And he learned from his mistakes. While Custer's commands had high casualty rates, his men never had the sense that their efforts and the deaths of their comrades had in effect been for nothing. In addition, he did not ask his men to do anything, or to take any risk, that he was not willing to do or take himself. Kilpatrick, on the other hand, generally commanded from the rear. While Custer cried: "Follow me!" and was generally the first man to hit the enemy, Kilpatrick's order was invariably: "Charge! God damn them!" while he stayed safely in the rear.

Kilpatrick, although he was usually not willing to expose himself to possible harm, had no qualms about ordering others into certain death. His penchant for ordering charges, which resulted in inordinate, and often needless, casualties, was mostly what earned him the nickname of Kill-Cavalry.[5]

(Custer's command style was well fitted to what the soldiers in the American Civil War demanded of their leaders. An important factor in Custer's success on the battlefields of the American Civil War was that he was commanding volunteers in the truest sense of the word. They were risking their lives because in the end they wanted to be there. After the American Civil War, Custer no longer commanded such motivated volunteers. Immediately after the war he commanded volunteer — troops along the Rio Grande in a show of force aimed at French Emperor Napoleon III and his puppet government in Mexico — who simply wanted to go home and who therefore clashed with whoever had to keep them there, causing in effect the beginning of the end of the popularity he had always previously enjoyed. The 7th U.S. Cavalry Regiment, of which Custer assumed tactical command when it was formed in 1866, consisted of embittered time-serving regulars, who in many cases were in the army because there was no place for them in civilian life. They were men who were looking for survival, not inspiration. Thus, Custer's reputation among the men he commanded continued to suffer.)

In the Second Battle of Brandy Station, Kilpatrick performed well, but most of the credit went to his subordinate, Custer, who was lightly wounded while attacking and overrunning a Confederate artillery battery with a handful of men from the 1st Vermont Cavalry Regiment. By this time the relationship between Kilpatrick and Custer had definitely soured, due primarily to what had happened during the Battle of Gettysburg. Custer apparently had no respect for Kilpatrick and seemed to consider him to be incompetent, especially after Farnsworth's death, while Kilpatrick considered Custer to be both a rival and insubordinate. In addition, shortly thereafter Kilpatrick led his division into an ambush, near the town of Buckland, disregarding Custer's apprehensions. Custer managed to extricate his brigade as they fought their way out of the trap, while Kilpatrick and his other brigade, now under the command of Brig. Gen. Henry E. Davies, were forced to run for their lives in a disgraceful rout under close pursuit by Stuart's cavalry, in what became known as the Buckland Races.

After this fiasco, Custer felt that he simply could not trust Kilpatrick in battle. There were other, more private, problems between them as well. Kilpatrick had married shortly after graduation from West Point. Custer had also married during the winter of 1864. The problem was that Custer was faithful to his wife, despite certain rumors to the contrary, while Kilpatrick was a notorious womanizer to the point of having various mistresses with him in the field providing "horizontal duty" and "sack drill." This behavior continued before, during and after Kilpatrick's first wife fell ill and died.

Most of the rumors of Custer's infidelity — on the other hand — can be traced to one man's hatred (that of Frederick W. Benteen), the capture of certain letters by the Confederates (which they believed to be from Custer's mistress but which were actually from his wife), and to an investigation into the activities of a certain Annie Jones.[6] Miss Jones was one of Kilpatrick's many mistresses. She had first shown up as Kilpatrick's companion in August of 1863. Kilpatrick provided her with a horse, a major's jacket and cap and a pass to sightsee the camp. She played havoc with inlaying and outlying pickets, exposed herself to rebel snipers, and then hightailed it over to the rebel lines for a purported two-night stand with then Maj. John S. Mosby. When she returned Kilpatrick sent her packing.

In an effort to get back at Kilpatrick (who had transferred his affections to certain other camp followers), she claimed to have shifted her attentions to Custer, which Custer denied during an investigation into her activities in March of 1864 when she was accused by another female camp follower, who was jealous of her, of being a Confederate spy. Custer, instead of inviting her into his bed, had in September of 1863 barred her from the 3rd Cavalry Division's camps at a time when he was temporarily in command as senior officer present due to Kilpatrick's absence. This in spite of passes from the War Department, the surgeon-general of the Army of the Potomac, and Maj. Gen. Gouverneur Kemble Warren, II Corps commander, allowing her to visit the army as a "sister of mercy" and her claims to have been officially placed as a hospital nurse with the 3rd Cavalry Division.

In November of 1863 and into January of 1864, Kilpatrick was again away from the 3rd Cavalry Division in Washington on furlough (supposedly due to the death of his first wife and then the death of his son) during which he sought to bring political influence to bear so that he could get permission to launch the Kilpatrick-Dahlgren Raid upon Richmond, since George Gordon Meade, as commander of the Army of the Potomac, and Alfred Pleasonton, as commander of the Cavalry Corps, both disapproved of the proposed raid.

(The raid was apparently the brainstorm of Elizabeth Van Lew, who headed a major Union spy network in Richmond, Virginia. She provided information as to the location of various Confederate prisoner of war camps located in and around Richmond and the number of prisoners being held there. According to Van Lew's information there were 1,000 officers being held in Libby Prison, 6,300 enlisted men on Belle Isle in the James River, and 4,300 more enlisted men in various other locations in and around Richmond. She recommended that a raid be organized to free the prisoners and Kilpatrick appropriated the idea as his own.)

Kilpatrick received permission for his raid from President Abraham Lincoln and Secretary of War Edwin M. Stanton during the winter of 1864, going over the heads of Meade and Pleasonton. (Meade had accepted the inevitable, but Pleasonton loudly did not, to the eventual detriment of his tenure in command of the Army of the Potomac's Cavalry Corps. In addition, Kilpatrick and his second-in-command, Col. Ulrich Dahlgren, also planned to decapitate the rebellion by capturing and killing Confederate President Jefferson Davis and his cabinet while setting fire to the city of Richmond to cover their retreat.

Kilpatrick, according to at least one biographer, had a reputation as a talker, a braggart, and on the way to Richmond, Kilpatrick, according to this biographer, most probably oozed confidence and most likely bragged to whomever would listen to him concerning what he was about to do to the enemy in Richmond.[7] But, when he arrived at the outskirts of the Confederate capital, Kilpatrick's nerve failed him. Once he had arrived at the defenses of Richmond there was no obvious place of safety. Behind him were Confederate troops, under the command of Wade Hampton, gathering to pursue his raiders. Before him were the defenses of Richmond, which were manned with men who he perceived were out to kill him.

Kilpatrick's personally "safest" option — if he were to actually assault Richmond — would have been to charge ahead with his men straight at the Confederate garrison of Richmond, in effect attacking men who, in Kilpatrick's perception, would only have had to wait there behind their defenses for a chance to shoot him down. (At that time they were actually mostly little or totally untrained militia, who had been recruited primarily from amongst Confederate government clerks.)

Instead Kilpatrick ordered a retreat to the northwest toward the haven of the Union Army of the James. He abandoned Dahlgren — who had been detached with a small force to conduct a diversionary attack — to his fate and ran for safety. Kilpatrick lost 340 officers and men — killed (including Dahlgren), wounded, and prisoners — along with 583 horses and achieved worse than nothing. Kilpatrick and Dahlgren's plans for Davis, his cabinet, and the city of Richmond itself were found in papers on Dahlgren's body. There has been speculation that certain attempts to kill or capture Lincoln (including John Wilkes Booth's successful assassination attempt) were inspired by what the Dahlgren Papers revealed.

The problems in their relationship caused Kilpatrick to make sure that Custer did not come along on the Kilpatrick-Dahlgren Richmond Raid, although he was relegated to conducting a diversionary raid, which nearly everyone, including Custer, considered to be a forlorn hope. (The solid core of the force Kilpatrick took with him, however, consisted of drafts from the regiments of Custer's Michigan Cavalry Brigade.) Custer, with a scratch force drawn mainly from the regulars of the Reserve Cavalry Brigade and Gregg's 2nd Cavalry Division, conducted what Maj. Gen. George G. Meade, commander of the Army of the Potomac, called a perfect cavalry raid. Kilpatrick had lost his nerve and failed when faced by the defenses at Richmond. Custer and his hastily gathered force, on the other hand, had accomplished their mission, during which they had covered 100 to 150 miles in 48 hours, destroyed an important bridge over the Rivanna River along with three large mills filled with grain and flour, and captured six Confederate artillery caissons, two forges and other military supplies. Custer's command also captured 50–60 prisoners, one flag, and 500 horses. Finally, his troops freed 100 slaves whom they took with them back to the Union lines. In addition, not one of Custer's men was killed or captured and only a very few were even lightly wounded.

In the aftermath of the dismal results of the Kilpatrick-Dahlgren Richmond Raid, Kilpatrick was removed from command of the 3rd Cavalry Division and Pleasonton was removed from command of the Cavalry Corps. The additional controversy over the Dahlgren Papers, whose documentation of Kilpatrick's alleged intention to capture and assassinate Jefferson Davis — which everybody (including Kilpatrick) disowned — may have actually saved his career. They showed Kilpatrick to be an adherent of total war, which may have influenced Maj. Gen. William Tecumseh Sherman to ask for Kilpatrick to be assigned to his command for the Atlanta Campaign and to assign Kilpatrick to be his chief of cavalry during both the March to the Sea and the March Through the Carolinas. [8]

After the departure of Pleasonton and Kilpatrick, Custer found in Maj. Gen. Phil Sheridan a chief he could follow without question, despite his personal disappointment at not receiving command of the 3rd Cavalry Division, which went instead to Grant's pet, James H. Wilson, who had never before commanded troops in battle.

(Finding a place for Wilson had required a bit of rearranging in the Cavalry Corps hierarchy. Both Custer and Brig. Gen. Henry Davies were senior to Wilson, therefore it would have been awkward for them to serve under Wilson's command. As a result, Custer and his entire brigade were transferred from the 3rd Cavalry Division to the 1st Cavalry Division, while Davies was transferred to command of a brigade in 2nd Cavalry Division. To avoid similar friction by promoting either Custer or Merritt — who were rivals — to divisional command, Alfred T.A. Torbert, previously an infantry division commander, was brought in to command the 1st Cavalry Division.)

Still Custer distinguished himself throughout 1864. During Sheridan's

Richmond Raid it was a charge by Custer's Michigan Cavalry Brigade which broke Stuart's defensive position at the Battle of Yellow Tavern. It was also probably one of Custer's men who fired the shot that killed Stuart that day. At the Battle of Haw's Shop, Custer's Michigan Cavalry Brigade rescued the 2nd Cavalry Division, which had been badly handled while attacking Confederate cavalry who outnumbered them in entrenched positions. In the Battle of Trevilian Station, which occurred as part of a raid upon the Army of Northern Virginia's supply lines, Custer got into the rear of the Confederate cavalry under the command of Hampton (who eventually succeeded Stuart as Lee's chief of cavalry). Hampton, reacting with speed and skill, managed to cut off Custer's Michigan Cavalry Brigade, which for hours had to fight for its very existence.

Gregory J.W. Urwin in *Custer Victorious* noted that no one was really to blame for the fiasco. He credits Custer with saving his command. Eric J. Wittenberg, in *Glory Enough for All: Sheridan's Second Raid and the Battle of Trevilian Station,* on the other hand claims that Sheridan had mismanaged the battle. Wittenberg maintains that the battle was an out and out victory for Wade Hampton and the Confederate cavalry despite the fact that Sheridan claimed it as a victory, a claim which was accepted by Grant and was supported in his memoirs. According to Wittenberg, Sheridan failed in all of his objectives. In addition, Wittenberg ranked Custer's performance on this day as spotty. He faulted him for "reckless abandon" which resulted in his brigade being caught in a trap and nearly annihilated. However, Wittenberg does not take into account the fact that the so-called trap was entirely unintended.

However, Sheridan did manage to accomplish the only objective that truly mattered to Grant. His raid had so distracted General Robert E. Lee that he remained totally oblivious to Grant's crossing of the James River to strike at the Confederate railroad hub at Petersburg. The attack on Petersburg failed due to a major blunder of a subordinate commander along with exhaustion and inertia on the part of the Union soldiers sent against the town.

In addition, in regards to Custer, Wittenberg's interpretation rests on equating recklessness with boldness. From a sufficient distance in time and space, boldness and recklessness can look to be the same, but they are not. In addition, while boldness generally works, it can turn around and bite you, especially when your opponents (in this case Wade Hampton and

Matthew C. Butler) are every bit as bold as you are. (This is also basically what happened to Custer at the Battle of the Little Big Horn.)

Being bold is defined as showing a readiness to take risks or face danger while accomplishing an objective. Boldness is best epitomized by the mottoes "No Guts, No Glory" and "He Who Dares, Wins." The essence of boldness lies in the idea of the calculated risk, whether the calculation is made on an intellectual basis or upon an intuitive basis. Custer calculated his risks on an intuitive basis, which gave him the great advantage of usually being the one who moved first. Being reckless, on the other hand, is defined as not regarding consequences, being headlong and irresponsible in the pursuit of one's objectives. Thus, the only time Kilpatrick ever bothered to calculate risk was whenever he was concerned about his own person.

What Custer attempted to do at Trevilian Station was to take advantage of what appeared to be a golden opportunity. In his attack upon the rear of Wade Hampton's Confederate cavalry division, he was doing exactly what a cavalry commander is supposed to do. Even Wittenberg admits that Custer was trying to carry out Sheridan's orders. He faults him for having too much audacity. Once again, it is a problem of perception and of the failure to recognize the difference between boldness and recklessness. The problem with most failed Union commanders — including Kilpatrick — was the simple fact that in the final analysis they did not have enough boldness, enough audacity.

The very worst that can be said of Custer was that he had all the vices of his virtues and that every once in a while they could turn on him, as they did at Trevilian Station and upon the Little Big Horn.

It is doubtful whether one can have too much audacity. As one Frenchman, Georges Danton, put it during the French Revolution, "Audacity! More Audacity! Always Audacity!" Audie L. Murphy, the most decorated American combat soldier in World War II, had this to say about the value of audacity: "If I discovered one valuable thing during my early combat days, it was audacity, which is often mistaken for courage or foolishness. It is neither. Audacity is a tactical weapon. Nine times out of ten it will throw the enemy off balance and confuse him. However, much [as] one sees of audacious deeds no one really expects them."[9] While audacity may not be the same thing as courage, both physical and moral courage are necessary to use audacity. It could be said that the essence of boldness is the combination of courage and audacity.

126

Then Custer was sent with Sheridan to the Shenandoah Valley. Here Custer distinguished himself at the Third Battle of Winchester (or Opequon Creek), the Battle of Tom's Brook, the Battle of Cedar Creek (where his 3rd Cavalry Division and Merritt's 1st Cavalry Division both helped avert the total collapse of Sheridan's Army, holding it together with the VI Corps until Sheridan could return, reorganize his army, counterattack and turn defeat into victory) and Waynesboro (where Custer and his division alone destroyed the remnants of the Valley District Army and ended Sheridan's Shenandoah Valley Campaign).

Custer was once again instrumental in the fighting during the Appomattox Campaign, fought from March 29 through April 9, 1865, beginning with the Battle of Dinwiddie Court House on March 31, which led directly to the decisive Battle of Five Forks on April 1. Custer was not present at the beginning of the Battle of Dinwiddie Court House, but his timely arrival was crucial in stopping the Confederates under Maj. Gen. George Pickett, who then, during the night, decided to retire back to their entrenched positions at Five Forks. The next day Sheridan was reinforced by the arrival of V Corps from the Army of the Potomac and Ranald Mackenzie's cavalry division from the Army of the James and went on to the attack.

The victory at Five Forks forced Lee to abandon his positions at Petersburg and evacuate Richmond. Lee attempted to retreat, trying to link up with General Joseph E. Johnston in North Carolina. Custer acted as Sheridan's spearhead in the pursuit of Lee, being highly instrumental in the cutting off and the destruction of almost half of what remained of the Army of Northern Virginia at the Battle of Sayler's Creek. At Appomattox Station, Custer and his division took four trains, which were awaiting Lee's army, and snapped shut the final escape route of the remainder of Lee's army. Then on the morning of April 9, 1865, Custer personally accepted a flag of truce that resulted in a cease-fire, which in turn led to Lee's meeting with Grant at the McLean house and the final surrender of Lee's Army.

Kilpatrick was also very busy during this same period as the commander of one of Sherman's cavalry divisions during the Atlanta Campaign and as Sherman's chief of cavalry during the March to the Sea and the March Through the Carolinas. During the Atlanta Campaign, Kilpatrick's efforts, while vigorous, were not particularly successful.[10] However, when compared to Sherman's other cavalry commanders, such as Brig. Gen.

127

George A. Custer led his 3rd Cavalry Division in repeated charges, capturing and destroying wagon trains and capturing about a third of Lee's remaining army at the Battle of Sayler's Creek (sketch by Alfred R. Waud, Library of Congress, Prints and Photograph Division).

Edward McCook, Maj. Gen. Lovell H. Rousseau, Maj. Gen. George Stoneman, and Brig. Gen. Kenner D. Gerard, Kilpatrick appeared positively heroic.[11]

During the March to the Sea, the Confederates assumed that Sherman's targets would be the cities of Macon, Augusta and Savannah and concentrated what forces they had available to defend these cities. Thus Sherman was able to march across Georgia without opposition. His infantry destroyed the railroads, bridges and factories between Atlanta and Savannah while Kilpatrick's cavalry and Sherman's infantry stragglers (the bummers) targeted ordinary civilians burning and looting their defenseless homes. In effect, most of the atrocities committed during the March to the Sea and remembered to this day by the people of Georgia can primarily be attributed to Kilpatrick. If the South had won the war and had captured Kilpatrick, he most likely could have been tried as a war criminal.[12] Sherman could have censured Kilpatrick for the outrageous conduct of both himself and the soldiers under his command, but Sherman chose not to.

General George A. Custer receives the flag of truce which halted the fighting between Union and Confederate forces just prior to Lee's surrender at Appomattox Court House (sketch by Alfred R. Waud, Library of Congress, Prints and Photographs Division).

In South Carolina, Kilpatrick fought only one actual battle when he walked into a Confederate ambush at Aiken and was routed. Otherwise his troops pillaged the countryside, burning homes, openly stealing from their victims, and even desecrating churches.

In North Carolina, Kilpatrick was again surprised and his troops routed by Confederate cavalry who attacked his camp at Monroe's Crossroads. (Kilpatrick, who at the time the attack began had been dallying with one of his mistresses, escaped in his underwear by directing Confederate troops after someone else, then grabbing a horse and fleeing as fast as the horse could run, leaving the mistress behind.) At the beginning of the Battle of Bentonville, the final battle in North Carolina, Kilpatrick had galloped up from the left and reported to the senior officer on the field, Maj. Gen. Henry W. Slocum, who was preparing to assault Confederate defensive positions, that his cavalry "was on the field ready and willing to participate in the battle." Slocum sent Kilpatrick and his horsemen to the rear out of the way of the infantry.[13] It was a terrific snub. One could even call it an insult. By this time Sherman may have begun to realize that his chief of cavalry was somewhat less than he appeared to be.

In contrast to Kilpatrick's behavior in Georgia, South Carolina, and North Carolina, it is instructive to take a look at Custer's reactions when he stumbled upon an atrocity of the minor kind.[14] The incident in question occurred on Saturday, April 8, 1865, while Custer was on his way to Appomattox Station to intercept the trains, which were at that moment awaiting the arrival of Lee's entire army. Custer and his division were on the Southside Road, only two miles southeast of Appomattox Station. With Custer in the lead the division moved a mile up the road toward Appomattox Station and the trains waiting for Lee, coming to a large, elegant plantation mansion. As Custer and his men approached the house, two young women came running down the lane leading to the road.

"They're robbing us!" one of the women screamed, her dress hanging in shreds from her naked body. Apparently she had been in the process of being raped when Custer and his division arrived. "They're murdering us!" screamed the other woman. Custer immediately drew rein, jumped from his horse and ran to the house, with the two women on his heels screaming: "We've been outraged! Oh, God in Heaven, help us!"

Custer bounded up the steps to the house, just as a Union infantryman came barreling out the front door, his arms loaded with loot from the house. Custer thereupon struck the man down with one blow from his fist and charged through the house. He collared another bummer heading out the back door. There was a short struggle with the bummer managing to twist away from Custer's grip. When he lost his grip on the bummer, Custer grabbed an axe, which was standing next to the stove, and heaved it out the back door after the fleeing bummer, catching him on the back of the head, apparently with the flat of the axe head's blade, knocking him out cold.

Shortly thereafter he remounted his horse and before heading out after his division he ordered his provost marshal to place a guard upon the house and had the two bummers hanged by the side of the road as a deterrent. The difference from the Front Royal executions was that these two men were Union soldiers, not Confederate prisoners of war, who had been caught red handed while in the commission of a number of crimes, including rape, against civilians. No one, Union or Confederate, ever questioned Custer's actions in this case.

One final area which should be examined is the question of ambition. Kilpatrick had a definite plan for himself, the origins of which date back to before his days at West Point. It included entering and graduating from West Point, winning military glory, then running for public office (specifically seeking the governorship of New Jersey), and using that public office as a springboard for seeking election to the presidency of the United States. In point of fact, Kilpatrick's misdeeds and malfeasance kept him from winning elective office, although he did serve as U.S. ambassador to Chile twice as well as being a successful farmer and lecturer.

Custer, who remained in the army after the war, was also accused of exhibiting excessive ambition. It was alleged that his political ambitions (he too was supposed to be considering running for president) were a factor in his behavior and actions which led to the disaster at the Little Big Horn. Custer was accused of hurrying to the Little Big Horn so that news of his anticipated victory would reach the Eastern United States in time for the Democratic Party's 1876 national presidential nominating convention. However, Custer's supposed presidential ambitions are to be found only in second hand accounts of conversations by Custer with persons who also died at the Little Bighorn (such as Custer's favorite Indian scout, Bloody Knife). The reports of these alleged conversations also postdated Custer's death.

In considering whether or not Custer was capable of ordering prisoners to be executed, it would be well to consider his immediate reactions when actually confronted by an atrocity, that of the rape and robbery of female Confederate civilians by Union bummers, which he came upon during his march to Appomattox. He could have ignored it; he would even have been justified in leaving any action to his provost marshal. Instead he took personal action to stop this atrocity and to punish the Union soldiers who were directly responsible for it.

Looking at Custer's character as revealed by his actions, I think it would be safe to say that if he had been ordered to execute the Confederate prisoners from Mosby's Rangers at Front Royal, he, like Lowell, would have followed those orders, although he may have found it as personally distasteful as Lowell did. He would have done it, but like Lowell, it would most likely have been done under protest and with a certain amount of grumbling. It must, after all, be admitted that he was definitely willing to follow Sheridan's instructions for the burning of the town of Dayton in retaliation for the death of Lt. John R. Meigs.

While on the one hand it is conceivable that he could have, if ordered, participated in the executions, given the provocations provided by Mosby and his rangers (whether or not he knew about Grant's August 16, 1864, directive that Mosby's men, if found, were to be executed without trial), on the other hand, I do not believe that it is at all likely, given his live and let live character, his sympathy for the South in general, and his friendships with many Confederate officers (such as West Point classmates Steven Dodson Ramseur and Thomas Lafayette Rosser), that he would have executed those men, or would have participated willingly in the executions, on his own initiative.

POSTSCRIPT:
CUSTER EXONERATED?

Over the course of writing this book, I would go online occasionally to check for new information concerning the atrocity at Front Royal. On all other previous attempts I found nothing online that I did not already know.

But, on one particular day I decided to search under *Front Royal executions*. What I found was an excerpt from the Southern Historical Society Papers, Volume 27, January to December 1899, posted on the Internet by the Lower Shenandoah Valley Civil War Roundtable, concerning the dedication of a monument in Front Royal to the seven members of John S. Mosby's 43rd Virginia Battalion of Partisan Rangers who were executed in 1864 after being taken prisoner. What I read almost caused me to fall out of my chair.

On September 23, 1899, the monument was dedicated to the six men who were executed in and about Front Royal and a seventh man who was hanged soon afterwards in Rappahannock County, Virginia, 35 years earlier. The reportage of the event and its aftermath was taken from the *Richmond Times* newspaper for the dates of September 24, 1899; November 12, 1899; December 8, 1899; and December 24, 1899. It quotes from the keynote address made by Judge Adolphus (Dolly) E. Richards, a former major in the 43rd Virginia Battalion of Partisan Rangers, who served as one of Lt. Col. Mosby's two sub-commanders. At the time of the dedication Maj. Richards was a lawyer then residing in Louisville, Ky. The dedication was part of the annual reunion of the veterans of Mosby's Rangers. Mosby himself, who resided at this time in California, did not attend.

The bulk of the material was very familiar to me. After being a small town journalist for 30 years I had written literally dozens of stories like it concerning very similar events of commemoration and remembrance. It was in the middle of Maj. Richards' keynote address that he dropped his bombshell: he now believed that George Armstrong Custer was in no way responsible for the events in and about Front Royal on September 23, 1864. Maj. Richards said:

> It was then thought that this was done by the order of Gen. George A. Custer, as the citizens reported he was seen at the time passing through the streets of the town; but from the disclosures in the official record of the war, we are of the opinion that he had nothing to do with it. Both Gen. Torbert, the commander-in-chief of the cavalry, and Gen. Merritt, the division commander, report that it was the Reserve Brigade of Merritt's division that was engaged in the fight. The records show that this brigade was commanded by Col. C.R. Lowell, and was composed of the 2nd Massachusetts, the 1st, 2nd and 5th United States regular cavalry. [The brigade also included the 6th U.S Cavalry Regiment but it had been so badly smashed during the Gettysburg Campaign that it was relegated to being the brigade's headquarters guard.] We also find the official record of Col. Lowell's report of the engagement, while it is not mentioned in any of Custer's reports. It was Lowell's brigade that was engaged in the fight. The officer and men who were killed on the Federal side were members of his brigade. He was personally in command at the time, and we may reasonably conclude that it was under his immediate supervision, and not Custer's, that our men were executed. Neither Col. Lowell, nor Gen. Torbert, nor Gen. Merritt, in reporting the engagement, mentions the fact that our men were executed after they surrendered, but content themselves with the statement that they were killed.
>
> In less than three weeks thereafter, Col. William H. Powell, commanding a brigade of Federal cavalry [actually it was a small division of two brigades], crossed the mountains into Rappahannock County. A detail of Mosby's men were at the same time escorting some Federal prisoners to Richmond, when they encountered Col. Powell's command. One of them, A.C. Willis, was captured. Under the order of Col. Powell, he was hung the next day.

Maj. Richards blamed the executions on the fateful directive sent by Union General-in-Chief Ulysses S. Grant to Maj. Gen. Philip H. Sheridan, commanding the Army of the Shenandoah, on August 16, 1864, which read in part: "When Mosby's men are caught, hang them without trial."

Needless to say, Maj. Richards' comments sparked at the time a firestorm of controversy, particularly since the commander of the 43rd Virginia was convinced of Custer's responsibility for the execution in Front Royal and remained convinced until the day that he died.

Shortly after the event, the *Richmond Times* received a communication from Mosby expressing his outrage that any of his men would ever attempt to rehabilitate Custer. His message to the newspaper is as follows:

> Editor of the Times:
>
> Sir — In his address at the unveiling of the monument at Front Royal to the seven men of my command who were hung and shot in the Shenandoah Valley campaign in 1864, when they were prisoners of war, Maj. Richards says: "We now know it was in strict compliance with an official order of the commanding general of the Federal armies;" and he quotes in proof of it the last line from the following dispatch from Gen. Grant, who was in front of Petersburg, to Sheridan, who was 200 miles away.
>
> CITY POINT, August 16, 1864 —1:30 P.M.
(Received at 6:30 A.M. 17th)
>
> MAJOR-GENERAL SHERIDAN,
> Commanding, &c., Winchester, Va.
>
> The families of most of Mosby's men are known and can be collected. I think they should be taken and kept at Fort McHenry, or some secure place as hostages for the good conduct of Mosby and his men. Whenever any of Mosby's men are caught, hang them without trial.
>
> U.S. GRANT
Lieutenant-General

As Harpers Ferry was the nearest telegraph station, Mosby stated in his communication to the *Richmond Times*, this dispatch must have been forwarded by a cavalry escort to Sheridan, who was 50 miles up the valley at Cedar Creek. Early was three miles farther south in line of battle at Fisher's Hill. Grant's instructions were: "Bear in mind — the object is to drive the enemy south; and to do this you want to keep him always in sight." The real objective point at which Grant aimed was Lee's lines of supply. Their destruction meant the fall of Richmond.

Of the same date (August 16, 1864) as Grant's dispatch is one from Sheridan to Maj. Gen. Henry Halleck, chief of staff, at Washington, saying: "Nothing from Gen. Grant later than the 12th." At 7:30 P.M. on the 13th, Sheridan had written Grant, "I was unable to get south of Early, but will push up the Valley," and at 10 P.M. the same day he sent Grant another dispatch saying: "Mosby attacked the rear of my train this morning en route here from Harper's Ferry and burned six wagons." This dispatch was not received until the 16th, and, according to Mosby, no doubt was the cause of the one sent by Grant on that date, which Sheridan did not receive until the 17th. He had been waiting at Cedar Creek for his supply trains.

After hearing of the attack on the train at Berryville there is a sudden change in the confident tone of Sheridan's dispatches and he had evidently become demoralized, Mosby wrote. On the 12th Sheridan had declared his intention to push Early up the Valley, yet on the 14th he says to Halleck, "I have taken up for the present the line of Cedar Run, but will at my pleasure take position at Winchester. This line cannot be held, nor can I supply my command beyond that point with the 10 days rations with which I started. I expected to get far enough up the Valley to accomplish my objects and then quickly return."

But Grant's instructions did not contemplate his return. Although Grant had ordered Sheridan to drive the enemy south and to keep in sight of him, he quietly retreated on the night of the 16th and did not stop until he got to Halltown, near Harpers Ferry, where he had taken command two weeks before on August 7. Mosby noted the *Times* on January 27, 1895, had published a review by Mosby of the Shenandoah campaign that said: "During the time that Sheridan was in the Shenandoah Valley, this [my] partisan corps was the only Confederate force that operated in his rear, or in Northern Virginia, east of the Blue Ridge. Sheridan affected to call us guerillas, but never defined what he meant by the term."

To emphasize this point Mosby included a number of communications between Grant and Sheridan. Sheridan wrote to Grant at Berryville, Va., August 17, 1864 at 9 P.M.: "Mosby has annoyed me and captured a few wagons. We hung one and shot six of his men yesterday." Mosby noted in his communication to the *Richmond Times* that two days before this he had dispatched 300 prisoners to Richmond.

Sheridan wrote to Grant on August 19: "Guerillas give me great annoyance but I am quietly disposing of numbers of them." Mosby commented that everybody would understand what "quietly disposing" of a man meant, especially when read in the light of Sheridan's former dispatches. According to Mosby the last dispatch suggested "the quiet operations of Jack the Ripper."

* * *

Sheridan to Grant, Halltown, August 22: "We have disposed of quite a number of Mosby's men." "Disposed of," Mosby notes, is not the usual language in which military reports state the casualties of war.

Sheridan to Grant, September 11: "We have exterminated three officers and twenty-seven men of Mosby's gang in the last twelve days." "We have exterminated," according to Mosby, was the language of the "Master of the Stair" when he announced the massacre of Glencoe. "Not one-third of my command was from that section of Virginia," Mosby said. "A great many were Marylanders. Even if it had been an unorganized body of citizens defending their homes, they would have only been doing what Governor Curtin and Gen. Couch urged Pennsylvania people to do when threatened with invasion [Early's invasion of the North prior to Sheridan's Shenandoah Valley Campaign]."

To illustrate his point Mosby included the following proclamation issued by Maj. Gen. D.N. Couch:

Pittsburg, Pa., August 4, 1864

To the people of the southern tier of counties of Pennsylvania:

Your situation is such that a raid by the enemy is not impossible at any time during the summer and coming fall. I therefore call upon you to put your rifles and shotguns in good order, and also supply yourselves with plenty of ammunition. Your cornfields, mountain forests, thickets, buildings, etc., furnish favorable places for cover; and at the same time enable you to kill the murderers, recollecting that if they come it is to plunder, destroy and burn your property.

D.N. Couch,
Major-General Commanding

Mosby took pains to note that this appeal to Pennsylvanians to turn bushwhacker was signed by a graduate of West Point and an officer of the regular army who once commanded a corps in the Army of the Potomac. It does seem rather ironic that a Northern military officer would issue a proclamation asking the people of the state of Pennsylvania rise up and defend their homes as guerrillas to combat a Southern invasion, particularly since the people of the Shenandoah Valley were more or less doing the same thing in attempting to defend themselves from an invading Northern army.

"I was a soldier of a great military power; in the Forum of Nations I was Sheridan's equal," Mosby said. "I had every right of war that he had. The Southern Confederacy like the empires of Alexander and Charlemagne has passed away, but that does not change the fact that it once existed."

Mosby contended that from the communications sent from Sheridan to Grant, Sheridan had begun hanging Mosby's men before he ever received Grant's dispatch of August 16. At Berryville on August 17, Sheridan said he had hung one and shot six on the day before. But, Mosby argued, Sheridan did not receive Grant's August 16, 1864, dispatch until 6:30 A.M. on August 17, so the "murders" could not have been committed in compliance with Grant's orders.

Furthermore, Mosby noted that all of the reports and correspondence during Sheridan's 1864 Shenandoah Valley Campaign had, by 1899, been published. Mosby said that in all of those orders and correspondence there was no imputation on the conduct of any of his rangers except for the statement in Merritt's report on the incident at Front Royal about the killing of Lt. McMaster. Mosby said that according to Sheridan's communications, Sheridan had begun hanging prisoners on August 16, and the only reason given for it is "Mosby has annoyed me."

To that Mosby pled guilty.

However, he disputed newspaper accounts during the war that said his rangers went about in disguise. "Mine was the best uniformed body of men in the Confederate army," Mosby said. "Every officer wore his insignia of rank. Sheridan speaks of having 'exterminated' three of my officers; but how could he have distinguished officers from privates if they were not in uniform?"

Mosby also said there could be no doubt that Grant's directive of August 16, 1864, was suggested by the receipt of Sheridan's dispatch concerning the Berryville Raid. In that dispatch Sheridan informed Grant that "Mosby attacked the rear of my train this morning en route from Harper's Ferry and burned six wagons." Mosby said that this dispatch deceived Grant on two counts: first, as to the magnitude of the disaster, and second, of the attacking force. The question Mosby asked was, why should Sheridan trouble Grant about the loss of six wagons? According to Mosby, the impression that it conveyed was that a few professed non-combatants, living in their homes in the Valley, in the guise of peace, had caught six wagons without a train guard and burned them. If Sheridan had told the whole truth about the destruction of the convoy, Grant would not have sent him such an order, maintained Mosby, because Grant would have known that a band of marauders could not have performed such a feat.

(It must be admitted that Sheridan had a tendency to shade his reports to Grant depending upon the impression he wanted to make as well as his agreement or disagreement as to what Grant wanted Sheridan to do. As far as hanging prisoners at this time, it apparently did not happen and that

Sheridan was writing this for whatever effect it might have on Grant. In all likelihood there were actually no executions of prisoners before the Front Royal Incident. Sheridan's behavior, as seen in many of his communications, most especially to Grant, could border on insubordination as well as to cross that line on more than one occasion. For whatever reason Grant tolerated this behavior, most likely because Sheridan was one of the very few officers who agreed wholeheartedly with Grant's concept of total war, which was used eventually to batter the Southern Confederacy to pieces.)

"It is a coincidence," Mosby said, "that the order is of the same date as the dispatch from Gen. Lee announcing the Berryville Raid to the Confederate War Department."

> Chaffin's Bluff, August 16, 1864
>
> Colonel Mosby reports that he attacked the enemy's supply train near Berryville on the 13th; captured and destroyed 75 loaded wagons and secured over 200 prisoners, including several officers, between 500 and 600 mules, upwards of 300 beef cattle, and many valuable stores. Considerable number of the enemy killed and wounded. His loss, two killed and three wounded.
>
> R.E. Lee, General
> Hon. J.A. Sedden, Secretary of War

This telegram, according to Mosby, was published the next day and was seen by Gen. Grant, as newspapers were generally exchanged between the lines. According to Mosby it informed him of the status of his command and it was the first public, official notice of Mosby and his 43rd Virginia Battalion of Partisan Rangers by Gen. Lee since Gen. Grant came to Virginia. The Berryville Raid was also the first Mosby ever reported to Lee by telegraph.

Mosby said the news was sent in haste because Mosby knew about Gen. Lee's anxiety about Sheridan's movement up the Valley, and that it would relieve Lee to hear that some kind of a blow had been struck against it. In Mosby's view Lee's dispatch to the War Department showed the importance that Lee attached to the Berryville Raid and that Lee foresaw the effect it would have upon Sheridan.

"It is a mystery," Mosby said, "Sheridan does not explain why he stopped talking about hanging my men. It was not because their manners had improved, or that they had ceased to annoy him. He gives no reason why there should be a difference between the treatment of my men and other Confederates."

Concerning his relationship with Lee, Mosby noted that there was no regimental officer in the Confederate army that was in as close a relationship with Lee than he was. Mosby said that he reported directly to Lee and received instructions directly from Lee. Generally, Lee commanded his army through his corps commanders, with Mosby's battalion being the only exception. "Although operating in the Valley," Mosby explained, "my command was independent of Early's army. Early was in front of Sheridan — I was behind him."

Mosby noted that after September 11, Sheridan's dispatches were silent on the subject of Sheridan's hanging his men as guerrillas. "If he ever hung anybody he kept it a secret," Mosby wrote. "I never heard of it until I read it in the war records. I am sure nobody else ever did; the war correspondents never mentioned it. When I retaliated for the massacre of my men at Front Royal, I wrote him a letter telling him what I had done, and published it in the newspapers.... If he had hung any citizen of the Valley, their families and friends would have known about it, and we would have heard of it. The only justification of punishment is to act as a deterrent; if it is secret it can have no such effect, and is criminal revenge."

Mosby further notes that during this time period not over half a dozen of his Rangers had been taken prisoner. These men were sent to a Northern prison. "If Sheridan hung them there was a resurrection," Mosby noted, "for they returned home after the war, and I know some of them are living now [in 1899]." Mosby also noted that during this time period he lost only one officer, Lt. Frank Fox, who was mortally wounded, not the three that Sheridan spoke of "exterminating." According to Mosby, "Sheridan was not as black as he painted himself."

Mosby defended his actions when he forced Union prisoners to draw lots with the intention of executing the seven losers. He actually succeeded in hanging only three men. Two others escaped outright and the remaining two (who were shot) were wounded, feigned death and also escaped.

"If I had not retaliated," Mosby maintained, "the war in the Valley would have degenerated into a massacre. We were called guerillas and bushwhackers. Now while bushwhacking is perfectly legitimate war and it is a fair to shoot a man from a bush as behind a stockade or an earthwork, no men in the Confederate army less deserve these epithets than mine, if by them is meant a body of men who fought under cover and practiced tactics and stratagems not permitted by the rules of regular war.

140

Sheridan certainly makes no such charge against us. A bushwhacker shoots under shelter with a long gun; the Northern cavalry knew by experience that my men always fought in a mounted charge, with pistols. The fact that we were called rebels gave the enemy no rights as combatants that we did not equally enjoy. As belligerents we stood on the same plane. One side could not command what it did not concede to the other."

Mosby commented that when Gen. Grant came east to take over direction of the Northern war effort, joining the Army of the Potomac in its camps at Culpeper, south of the Rappahannock River, he moved toward Richmond, crossed the James River, and was in front of Lee at Petersburg. Mosby's Rangers remained in northern Virginia to threaten Washington and the border area. Mosby said his rangers operated along the Potomac in the Shenandoah Valley and did not come in contact with that portion of the army which Grant accompanied. Thus, Mosby contended that Grant only knew about Mosby's Rangers by report and that he no doubt believed that Mosby and his men were the equivalent to the Western bands of outlaws whose deeds the Confederate government disowned, and that he shared the general belief of Northerners that Mosby was a leader of "banditti"—a chief of brigands.

"Grant's dispatch [of August 16, 1864] bears internal evidence, and read between the lines, shows the delusion he was under in regards to my men," Mosby commented. "He says—'the families of Mosby's men are known and can be collected'—which implies that their homes were in Sheridan's lines, where in fact they were scattered all over the South, and some states in the North. Sheridan made no attempt to enforce this order, because it was impossible. I wish he had; it would have been the most effective way of destroying his army. He would have had to have dispersed it over half a dozen states, catching and corralling women and children."

Mosby maintained, but provided no proof or evidence of his assertion, that only one of the six men who were hanged at Front Royal was from the Valley (that would had to have been Henry Rhodes, who lived in Front Royal and was not a member of Mosby's 43rd Virginia but in a surge of youthful exuberance he had joined the Rangers on their way through the town to attack the Union wagon train that day) and one was from Georgia. According to Mosby, while Grant evidently thought that his men lived within a few square miles, that was not correct, and Sheridan knew better. Mosby said that Grant's August 16 dispatch reflected the idea that prevailed in the North during the war and that continued up to and beyond the dedication of the monument to his men at Front Royal as "bluebeards" and "Jack-the-Giant-Killers." According to Mosby this conception was purely the creation of war correspondents.

"But Gen. Grant," Mosby continued, "admits in his memoirs the erroneous impression he once had of me; of course it equally applies to my men. Some may say the change was due to politics. But his conduct at the surrender when he voluntarily offered us the same parole he gave to General Lee, after Stanton had proclaimed me an outlaw, showed that the change came about before the close of the war. The friendship that afterwards grew up between us should be viewed with indulgence by Southern people, as it was certainly disinterested on his part, and hurt no Southern men."

Personally, Mosby acquitted Sheridan of all responsibility for the deed at Front Royal. "The orders of a superior are no defense of a criminal charge," Mosby the lawyer noted. "It is a well settled principle of law that a principal is not responsible for the *malicious* act of his agent; the agent incurs a personal liability." Mosby doubted whether Sheridan had even heard about the executions at Front Royal before he received Mosby's letter.

Concerning the reported death of Lt. McMaster, who was supposedly robbed and shot after he surrendered, Mosby noted that this story is only mentioned in Merritt's report. Mosby maintains that McMaster was never a prisoner. That instead he was overrun and killed. "While Torbert's, Merritt's and Lowell's reports betray the consciousness of a crime committed by someone, they do not disclose who did it," Mosby said. "Even admitting that McMaster offered to surrender when killed, there is a vast difference in refusing quarter in the excitement and *brevis furor* of a cavalry combat and killing in cold blood and under official sanction when combat is over."

(*The Official Record of the War of the Rebellion* is not the sole repository of records. There are other reports in letters, memoirs, regimental histories, etc. which do offer some confirmation of McMaster and his fate, as noted in Merritt's official report.)

In addition, Mosby notes that Torbert, Merritt and Lowell's reports contradict each other, first in regard to the number killed (Torbert claimed they killed two officers and nine men, Merritt says they killed 18 and

Lowell that they killed 13). Second, they said nothing about any wounded, which Mosby found significant since the usual proportion of killed to wounded is generally three or four to one. Third, they made no mention of prisoners. "As the prisoners were murdered they wouldn't have acknowledged that they took any," Mosby commented.

Mosby claimed that he did not believe Sheridan ever instructed his subordinates to execute Grant's directive of August 16, because he knew that Mosby could hang 500 of his men, where he could only hang one of Mosby's. Mosby reiterated that none of his men were hung before September 23.

Concerning Custer, Mosby admits that his men were not involved in the fighting at Front Royal, so of course Custer makes no mention of it. "But," Mosby maintained, "There is no evidence that he had nothing to do with the hanging — he was on the ground. As none of the reports speak of the hanging, they would equally prove the innocence of Torbert, Merritt and Lowell — in fact, of everybody. They were all ashamed of it as a blot on the fame of Sheridan's army. It is of no concern of mine whether only one or all the generals participated in the crime; they may all have been *in pari delecto*. They can settle that question among themselves. The people of Front Royal considered Custer the most conspicuous actor in the tragedy, and so I stated in my letter to Sheridan. Custer never denied it."

Mosby also cited a report by Capt. Richard Blazer of Blazer's Scouts, a special unit of picked men, who reported being in the vicinity of Front Royal about two days later. "In another affair below Front Royal," Blazer reported, "I left eight of his [Mosby's] murderers to keep company some that [were] left by Gen. Custer." While Mosby admits that Blazer's language was obscure, he interpreted it to mean that Blazer had killed eight of his men "to accompany those Custer had hung and shot at Front Royal." Mosby maintains that the eight men Blazer claimed to have killed were "as pure phantoms as those Sheridan said he had hung." But, Mosby said, Blazer gave Custer all of the credit for what was done at Front Royal. (Blazer's Scouts were later destroyed in an action with a portion of Mosby's Rangers. In later communications Mosby noted that he was not present at this action and gives all credit for this achievement to Maj. Richards, who was serving at the time as one of his two sub-commanders.)

Mosby also maintained that Custer had a grudge against him and his men. Mosby claimed that his men caught a party of Custer's men burning houses in the vicinity of Berryville and that Mosby's orders were to bring in no prisoners caught in the act of house burning. Mosby said that no quarter was shown and about 25 men were shot to death and, although horses were captured, there were no prisoners. Mosby concluded:

> This has been written in justice to a great soldier who was my friend, as well as to the men who were actors with me in the great drama along the Shenandoah, and especially to the seven whose names are inscribed on the monument in Front Royal. The granite shaft perpetuates the fame of a glorious band — 'a remnant of our Spartan dead.' About the affair in which they were sacrificed to the bloody moloch of revenge, I feel now as I have always felt. A highlander is not asked or expected to forgive or forget Glencoe or Culloden. It will always be a proud satisfaction to me that, in the presence of their executioners, these martyrs did not imitate the despairing cry of the gladiator in the arena — Caesar *morituri salutamus* [Caesar, we who are about to die salute thee] — but with heroic confidence, foretold they would have an avenger. The prophecy was fulfilled. Those who committed the great crime have not escaped the Nemesis, who adjusts the unbalanced scale of human wrongs.

Mosby's response to Maj. Richards' keynote address was dated October 31, 1899. On December 3, 1899, Richards wrote his reply to Mosby's comments as follows:

> Editor of the Times:
>
> SIR — In my address at the unveiling of the monument erected at Front Royal to the memory of Mosby's men who were executed after they surrendered, I stated two conclusions drawn from the official records of the war, which seem to have attracted particular attention and elicited some discussion. The interest thus evidenced encourages me to give the facts supporting those conclusions.
>
> The Front Royal tragedy occurred on September 23, 1864. At that time we did not know that Mosby's Rangers, embracing only eight companies of cavalry [actually there were only six companies at that particular time], had attracted, or rather distracted, the attention of Gen. Grant, who was at that time commanding general of the United States armies. But the official records, now published, indicate that he stopped "Marching on Richmond" long enough to send implicit instructions to Gen. Sheridan in regards to his campaign against Mosby's men.

Richards then proceeded to reiterate and review Grant's directive of August 16, 1864, and Sheridan's answer of August 17. According to Richards, up to the time of the receipt of Grant's August 16 directive, Sheridan never claimed to have executed any prisoners from among

Mosby's Rangers. Richards noted that it was significant that after receiving Grant's August 16 directive, he responded with the claim that he had hung one of Mosby's men while shooting another six.

Richards agrees with Mosby that this incident existed only in Sheridan's imagination, and it was only mentioned in the dispatch from Sheridan to Grant dated August 17. "But," Richards noted, "the correspondence shows he was answering Gen. Grant's message containing the order for the hanging of our men; and we can only conjecture his motive for reporting that he had already commenced the hanging."

On the following day, August 18, Sheridan received instructions from Grant: "If you can possibly spare a division of cavalry," send them through Loudoun County to destroy and carry off crops, animals, wagons, and all men under 50 years of age capable of bearing arms. Grant stated that "in this way you will get many of Mosby's men."

Grant further suggested in a dispatch dated November 9, 1864, that all citizens living east of the Blue Ridge be ordered to move north of the Potomac River with all of their stock, grain and provisions so that they will not support Mosby's Rangers and as long as the war lasts that these citizens be prevented from raising another crop in as much of the valley as was controlled by Union troops.

Richards conceded that on August 19, August 22, and September 11, Sheridan sent to Grant communications, cited by Mosby, describing his "progress" in the process of "exterminating" Mosby's men. A fourth dispatch, dated September 29, was in regards to the devastation of the countryside, which became known as "The Burning."

This dispatch noted that Merritt's and Custer's cavalry divisions had been ordered to sweep through the valley like a "dragnet" covering every foot of Mosby's Confederacy. The work of destruction went on day and night.

Richards recalled The Burning, noting: "I watched it from a point on the Blue Ridge Mountains, where I was bivouacking for the night, on our way to the Valley of Virginia with a few of our men. As far as the eye could see the whole country east of the mountains was lit up by the destroying flames, and the glare was reflected by the sky above. It was a sublime sight to the eye, but a sickening one to the heart."

According to Richards, Sheridan had been ordered not only to hang Mosby's men and devastate the countryside, but also to carry off the families of Mosby's Rangers and to imprison them in Fort McHenry. Richards noted that Sheridan did not carry out this order and that the records do not state why he did not carry out this order. However, Richards maintained that it was not because they were out of his reach. "There was scarcely a family in all that section that did not have some member in Mosby's command," Richards said.

Mosby's reply was that if this was true, than he, Mosby must have had a larger army than Sheridan's. This response is facetious. The Shenandoah Valley was the source of a large number of Confederate troops. The Stonewall Brigade, the Laurel Brigade and Mosby's own 43rd Virginia Battalion of Partisan Rangers were only a few of the units to be recruited in whole or in part from among the residents of the Valley, thus by 1864 greatly reducing the pool of possible recruits.

Richards noted that Mosby himself had married a resident of Farquier County, and many of the other officers and enlisted men had families within the condemned territory. Richards said that had Merritt and Custer been ordered to arrest the families of Mosby's men during The Burning, it could have been easily accomplished. "It would have been the most severe and cruel blow of all — its paralyzing effect could only be fully realized by those of us whose loved ones were still sheltered by the old homesteads in Loudoun and Farquier."

In response, Mosby, stated that moving his soldiers' families to Fort McHenry would have been a more humane way of eliminating his command than killing his men. "Sheridan," Mosby stated, "knew that if he did anything of the kind it would stimulate the activity of my men; so he didn't try it. As for our lieutenant colonel [Mosby referring to himself], who, as Maj. Richards says married in that section, I think that, if Sheridan had captured his wife and mother-in-law and sent them to prison, instead of going into mourning, he would have felt all the wrath and imitated the example of the fierce Achilles when he heard the Patroclus, his friend, had been killed and his armor had been captured. 'Now perish Troy!' he said, and rushed to fight."

Despite these directives from General Grant, Richards still credited Grant with being essentially a soldier and a great leader. "Like Gen. Forrest, of the South, he knew that 'war meant fighting, and fighting meant killing,'" Richards said. Grant's aim, according to Richards, was to end the fighting as soon as possible and the way to do that was to capture

Richmond and to destroy Lee's army. What Grant was doing, Richards realized, was urging Sheridan to conclude the Shenandoah Valley campaign as soon as possible so that the bulk of his infantry troops could be transferred to assist in the siege of Petersburg, the seizure of Richmond, and the final destruction of Lee's army.

According to Richards, Grant realized that Mosby and his rangers were an obstruction to his plans and that they had already disrupted Sheridan's line of communications and supply, forcing him to fall back from his advanced position. "The Manassas Gap Railroad could neither be repaired or operated as long as we held our position in Loudoun and Farquier counties," Richards commented. "So the orders went forth for the extermination of 'Mosby's gang.' Our men were to be hung, our country devastated by fire, and our families imprisoned."

Richards fully admits that Grant was misinformed about the nature of Mosby's Rangers, as Grant states in his memoirs. Richards blames this mostly upon Sheridan since he characterized Mosby's men as "guerrillas" or worse. However, by the end of the war this misinformation was corrected, with Grant realizing that the 43rd Virginia Battalion of Partisan Rangers was a regularly organized unit of the Confederate army, receiving orders from and reporting directly to General Lee. Richards said that despite much discussion he was more convinced than ever that General Custer had not directed the executions at Front Royal.

According to Richards, what had actually happened was that Torbert, in command of four brigades of cavalry from two divisions on September 21, 1864, had gone up the Luray Valley under orders to cross over to the main valley and attack Early's flank and rear. After a skirmish with an inferior force of rebel cavalry, he had retreated, much to Sheridan's disgust, and he had returned through Front Royal on September 23.

On approaching Front Royal, Wesley Merritt's division was in the lead. Taking the van was Col. Lowell's Reserve Cavalry Brigade and following behind was Gen. Custer's Michigan Cavalry Brigade. Capt. Chapman of Mosby's Rangers attacked the wagon train in front of the column and the remainder of Lowell's brigade closed in on Chapman's men, capturing the six who were later executed. In the fighting one of Lowell's best officers and several men were killed. Afterwards the six prisoners were executed, although none of the official reports mention this fact.

Richards agreed with Mosby that the Union commanders involved were ashamed of the incident. But, Col. Lowell did report that he had made the fight and "killed" the men. General Merritt, the division commander, reported that Lowell's command fought the skirmish and "killed" the men. General Torbert reported that Merritt's division had "killed" the men.

"We had always thought that Gen. Custer had directed the execution," Richards stated.

> We had gotten this impression from the citizens of Front Royal. Custer's brigade was marching next to Lowell's, and had arrived before the execution. Gen. Custer was a conspicuous figure, in his velvet uniform, with his long golden curls. The citizens of Front Royal had learned to recognize him. Seeing him in their streets at the time, it is not surprising that they should have reported him in command. But it would have violated all military rules for one brigade commander to have taken the prisoners from another brigade commander and ordered their execution, especially when the divisional commander was within reach.

Richards wanted to be certain that his conclusions about what had happened in and around Front Royal on September 23, 1864, were correct. Therefore he had written to Confederate Maj. Gen. Thomas L. Rosser seeking a statement. Richards sought a statement from Rosser because he knew that Custer and Rosser had been friends before the war, and although they fought on opposite sides, their friendship had never wavered and the two men had renewed their friendship after the war.

Rosser's reply is as follows:

> Charlottesville, November 23, 1899
>
> Major A.E. Richards, Louisville, Ky.:
>
> My Dear Major — I saw a great deal of Custer while I was constructing the Northern Pacific R.R., in the Northwest, in the seventies, and had many talks over the war with him; and he often stated that he was in no way responsible for the execution or murder of those men.
>
> I have no doubt of Custer's innocence, for he was not in command, and his superior officer was present; and it is not probable that such a matter would have been turned over to Custer under the circumstances.
>
> Yours most truly,
> Thomas L. Rosser

"This statement of Gen. Rosser," Richards maintained, "supported as it is by the official record, seems to me to be conclusive, and the future historian must exonerate Gen. Custer from the responsibility of the Front Royal tragedy."

"I don't care a staw," Mosby wrote in response to Maj. Richards' exoneration of Custer, "whether Custer was solely responsible for the hanging of our men or jointly with others. If we believe the reports of the generals, none of them even heard of the hanging of our men; they must have committed suicide. Contemporary evidence is against Custer. I wonder if he also denied burning dwelling houses around Berryville."

Personally, I was astounded that no hint of this exoneration of Custer by a member of Mosby's Rangers, not to say by one of Mosby's two subcommanders, was to be found in any of my previous research for this book.

Moreover, it is my opinion that Mosby's comments in these communications and correspondence sounds very much like that of a man who finds it impossible to admit that there may have been a possibility, however slight, that he might have been wrong to place the blame for the execution of his rangers at Front Royal solely upon the shoulders of George Armstrong Custer.

In addition, Mosby's absolution of Grant from having any responsibility for the executions even though he did issue the infamous August 16, 1864, directive reinforces this impression of Mosby's character, since Mosby and Grant had become friends after the war. If Mosby and Grant were to be friends then Grant had to be absolved, in Mosby's mind, of any of the guilt in what Mosby saw and continued to see to the end of his days as the murder of his men. I find it sad that John S. Mosby, one of the true heroes of the American Civil War, spent the last 50 years of his life heaping slander, libel and dishonor upon the name of another hero of the American Civil War, albeit a hero from the other side.

Finally, after researching and writing this book about the Front Royal Incident and its aftermath, I have reached three conclusions about George Armstrong Custer. These are as follows:

- First: Hugh Judson Kilpatrick was everything that George Armstrong Custer was ever accused of being and was not.
- Second: The only thing that can truthfully be said against Custer was that he had all the vices of his virtues.
- The major failing of most Union generals was that they did not have enough audacity and that in final analysis there is no such thing as too much audacity.

Appendix I

GEORGE ARMSTRONG CUSTER: HERO OR GOAT?

"If there is anything truly heroic about [George Armstrong] Custer it must be read in the Civil War," the late military historian S.L.A. Marshall once wrote.

Marshall's comment represents a prevailing opinion that George Armstrong Custer was an exceedingly rash, if not reckless — and a somewhat incompetent military commander. However, a close examination of the record, Custer's American Civil War record, reveals that while he may not have been the greatest strategist or tactician ever to come out of West Point, he was still an outstanding battlefield commander with the talent to take in a military situation at a glance, in an instant determine his own course of action, and then follow through, his movements occurring with a speed and determination that often dazzled his Confederate opponents.

The two years Custer spent as a brigade and divisional commander in the Army of the Potomac tells a story that is today largely unknown. From the primary sources — the diaries, letters, and regimental histories of the men he commanded — it can easily be seen that these two years were the most successful of Custer's entire life. Ironically, today, this period of his life is frequently ignored while his later career as an Indian fighter and the disaster at the Little Big Horn receive all the attention.

Gregory J.W. Urwin, another military historian, believes Marshall's verdict on Custer "is the result of shoddy scholarship, superficial thinking, unforgivable prejudice, and a desire of literary popularity." And yet, despite all of these shortcomings, Urwin admits, Marshall still has managed to strike his nail squarely upon the head, for it is during the American Civil War that Custer most outstandingly demonstrated his ability. It cannot be stressed enough that in order to understand Custer, you must understand that the American Civil War was the most important event of his life, and everything else, even the "Last Stand" at Little Big Horn, was nothing more than anticlimax.

A comparison of Custer's record during the American Civil War and his later career as an Indian fighter shows a strange split personality. It is almost as if you are talking about two entirely different men. During the American Civil War the men of the Michigan Cavalry Brigade and later the 3rd Cavalry Division idolized and admired him to the point where they consciously imitated him in both dress and manner. But after the war, there was a change. The enlisted men no longer admired Custer. In fact, his 7th U.S. Cavalry Regiment had a huge problem with desertion. The officers were divided into pro- and anti–Custer factions.

Perhaps the best explanation for this split personality was that something had changed, and it wasn't Custer. What had changed was the military environment that he found himself in. That had changed, drastically.

The men Custer had commanded during the American Civil War were volunteers in the truest sense of the word. In the final analysis these men were there in the Michigan Cavalry Brigade and the 3rd Cavalry Division because they wanted to be there. For the most part they were not draftees and they were not fleeing economic hardships. Instead, they voluntarily chose the hardship of leaving their homes to enlist in the army, sacrificing at least three years of their lives if not life itself. They also risked terrible wounds and the

Bvt. Maj. General George A. Custer as photographed at the end of the American Civil War; the primary question historians have sought to answer about him has been: was Custer the hero of his own life, or was he the goat? (Library of Congress, Prints and Photographs Division).

possibility that instead of dying on the battlefield they would either die in a hospital or live minus an arm and a leg. In addition, for every man who died on the battlefield, at least another man died in a sickbed. These men were fighting for the continuation of their country and to make that country become a place where one man could not own another man.

The end of the American Civil War brought great changes, or more properly, a return to normalcy within the U.S. Army. From its peak of 500,000 during the Civil War, the U.S. Army decreased to an authorized strength of 25,000 by 1869. Such a low strength level made the U.S. Army just barely adequate for policing the Indian territories of the West. And, much of the time the U.S. Army was considerably below its authorized strength. Custer himself reverted from his wartime rank of brevet major general of volunteers to his regular army rank of captain. Later, he was promoted to lieutenant colonel, being made the executive officer and de facto commander of the brand new 7th U.S. Cavalry Regiment.

Gone were the volunteers who had fought the American Civil War. In their place were the "regulars" — generally men recruited from the dregs of society, or just off the immigrant boats, or men fleeing from economic hardships or other problems, for the Army was the employer of last resort and they got very little if any respect.

And Custer, who went straight from West Point to the battlefield of Manassas/Bull Run, was ill equipped to handle this sudden state of affairs. His entire experience had been in the Army at war — not the Army at peace. And in peacetime, even with the various Indian wars, there was considerably less chance for Custer to excel in the way he had during the American Civil War.

During the 11 years from end of the American Civil War in 1865 to his death in 1876 he fought just two major battles against the Indians. The first was the Battle of the Washita in 1868 and the second was his final battle at the Little Big Horn in 1876, both of which are today covered in controversy.

Here, however, we are mostly concerned with Custer's American Civil War record.

During the American Civil War those officers who succeeded in winning the respect of their men were the ones who led from the front (which was the style of leadership that definitely suited Custer perfectly), rather than commanding from the rear (which was rather more in Kilpatrick's style of command).

Custer made himself conspicuous in appearance and battlefield behavior on purpose. He deliberately demonstrated his courage (or fearlessness), courting danger, on purpose, to allay his soldiers' natural fear. He wore an outlandish uniform to ensure they would always know exactly where he was in the thick of any fight. (There are some people, adrenalin junkies, who do not feel fear and who are excited by the prospect of danger. That is fearlessness. There are also people who use their fear and/or rise above it. That is being courageous. There is no way of knowing now exactly which Custer was; but either works, so in the long run, who cares?)

True, it was not long before every newspaper correspondent with the Army of the Potomac knew him by sight. But, so did every one of the soldiers he was commanding and a great many of the Confederate soldiers he was fighting against. During Sheridan's Shenandoah Valley Campaign of 1864 the Confederate Army paid him a backhanded complement. They detached an entire company of sharpshooters and gave it a single order — Kill Custer! An enemy certainly does not bother to do this when faced with an incompetent.

Now that Custer was finally a general, how did he conduct himself as a military commander?

In his first skirmish as a general, he has been accused of being rash and reckless at Hunterstown, personally leading a decoy party to lure the Confederates onto his killing ground. Although the decoy party lost nearly half its number and Custer himself was almost killed, the diversion did succeed in that Confederates pursuing the party were decimated, with at least one of Hampton's units losing almost all of their officers. Custer, however, made it a practice to never repeat his mistakes. At Gettysburg, Custer disregarded orders and thus was instrumental in stopping Confederate Maj. Gen. J.E.B. Stuart from getting to the rear of the Union Army.

In Judson Kilpatrick's failed raid on Richmond, Custer's part was successful. He was to cut a railroad line, destroy a supply depot and divert Stuart, all of which he carried out without losing any men and meanwhile securing 50 prisoners and freeing 100 slaves. Custer continued to provide successes when he and his brigade were transferred to the 1st Cavalry Division.

At Yellow Tavern it was Custer's Michigan Cavalry Brigade that broke J.E.B. Stuart's line and it was undoubtedly one of Custer's horse soldiers who fired the shot that killed Stuart. At the Third Battle of Winchester/

Opequon Creek it was Custer's Michigan Cavalry Brigade that sent the Confederate Valley District Army "Whirling through Winchester."

When Wilson, who proved to be a lackluster commander, was transferred back to the Western Theatre, Custer was given command of the 3rd Cavalry Division, although the Michigan Cavalry Brigade remained with the 1st Cavalry Division. It was not long before the men of the 3rd Cavalry Division emulated the men of the Michigan Cavalry Brigade with every man outfitting themselves with a bright red tie. Thus the men of the division quickly became known as "The Red Tie Boys."

And Custer just kept on repeating his successes.

At the Battle of Tom's Brook, Custer opposed a Confederate cavalry division commanded by an old friend from West Point, Brig. Gen. Thomas Lafayette Rosser. Rosser was determined to best Custer and had placed his three brigades on the high ground. Custer arrived with but two brigades and formed them for battle. When everything was ready — knowing that Rosser was in command of the Confederate cavalry — he rode out in front of his men and bowed in his saddle to his opponents.

Custer's actions were more than a simple gesture of respect. What he was actually doing was scanning the enemy's position looking for a weakness, and he found one. After determining where Rosser was vulnerable, he returned to his own lines and attacked, routing Rosser's cavalry, chasing it for 12 miles in what became known as the "Woodstock Races."

At Cedar Creek when a surprise attack by Early's Valley District Army routed two-thirds of Sheridan's Army of the Shenandoah, Custer and Merritt threw their two cavalry divisions in the path of the victorious Confederates to hold the Union left and center together, buying time for Sheridan to arrive from Winchester. During his famous ride, Sheridan managed to put his army back together as he literally rode to the sound of the guns.

That day at Cedar Creek, Sheridan managed to do something that no one else did in the entire war. He took an army that had been beaten in the morning and in the afternoon of that same day he turned it loose upon its tormentors and drove them from the field. He was able to accomplish that miracle at least in part because Custer had held the line.

In the final campaign of the war in the East, after the fall of Petersburg and Lee's evacuation of Richmond, Custer's division was often used as the spearhead of the pursuing Army of the Potomac. At Five Forks,

Custer's division smashed through Confederate entrenchments to join hands with the infantry of V Corps to trap 5,000 Confederate soldiers, who were forced to surrender. The Battle of Five Forks allowed Sheridan to cut the Danville and Southside railroads, Richmond's final lifelines. Altogether the Confederates lost more than 6,000 men at Five Forks. The loss of Five Forks and those 6,000 men meant than Lee no longer had the soldiers and supplies to continue to hold out at Petersburg. Skillfully Lee evacuated both Petersburg and Richmond and began his final retreat.

At the Battle of Sayler's Creek when George Crook's 2nd Cavalry Division was stopped cold by Lee's rear guard, Confederate infantry under Richard Anderson and what remained of the Richmond garrison under Richard Ewell, it was Custer's division that sliced through Lee's rearguard and cut off roughly a third of Lee's remaining troops, holding them in place until the arrival of VI Corps forced their surrender. A number of generals (including Lee's youngest son, George Washington Custis Lee, Anderson, and Ewell) and most of Lee's wheeled transport were also captured.

And it was Custer's division that dashed Lee's last hope of continuing the war by capturing four trainloads of desperately needed supplies at Appomattox Station and a full battalion of artillery consisting of 24 cannons, which attempted to stop him. He then pushed on to Appomattox Court House, driving Lee's advanced pickets back into Lee's camp and placing his division squarely across Lee's line of retreat. Thus Custer stopped Lee's retreating army in its tracks at Appomattox Court House and held them in place long enough for the rest of the Army of the Potomac and the Army of the James to come up and for Grant to effectively end the war with Lee's surrender.

Custer's record during the American Civil War has long been overshadowed by what came after it — the anticlimax that formed the rest of Custer's life and which ended on that Montana ridge, the site of Custer's Last Stand. Most of Custer's biographers and a good many historians have fixed their sights upon the Little Big Horn at the expense of the rest of Custer's life and accomplishments. As at least one historian (Gregory J.W. Urwin) has put it: "This is like basing your entire understanding of a man, solely upon the last day of his life, about which you know practically nothing."

A final point to remember is that the Battle of the Little Big Horn occurred on June 25, 1876. This date is of extreme importance in order to understand what occurred after the battle. Not only was it the centennial of American independence — it was also a presidential election year. And in American politics everything that goes wrong in an election year is blamed upon the incumbent administration.

Grant was now president, although he was not running for re-election. Still, he had enough problems in overseeing what was probably one of the most corrupt administrations in American history. He did not need another scandal and the Army, ever sensitive to the political implications and desires of its civilian masters, accommodated them.

The disaster was quickly blamed upon Custer's "rashness and recklessness." After all Custer, was safely dead and was unable to defend himself and what are a few minor deceptions when it came to protecting the living and the reputation of the Army. Today such behavior is known as covering your arse.

Granted, Custer made mistakes at the Little Big Horn and he was ultimately responsible for his own doom. Yet his were not the only blunders that were made in that campaign. There were some who lied from the beginning to protect their own careers (such as John Gibbon, who, if only he had exerted himself and obtained precise information, which was readily available, about the exact location of Sitting Bull's winter roamers before they were joined by the summer roamers from the reservations, might have prevented the disaster), and Custer was such a convenient scapegoat. Others changed their stories as time went on, incriminating details were deleted, unimportant incidents became inflated, and some were even fabricated, especially during the only official investigation into what had happened, the Reno Court of Inquiry.

Historian John S. Grey, author of *Centennial Campaign: The Sioux War of 1876*, believes Custer was misled by faulty intelligence, which indicated he would encounter far fewer Indians than he actually did and by the belief that the Indians would flee rather than stand and fight. From the beginning of the campaign each of the officers involved in planning it and executing it were most concerned with how to catch the Indians, not with how to fight them once they were caught.

When he finally learned how big the village actually was (Custer had the misfortune of attacking the Indians at their peak strength, if he had attacked a few days earlier or a few days later he would not have been so heavily outnumbered) and that the Indians were not going to run away, but were going to stand and fight. (Custer never did learn that over a week earlier the Indians had defeated and turned back another column led by George Crook, who then went fishing.) Once Custer found out how many Indians there were and that they would stand and fight, it was too late, even for a master battlefield improviser such as Custer. His regiment was divided in an attempt to locate the Indians and one portion of it was already engaged.

From the evidence it appears that Custer attempted to strike a diversionary blow and thus reconcentrate his command. He failed and he died.

Consider the record established by Custer in his American Civil War service, compare it to his later days as an Indian fighter and to his demise at the Little Big Horn and ask yourself if this is the record of a fool, of a rash, reckless, and incompetent commander? Is Custer the hero of his own life, or like Charlie Brown in the Peanuts comic strip, is he the goat?

Appendix II

AUTIE AND LIBBIE: ROMANCE OR SHAM?

Many historians have considered the relationship between George Armstrong Custer (Autie) and his wife, Elizabeth Clift Bacon Custer (Libbie), to be one of the great romances of American history. Then there are those who consider their marriage and relationship to be one of the great shams of American history.

Custer, in one of the most important relationships of his entire life, has been accused of numerous and great infidelities. Elizabeth, herself, in at least one TV/film treatment, *Son of the Morning Star*, has been accused of either being or becoming sexually cold and as a result driving her husband to at least one infidelity with a Native American woman. In addition, Libbie has also been accused of encouraging the advances of other men, causing Autie in a jealous rage to abandon his command and conduct a hellish march to confront her and her "supposed" lover.

But, if one takes a close look at the record, specifically at the incidents that have given rise to these accusations, it will become clear that they are baseless and without support. The story of Autie's supposed infidelities are generally based upon what we will call the Annie Jones Incident, the Captured Letters Incident, and the Cheyenne Squaw Incident. The charge that Libbie was sexually cold has generally been based upon the observation that she and Autie had no children. In addition, it has been charged that she tolerated Autie's infidelities and that she may have even had a few of her own. These charges have been based upon the letters and statements of Capt. Frederick W. Benteen, who was the senior captain of Autie's 7th U.S. Cavalry Regiment, and which can be shown to be nothing more than bald faced lies — the ramblings of a man who hated and detested Autie and everything that he stood for.

First, let us examine the likely reason why Autie and Libbie were with

159

General George A. Custer and his wife, Elizabeth Bacon Custer. Another question for historians: was their relationship one of the great romances of American history, or was it only a Victorian Era sham? (Library of Congress, Prints and Photographs Division).

out children. The explanation is quite simple: George Armstrong Custer was most probably sterile.

Jeffry D. Wert, in his book *Custer: The Controversial Life of George Armstrong Custer,* notes that Autie received his first summer furlough from West Point in 1859, at the end of his second year, most of which was spent at his family home at New Rumley, Ohio, and that he reported back to West Point on August 28, 1859. On August 29, 1859, Autie was admitted to the academy's hospital, where he was diagnosed as suffering from gonorrhea. Gonorrhea is a venereal disease that causes a painful urethral discharge in men. Autie apparently became infected while on furlough, most likely contracting the disease from a prostitute while passing through New York City on his way back to the academy. According to academy records, during this time gonorrhea was a common malady among cadets returning from furlough.

In 19th Century medicine there was no effective cure for gonorrhea and what treatments were available were only palliative at best. Some victims suffered little or no lasting harm. But, since the treatments that were available did not destroy the bacterium causing the disease, which lodged in the prostate, seminal vesicles, and vas deferens, a victim could be rendered sterile by scarring and fibrousness of the urethral tract and of the sperm passageway. Where fibrousness was severe and persistent, a surgeon inserted a metal rod and scraped the tract.

Concerning Autie's infection, there is no way of determining how severe it was. However, in one letter home he wrote that he had been ill for some time, being detained in hospital during the beginning of the term. He does not seem to have shared just what the diagnosis was. Once the gonorrhea ran its course he would be free of it. If the illness persisted, as his letters seem to indicate, the possibility of the infection causing sterility increases significantly.

Therefore, the fact that Autie and Libbie never had children had nothing whatsoever to do with Libbie and everything to do with Autie. Furthermore, it can be easily demonstrated that Autie and Libbie were anything but sexually cold or indifferent to each other. Nor can Autie visiting a prostitute at this time in his life be considered infidelity on his part, since it occurred at least three years before he and Libbie were even officially introduced.

Of a rather more serious nature, at least to gossips, was the Annie Jones Incident.

It began innocently enough for Autie in August 1863 when Autie's divisional commander, Brig. Gen. Hugh Judson Kilpatrick, a notorious womanizer, introduced Autie to his latest mistress, Annie E. Jones. As D.A. Kinsley, author of *Custer: Favor the Bold; A Soldier's Story* put it, Annie Jones did "sack duty and horizontal drill" with and for Kilpatrick for all of a week, while he presented his "morale booster" with a horse, a major's jacket and cap (complete with insignia), and a pass to sight-see the camp.

Armed with all this, she proceeded to play havoc with the inlying and outlying videttes, exposed herself to Rebel snipers, then hightailed it behind enemy lines for a purported two-night stand with Maj. John S. Mosby, leader of partisan rangers and the Grey Ghost of the Confederacy. When she returned Kilpatrick sent her packing. Autie declared at the time that Kilpatrick had finally shown good sense by getting rid of a dangerous nuisance.

Then, during the first week of September 1863, while Autie was in command of the 3rd Cavalry Division due to Kilpatrick's absence, Annie Jones returned. She showed up one evening at twilight in a wagon that rumbled to a stop outside of Autie's headquarters tent. Autie's first reaction was to immediately order her out of his camp. When she refused to leave, Autie threatened to have her forcibly expelled.

She thereupon produced a War Department pass, a pass signed by Dr. Jonathan Letterman, surgeon-in-chief of the Army of the Potomac, and a pass signed by Maj. Gen. G.K. Warren, commander of II Corps, giving her permission to visit the army as a "sister of mercy." She claimed to have been officially placed as a hospital nurse in the 3rd Division, Cavalry Corps, Army of the Potomac, to which Autie's Michigan Cavalry Brigade still belonged.

All this despite a general order issued by Maj. Gen. George Gordon Meade, commander of the Army of the Potomac, that no women were to accompany troops in the field unless they were directly attached to the medical department and were under the direct supervision of Dr. Letterman. These general orders had resulted from the amorous escapades of Kilpatrick and others, along with a truly alarming venereal disease rate among the soldiers and officers of the army.

Autie gave her back the passes and again demanded that she leave his camp. His position was that neither Gen. Warren nor Dr. Letterman had any authority in the 3rd Cavalry Division and there was no mention of the Cavalry Corps in her War Department pass. He told her that nothing but a direct order by Kilpatrick, approved by Maj. Gen. Alfred Pleasonton, Cavalry Corps commander, could allow her to remain with the division, but as far as Autie himself was concerned only his approval would allow her to remain with his brigade. "You will get none of these," he told her. "Now please leave, or else I shall be forced to turn you out like a common bummer." Autie ordered his adjutant to see that she went back to Gen. Warren at Centreville in the morning. However, that was not the end of Annie Jones.

After Autie ordered her out of his camp nothing more was heard of her until March 22, 1864, when a thick packet was delivered to Autie by one of Kilpatrick's aides. It was marked "Confidential" and contained what was titled *Report Respecting a Young Lady Calling Herself Annie Jones, Supposed to be a Rebel Spy* and *Statement In Regards to Her Adventures in the Camps of the Middle Department and the Army of the Potomac, and Her Connection With Various Officers Since August 1861*. The documents had been "respectfully referred to Gen. Pleasonton by Gen. Meade as commanding general of the Army of the Potomac," who "deems it due to Brig. Gen'ls Kilpatrick and Custer that they should have an opportunity to offer such explanation as relates to them." Pleasonton on receipt of this missive referred the matter to Kilpatrick, who submitted the same to Autie "for compliance with requirements for a full explanation." This is known as passing the buck.

This particular snowball started rolling when an unsigned letter, dated Falls Church, Jan. 18, 1863" (roughly eight months before Autie even met Annie Jones) was sent to Brig. Gen. Samuel T. Heintzelman (then commanding the defenses of Washington) with his headquarters at Alexandria, Virginia. According to the letter, Miss Jones was to all appearances "a Rebel spy who has in her possession (and has shown it to a number of persons) a pass anywhere within the Confederate lines.... She boasts of being the friend of some of the most prominent officers in the Southern Army.... She makes no hesitation of avowing her feeling for the South, saying that they are right and must eventually triumph. Her acquaintances among Union officers are numerous; and she is very well educated and intelligent, she easily interests and engages their attention, and might obtain from them the most important information."

An investigation was conducted by Lt. Charles H. Shepard, provost marshal, Fort Albany, Virginia, who "could not find any person who supposed her to be a spy." Lt. Shepard discovered she had first come to the Army with the 135th New York Volunteer Infantry Regiment as a "daughter of the regiment;" that "she denies ever having been South;" that "she has twice been arrested and accused of espionage," but has "proved her loyalty beyond question." Again Lt. Shepard stated: "I could not find any person who had ever heard her make any disloyal remarks."

Shepard concluded: "The letter containing the charges was evidentially written by a female who is jealous of her as her former lover is paying some attention to this Miss Jones, and I have found she was very anxious of having this Miss Jones out of the way. It was a very amusing investigation on the whole."

Notwithstanding Lt. Shepard's report, Gen. Warren had ordered her re-arrested in September 1863 (shortly after her visit to Autie's camp) for acting as a spy, giving information to Rebel raiders, "harboring and concealing enemies of the U.S.," and breaking her parole by entering Virginia.

She was sent to Old Capitol Prison in Washington, D.C., where she signed a statement noting her "intention of offering my services as a hospital nurse.... While in the various camps, I was furnished by the commanding officers with a tent, and sometimes occupied quarters with the officers." Her statement said she was a "guest" of Maj. Gen. John Pope and Maj. Gen. Franz Siegle and their staff officers at Centreville and Fairfax Court House, respectively. She matter of factly stated she remained with Gen. Julius Stahl (who commanded the 3rd Division, Cavalry Corps, Army of the Potomac, until Kilpatrick relieved him just prior to the Battle of Gettysburg) "when I joined Gen. Kilpatrick's command, and went to the front, as the friend and companion of Gen. Custer. We made our headquarters near Hartwood Church. While stopping at this point, Gen. Kilpatrick became very jealous of Gen. Custer's attentions to me, and went to Gen. Meade's headquarters and charged me with being a Rebel spy. I was then arrested and sent to Gen. Martindale, Military Governor of Washington, who committed me to Old Capitol Prison."

Her statement bore very little resemblance to the official records. Kilpatrick made no such charges to Gen. Meade, but merely ordered her (after her reputed rendezvous with Mosby) out of his command. She was subsequently arrested by order of Gen. Warren at Centreville for consorting with Confederate raiders in that area.

"I have spent two years and a half with the Union Army," her statement continued, "and during this time have been the guest of different officers: they furnishing me with horses, orderlies, escorts, sentinels at my tent or quarters, rations, ect.... I invariably wore Major's straps. I have repeatedly passed into Rebel lines, and was once captured by Mosby and ... detained one or two days ... during no part of the time I was with the Federal Army was I employed as ... a hospital nurse, but as a companion to the various commanding officers ... as a private friend or companion."

She also admitted that her release from Old Capitol Prison was greatly influenced by her becoming "intimately acquainted" with the assistant superintendent (who was subsequently discharged) and with the chief jailer. Her statement added: "During the entire time since my leaving home in 1861, I have led a very roving and very questionable life. I am now very unwell, owing to my long confinement and other causes (which may have included one or more abortions) and desire to be released from custody that I may return to my home and friends."

The entire incident had come out of the blue and landed in Autie's lap. Understandably, Autie was furious. If Annie Jones had been anyone's mistress in the Army of the Potomac, she had been Kilpatrick's and probably Warren's as well — not his. He responded with the following statement:

> Hd. Qtrs. 2nd Brig., 3rd Div.
> Cav. Corps, Army of the Potomac
> Mar. 22, '64

Statement of Brig.-Gen'l G.A. Custer in regard to Annie E. Jones

> She was at my Head-qrs. about one week, during which time she was never allowed to go outside my lines or even visit the outer posts, although she frequently expressed a desire to do so. Her whole object of being with the Army seemed to be to distinguish herself by some deed of daring. In this respect alone she seemed to be insane. It was only my disinclination to use force towards her that induced me to permit her to stay that short time I mentioned. So far as to her statements in relation to Gen'l Kilpatrick and myself goes, it is simply untrue. I do not believe she is or ever was a spy. This part of her reputation has been gained by her impudence.

> Respectfully Submitted,
> G.A. Custer
> Brig.-Gen'l

Autie in his reply was extremely circumspect. As a lifelong Democrat, he was already branded in some quarters as a copperhead. As a former "McClellan man" he was regarded with considerable suspicion by certain Radical Republicans in the Congress. In addition, Autie had been married to Libbie for just barely a month when he received the request to provide an official explanation about his relationship with Annie Jones. He suspected that the Annie Jones Incident was a setup designed to blackmail him or to compromise his own position. In addition, Autie's statement also disembarrassed Kilpatrick from a scandal he could ill afford after the recent debacle of the Kilpatrick-Dahlgren Raid he had led against Richmond.

Hopefully, the Captured Letters Incident will put to rest the supposition that Libbie was a typically sexually repressed woman of the Victorian Age. The Captured Letters Incident was one of the repercussions of the Battle of Trevilian Station. During this engagement Autie's Michigan Cavalry Brigade managed to get into the rear of the Confederate cavalry divisions of Wade Hampton and Fitzhugh Lee, but was cut off from the rest of the Union Cavalry Corps, the divisions of A.T.A. Torbert and David M. Gregg.

During the battle, Autie's headquarters wagon was captured by the Confederates. It contained, as he later put it, "my all — bedding, desk, sword-belt, underclothing, my commission as general, which only arrived a few days before; also dress coat, pants, and one blue shirt" not to mention an ambrotype of Libbie and a packet of her letters. Eventually he could joke about it. "Do you know what they captured from me? Everything but my toothbrush!"

The captured letters offered considerable titillation. According to Confederate Capt. William Blackford, chief engineer to the Confederate Army of Northern Virginia Cavalry Corps: "Some of the letters from a fair but frail friend of Custer's were published in the Richmond papers, and afforded some spicy reading, although most of the really spicy parts did not appear." The identity of that "fair but frail friend" was none other than Libbie Bacon Custer. The automatic assumption that these letters were from Autie's mistress in Washington is characteristically purely Victorian, for it was just not seemly that a husband and wife should indulge in what amounted to literary love making.

Autie himself was once again highly amused by the entire affair.

"Somebody," he wrote to Libbie, "thought her Boy intended to chide her a least little bit about her captured letters! Ha-ha, dear one, you did not know him if you supposed he intended to 'chide' his heart's idol. I only wished to impress on you the need for more prudence in writing. But, the effect was not lasting — for the very next letter would afford equal amusement for any Southern acquaintances as those now in their hands."

Eventually, after the Battle of Tom's Brook, Autie captured the headquarters of his old friend, Brig. Gen. Thomas Lafayette Rosser, and got Libbie's letters back.

After the war, Autie was reduced to the rank of lieutenant colonel and was assigned to the brand new 7th U.S. Cavalry Regiment. Autie became an Indian fighter and he and his regiment's most notable success occurred during Sheridan's 1868 Winter Campaign at the Battle of the Washita.

There were 53 captured Cheyenne Indian women and children from the battle, among them Meyotzi — also known as Mo-nah-se-tah — whom Autie used as both an interpreter and messenger to her people. Apparently Autie treated her with considerable kindness. The story among the Indians, the Cheyenne in particular, was that she was also Autie's mistress and that she bore him a son in late 1869 named Yellow Swallow or Yellow Tail.

There is no documentation that Meyotzi bore a child at the end of 1869. The tale of Autie's alleged infidelity is based upon three sources. These are the writings of Benteen, the memories of a scout named Ben Clark, and finally the Cheyenne oral tradition.

Benteen's and Clark's versions are highly suspect. Benteen hated Autie with a virulence that grew with the years and may have been tinged with guilt after June 25, 1876. Clark blamed Autie for him being dismissed from service as an Army scout. The Cheyenne oral tradition, while it is not tainted by this degree of animosity and is thus rather more credible in this particular instance, is still suspect, primarily because it does not get around the almost certain fact that Autie was sterile and could not have physically gotten anyone pregnant.

The Cheyenne oral tradition claims — with a certain amount of half-hearted pride — that Autie made Meyotzi his mistress. But, the main question to be considered is whether they confused Autie with someone else, his brother, Thomas Custer, who was also an officer in the 7th Cavalry, and who looked and dressed somewhat like his older brother. Tom Custer had a well-earned reputation as a hell raiser, due to his womanizing and drinking. The supposition that Tom Custer and Meyotzi did have a sexual liaison is supported by a number of sources among the officers of the 7th Cavalry. Apparently, the relationship between Meyotzi and Tom Custer was considered something of a standing joke, which may have been Tom Custer's intention from the beginning.

The relationship between Autie and his brother was very close. The two of them were well known for constantly playing practical jokes on each other. In addition, Autie (who had taken a temperance oath as a young man, which he never broke) and Libbie were always trying to get Tom to reform to stop womanizing and to stop drinking. It is possible that Tom may have used their resemblance to encourage rumors of Autie's infidelity among the Cheyenne. Thus if Meyotzi did bear a blonde child in late 1869, it is almost certain that the child was Tom Custer's, not Autie's.

Libbie herself met and got to know Meyotzi, but there is no inkling whatsoever in her writings on the subject of Meyotzi that she ever suspected that any kind of a special relationship, especially a sexual relationship, ever existed between Autie and the Indian maiden.

Finally, there is Autie's own statement about Meyotzi written shortly after she was introduced to Autie by Mah-wis-sa, sister of Black Kettle, who performed what amounted to a Cheyenne marriage ceremony between them, which may have given Tom the original idea for his practical joke. When his scout and interpreter, California Joe Milner, explained what was going on, Autie was highly embarrassed.

Autie later wrote concerning the incident: "Although never claimed as an exponent of the peace policy about which so much has been said and written, yet I entertained the most peaceable sentiments towards all Indians who were in a condition to do no harm or violate any law. And while cherishing these friendly feelings, and desiring to do all in my power to render our captives comfortable and free from anxiety regarding their future treatment at our hands, I think even the most strenuous and ardent advocate of that peace policy (which teaches that the Indians should be left free and unmolested in the simple gratification of his simple tastes and habits) will at least not wholly condemn me when they learn that this touching and unmistakable proof of confidence and esteem offered by Mah-wis-sa, and graciously and if not blushingly acquiesced in by the Indian maiden, was firmly, but respectfully declined."

It was Benteen who claimed "it was notorious" throughout the Cavalry Corps throughout the American Civil War that Autie "used to sleep with his cook." She was an escaped slave named Eliza Dennison Brown. Eventually she came to rule his headquarters with the Michigan Cavalry Brigade and later the 3rd Cavalry Division as effectively and firmly as Autie commanded both units in the field. After the war Eliza continued to be employed for some years by Autie and Libbie.

Benteen claimed he learned that Eliza was Autie's mistress from a "Virginia classmate of mine." Benteen's assertion is nothing more than malicious hearsay. He offers no primary knowledge, just what someone told him. Benteen also charged that Libbie knew about the extramarital relationship between Autie and Eliza. If there was such a relationship, and Libbie knew about it, she managed to conceal it with consummate skill. Libbie's own writings regarding Eliza describe her in the kindest and fondest of terms. More importantly, it is highly unlikely that Libbie would have retained in her household for six years a woman who shared a sexual relationship with her own husband.

Eliza was a servant. She could have been fired at any time. Even when she did leave Autie and Libbie's employ Eliza remained attached to both of them. "There's many folks," Eliza is recorded as telling Libbie, "says that a woman can't follow the Army without throwing themselves away, but I know better. I went and I came out with the respect of the men and of the officers."

In addition, no independent supporting evidence of Benteen's accusations has ever been found. Finally, his private correspondence concerning Autie positively drips with vitriol and is loaded with demonstrable falsehoods, half truths, and outright venomous lies against Autie and all of his works. Eliza's simple statement to Libbie seems to echo with much more credibility than those of a man consumed by so much virulent hatred.

Finally, there is Benteen's charge that Capt. Thomas Weir shared a relationship with Libbie during the summer of 1867. At the time that the 7th Cavalry was formed in the fall of 1866, Weir was a 28-year-old bachelor, whom women, including Libbie, found attractive despite his drinking problems.

During the summer campaign of 1867, Autie abandoned his command and went on a wild ride from Fort Wallace to Fort Hays, a distance of 150 miles in 57 hours, and then on to Fort Harker, where he boarded a train to Fort Riley to join Libbie. For leaving his command without permission and for hunting down and shooting deserters without trial, Autie was court-martialed, found guilty, and was ordered to be suspended from the Army without pay for one year.

Benteen later claimed that Autie began his ride in a jealous rage after receiving a letter from an officer who stated that Eliza was urging him to hurry back to Fort Riley to "look after his wife a little closer." Supposedly Libbie and Lt. Weir had been together too often to suit Eliza's sense of decorum. There is no evidence that Libbie ever did anything more than flirt with Weir, if she ever did even that. (On the subject of flirting, both Autie and Libbie were both incorrigible. They seemed to enjoy it and were not shy about sharing their activities as flirts with each other in their letters. There is absolutely no evidence that any of these flirtations ever went beyond looks and words.)

If Autie had ever really suspected Weir of improper conduct with Libbie, it is strange there is no record that Autie ever looked upon Weir with any resentment or anger. In addition, Weir's actions demonstrate that he was an especially loyal officer and was dedicated to Autie, always being counted as among the pro–Custer faction within the faction riddled 7th Cavalry. Although the existence of such a personal relationship between Libbie and Weir seems unlikely, Benteen may have had an ulterior motive for suggesting that there was such a relationship in the first place.

Benteen's motive may have laid in the fact that Weir in particular demonstrated his loyalty to Autie in the Battle of the Little Big Horn. In Autie's last battle Weir was the only officer in Benteen's battalion who was concerned enough about Autie to attempt to go to his support not just once, but twice.

That fateful morning Autie had detached Benteen and his battalion — consisting of Troops D, under Weir's command; H, under Benteen's command; and K, under Lt. Edward Godfrey — to make sure that there were no hostile Indians upriver from the village that Autie's Crow and Arikara scouts claimed to have found. In addition, Captain Thomas MacDonough's B Troop was detached to escort the pack train, which immediately began falling behind.

Near the village Autie detached Maj. Marcus A. Reno with Troops A, G, and M, along with the Arikara and civilian scouts with orders to charge the village and capture the Indians' pony herd. From some high ground Autie watched as Reno's attack first stalled and then sputtered out. Autie then took Troops C, E, F, I, and L, along with the Crow scouts to the north, where he apparently attempted an attack upon the village, possibly to relieve pressure against Reno and to reunite his command. If that was his purpose, he failed, and Autie's five-company battalion was wiped out to the last man.

At a watering spot for Benteen's Battalion, gunfire from Reno's abortive attack upon the village could be heard towards the valley. Although Benteen had been instructed by Autie to set as fast a pace as prudently possible, Benteen instead proceeded at a rather slow pace. Benteen's attack of the slows is documented in John S. Grey's *Custer's Last Campaign: Mitch Boyer and the Little Big Horn Reconstructed.* At the watering spot, upon hearing the gunfire and impatient with Benteen's slow pace, Weir, upon his own initiative, led his D Troop forward at a much faster pace and was followed by Benteen and his other two companies.

After meeting several messengers dispatched by Autie, Benteen finally quickened his own pace and arrived at Reno Hill just as the remnants of Reno's Battalion and the pack train were reaching the high ground. Soon after the two battalions and the pack train joined, heavy gunfire was once again heard, this time from the north. Reno and Benteen later denied hearing the gunfire, but the evidence provided by most of the other officers and certain of the enlisted men present is overwhelming that there indeed was audible gunfire coming from the north.

For the second time that day Weir tried to get to Autie. After a fruitless discussion with Reno and Benteen, Weir, without orders and upon his own initiative, ordered his D Troop forward. Seeing his troop leave, other troop commanders, believing he had been directed to find Autie, joined him. Reno and Benteen, who couldn't decide on what else to do, eventually followed with the rest of their force in Weir's wake. Weir halted to reconnoiter at a rise, Weir's Point (Custer's Hill, where Autie and his five troops were wiped out, is readily visible from Weir's Point). From this vantage point, Weir and his troopers could see dust and chaos originating from Custer's Hill and soon encountered opposition from the Sioux and Cheyenne. By the time Reno and Benteen arrived at Weir's Point, the number of hostiles between them and Custer's Hill soon convinced them to order a retreat back to Reno Hill.

Shortly after the battle, Weir wrote a very interesting letter to Libbie. In this letter he stated he intended to visit her and provide her with certain information regarding Autie's final battle. "I have so much to tell you that I will tell you nothing now.... I am coming to Monroe to see you all." A month later Weir again wrote to Libbie promising that he would be visiting her soon, stating that it was "my life business to vindicate my friends of that day." Unfortunately Weir died suddenly and unexpectedly before he could make the trip to Monroe, Michigan, and tell Libbie what he knew. (It was said afterwards that Weir's death was due to his drinking, but no direct evidence of this was recorded.) Is it possible that Benteen invented the story about the alleged relationship between Weir and Libbie in order to discredit any information Weir might have had about the Battle of the Little Big Horn? So much for Fred Benteen.

However, Shirley A. Leckie, a biographer of Libbie and believer that Weir was in love with Libbie, has contended that Weir most likely had no such information but found himself caught between Libbie and Frederick Whittaker, Custer's first biographer, of Maj. Marcus Reno's culpability at what happened at the Little Big Horn. However, if Weir did have nothing really to say, why did he contact Libbie, unsolicited by her, offering information, not once, but twice? If he did not want to hurt Libbie, then why contact her at all? Why provide her with false hope of some revelation?

All in all, I find what someone actually wrote to be more convincing about a person's opinion and state of mind than the hearsay evidence of another person's recollection of the subject's statements and state of mind, which is publicized only after the subject's death when he can no longer inform us about or verify exactly what his opinion and state of mind actually was.

Getting back to Autie's mad ride in 1867, that incident, which has never been adequately explained, may have been the result of a nervous breakdown brought on by stress created by the realization of just how much Autie's entire world had changed when the American Civil War ended. It is likely that Autie's view of himself revolved entirely around his Army career. But with the end of the American Civil War, the Army had rapidly changed.

The soldiers, officers and men, whom Autie had commanded in the American Civil War, had been volunteers in the truest sense of the word. The solid core of Custer's American Civil War commands were dedicated veteran volunteers. These men were fighting the war because they wanted to be there. But, the end of the war brought a return to normalcy within the Army.

Up until the end of the war, Autie had no experience with the peacetime Army. His entire experience, aside from facing off the French along the Rio Grande in Texas and in reconstruction duty in the South, was with the Army in the middle of a major war. The traditional normal state of the Army in America is to be small, weak, and almost totally inoffensive in the eyes of civilian politicians. Its peacetime purpose was to keep the Indians from making trouble. In the twinkling of an eye the U.S. Army went from a peak strength of 500,000 men when the American Civil War ended in 1865 first to an authorized strength of 50,000 and then down to just 25,000 a few years later, just 9,000 men above its authorized strength of 16,000 men prior to the American Civil War. As a matter of fact, Congress was preparing additional cuts when the news of Little Big Horn demonstrated even to Congress the abject stupidity of such an action. In addition, unless there was some kind of an emergency, the Army's actual strength never matched its authorized strength. The makeup of the troops was also different. Instead of motivated volunteers and regulars, commands consisted of those who could get jobs nowhere else or were fleeing their personal lives.

Autie's first major campaign against his new enemies in the West (the Indians or Native Americans) the Hancock Expedition, turned into an embarrassing farce for everybody concerned, except the Indians who had great fun playing hide and seek with the Army. It is quite possible that Autie, reeling from these multiple shocks was — in the end — running for reassurance from the one person who he could absolutely rely upon to be there for him no matter what: Libbie.

Perhaps the final word on the relationship between Autie and Libbie can best be provided by Libbie herself. In the half century between the Battle of the Little Big Horn and her own death, she never remarried. She dedicated herself instead to promoting Autie's memory, creating one of the Great Myths of America.

When Autie died he left her with a number of debts, totaling roughly $100,000 and incurred primarily through bad investments and gambling, something Autie was never able to abandon like he had the use of alcohol. In order to pay off those debts, and to support herself, Libbie became an author and lecturer. She was so successful that when she died she had paid off all of Autie's debts she left an estate of $100,000. She purposely devoted the rest of her life into making her husband an immortal American hero. Her devotion to Autie's memory attracted a number of supporters, including Frederick Whittaker, who wrote the first Custer biography, *A Complete Life of General Custer*. Autie's reputation was safe as long as she and her allies among the veterans of the Michigan Cavalry Brigade and the 3rd Cavalry Division lived to defend it.

It was only in 1934 — just a year after Libbie's death — when most of Autie's veterans were themselves also safely dead, that a novelist, Frederick F. Van de Water, began the attack upon Autie's reputation with the publication of what was billed as a historical biography, *Glory Hunter: A Life of General Custer*. It turned out to be Van de Water's most enduring work of fiction.

Van de Water has been accused by modern historians of dispensing with historical documentation, twisting the facts, and adding rhetorical

The caisson carrying Custer's remains, which were eventually removed from the Little Big Horn battlefield to the West Point military cemetery, at his funeral. Fifty-seven years after his death, his widow, Libbie, was finally laid to rest beside her "bright star" (Library of Congress, Prints and Photographs Division).

embellishments of his own in order to misinterpret everything Autie ever said or did, in order to depict Autie as an egomaniac, bully, braggart, and fabricated hero.

Libbie herself died on April 2, 1933, just six days prior to her 91st birthday. It was on that day that she was laid to rest at the U.S. Military Academy Cemetery at West Point beside her "own bright star."

Appendix III

CUSTER'S SECOND ATROCITY: THE WASHITA

During the fall and winter of 1868 George Armstrong Custer was seeking to redeem his military career. That he achieved, but in doing so he became associated with what many would call an atrocity, one that most particularly targeted the Indians or Native Americans.

The previous year he had participated in the Hancock Expedition against the Plains Indians and it was a complete and total fiasco. Winfield Scott Hancock, known as the Superb for his record during the American Civil War, knew nothing at all about Indians. The principal leaders of the Cheyenne, Arapaho, Kiowa, and Comanche wanted to avoid trouble, even if the cost of that avoidance meant the abandonment of *some* of their territory. However, the chiefs always had trouble keeping their young warriors off the warpath. This problem was greatly aggravated at the end of the American Civil War by the renewal of the western expansionist movement that had been restricted by the war and the advance of the railroads, particularly the new transcontinental railroad.

The menacing attitude of the Cheyenne Dog Soldiers, for instance, belied the protestations of the peace chiefs. To complicate the situation still further, bands of southern Brule and Ogallala Sioux of uncertain disposition had dropped down from the Platte and the Republican rivers to the north to mingle with the Cheyenne and Arapaho. Therefore, it was felt that the insolent threats from the young warriors and their scattered depredations, if allowed to continue, could definitely escalate into much more serious trouble. However, how to single out the few troublemakers from the majority who had no intention of making trouble was a problem that the U.S. Army would prove itself to be totally unable to solve.

Thus, on March 11, 1867, Hancock advised the Indian agents for the Cheyenne, Arapaho, Comanche and Kiowa that he intended to lead an army into the Plains as a show of force to demonstrate to the Indians that he could defeat them at any time he chose if they interfered with the rail-road and the other trails and roads that led through their territory. He noted his intention of talking with the chiefs, but that if they wanted war he fully intended to oblige them.

By April 7 at Fort Larned, Hancock had gathered his forces for the proposed expedition. These forces included 11 troops of Custer's 7th Cavalry, seven companies of the 37th Infantry and a battery from the 4th Artillery, a total of 1,400 men.

Hancock, as promised, talked first; specifically to a delegation from a village of Cheyenne Dog Soldiers and Ogallala Sioux on Pawnee Fork, 35 miles from Fort Larned. A snowstorm and a buffalo hunt delayed the meeting for several days; when the meeting was finally held only two chiefs, albeit important ones, and a dozen warriors attended to listen to a lecture from Hancock giving them their choice of war or peace and announcing that in the morning he would march up Pawnee Fork and deliver his message to the rest of the chiefs.

The next morning Hancock's advance up Pawnee Fork with his army so panicked the women and children that they stampeded en mass to the hills; Hancock camped about a half mile from the village and directed the chiefs to bring their people back. That night Hancock was told that the braves were also preparing to leave the village, so he ordered Custer to throw a cordon formed from his 7th Cavalry around the village. In the morning the village was found to be abandoned.

To Hancock this looked like war. The abandoned village was eventually destroyed and as the Sioux and Cheyenne fled north they were pursued by Custer and eight troops of the 7th Cavalry. The Indians scattered into small parties and left no trail large enough to follow. When Custer reached the Smokey Hill Road he found chaos. The stage stations had been burned, stock had been run off, and a number of civilians had been killed in raids. Custer headed for Fort Hays and was immobilized when it was discovered that badly needed forage for his horses that was supposed to have been stockpiled there had been delayed due to high water.

At additional conferences at Fort Dodge and Fort Larned with Arapaho and Kiowa chiefs, Hancock repeated his peace or war ultimatum. Hancock then set out for Fort Hays, which he reached on May 2, finding Custer still immobilized by lack of forage. As soon as the grass grew greener

Custer was directed to resume operations. Hancock then returned to his headquarters at Fort Levenworth.

While Custer waited for greener grass, the Sioux and the Cheyenne waged war between the Arkansas and Platte rivers. The Indians attacked stage stations, mail coaches, wagon trains, and railroad workers on the Platte, Arkansas, and Smokey Hill rivers. Railroad construction slowed to a crawl, and for a time stage coaches on the Smokey Hill Road ceased running at all. In western Kansas, Fort Wallace endured constant harassment, its garrison clashing several times with Indian war parties.

Custer on June 1 finally headed out from Fort Wallace with six troops of the 7th Cavalry, about 300 men. His mission was to search out the hostiles along a 1,000 mile stretch to the Platte, to the Republican, and back to the Smokey Hill. His progress was marked with inconclusive clashes with the Sioux. Finally, on July 13, he returned to Fort Wallace with his horses having mostly become unfit for further campaigning. During this march Custer had constant problems with desertions, groups as large as 20 or 30 men at a time breaking out. When he could catch them, Custer in desperation had shot some of the deserters out of hand.

Custer during the American Civil War had been used to the adulation of his soldiers; now they hated and despised him. The situation got so bad that it appears that Custer suffered some kind of a breakdown and went on as wild ride, covering 150 miles in 57 hours before catching a train to take him to his wife, Libbie Bacon Custer, the only person who was totally there for him and who helped him regain his equilibrium. However, for deserting his command Custer was called to account. He was court-martialed, found guilty, and sentenced to being suspended from the Army for one year without pay.

For the rest of the summer the Indians ran wild. The Indian agents for the Cheyenne, Arapaho, Kiowa and Comanche claimed that their charges had moved south of the Arkansas River to avoid various army columns, including Custer's. They blamed the continuing raids by hostiles on other Indians. The peace chiefs and the women, children, and old men may have gone south, but many of the warriors remained north of the Arkansas River and enjoyed an exciting and profitable raiding season. Thus, in the end all that the Hancock Expedition had actually done was to incite a bloody and likely totally needless Indian war.

Repercussions from the Hancock Expedition fiasco brought another totally and completely unwanted problem. The inability of regular troops to stop the headline-making raids on stage stations, the stage coaches themselves, and the railroad workers caused the governors of the states of Kansas, Colorado, and Minnesota (which had suffered a deadly Indian uprising in 1862), along with the Montana Territory to bombard the military with appeals for the authority to call out their militia or volunteers to assist the regulars. (In 1862 the Teton Sioux, under the leadership of a former peace chief, Little Crow, were starving to death due to disruptions and considerable delay in the arrival of gifts and money from the federal government caused by the American Civil War. During the uprising hundreds of citizens of Minnesota were killed. Its end was marked by the mass public hanging of 38 Indians condemned to death after court-martial for atrocities committed against Minnesotans. Originally over 300 had been condemned to hang, but President Lincoln commuted the sentences of all but the most clearly guilty.)

Nothing quite had the potential of complicating an Indian war than having raw, untrained and undisciplined militia volunteers swarming the countryside in a blind search for hostile Indians. Nobody wanted a repetition of what happened at Sand Creek in Colorado in 1864 (see below). Therefore, William T. Sherman, the general-in-chief in Washington, wanted absolutely no part of such "volunteers" in any way, shape, manner, or form.

His denial of those petitions made Sherman a target of scathing criticism in the newspapers, which Sherman loathed anyway, and in addition risked the occurrence of additional disasters that might be charged to his intransigence. Eventually he softened just enough to allow the governors to organize volunteers; but, they must provide the funding themselves with the hope that Congress might later reimburse them. Sherman knew that without the firm promise of federal funding merchants would not advance credit and that the civilians would not volunteer. However, it still remained a delicate issue because volunteers might actually be needed to put down the hostiles.

Thomas Francis Meagher, the acting governor of Montana Territory, adroitly used this very argument to persuade Sherman to sanction the muster of 800 volunteers. The resulting rank heavy battalion managed to run up costs of more than $1 million in June and July, half of which Congress eventually reimbursed to the territory.

The governors of Colorado and Kansas pressed their cases with fervor. Kansas finally obtained permission to raise the 18th and 19th Kansas Volunteer Cavalry Regiments. The 18th Kansas Cavalry actually performed creditable work in helping the regulars patrol the travel routes. The 19th Kansas Cavalry would be too late in arriving to join Custer's march upon the Washita, although it too performed creditably in the aftermath of that battle, when Custer persuaded many of the hostiles to return to their reservations the following spring.

Following the fiasco of the summer of 1867, Gen. Philip H. Sheridan, commander of all U.S. troops in the Department (and later the Division) of the Missouri, was busy creating a whole new strategy. He realized that the Plains Indians were too mobile to be chased down during the summer months. Instead he would wait until winter, when the Indians would be immobilized and tied down in their winter camps. During the fall Sheridan would place as many columns as possible in Kansas in a holding operation aimed at diverting the hostile Indians from raids into Kansas while nudging them south of the Arkansas River.

As part of this effort, Sheridan, like he had in the Shenandoah Valley during the American Civil War, organized a special force of scouts. They were organized in August and were comprised not of soldiers but frontiersmen. Sheridan placed them under the command of one of his aides, Maj. George "Sandy" Forsyth. They were armed with American Civil War surplus Spencer repeaters, the very best weapons available, and were turned loose.

On September 17, after discovering a hostile village on the north fork of the Arikara River in eastern Colorado, the scouts were pinned down in what became known as the Beecher's Island Fight. (Beecher's Island was named for the scouts' second in command, who was killed there early in the fight.) The 50 or so scouts beat back a number of attacks while losing about half of their own numbers. Casualties suffered by the Cheyenne were heavy, including at least one war chief, Roman Nose.

On October 13 an event occurred that incensed the entire state of Kansas. A party of warriors attacked a settlement in Putnam County. Four men were killed, two girls were raped, and a woman was carried off. When the news broke, the 19th Kansas Volunteer Cavalry Regiment was raised in three weeks and was dispatched to hunt down and kill every Indian they could find.

But all this was only the preliminaries — once the Plains winter was under way, Sheridan would hit them when they couldn't run and he had just the man in mind to carry out his new strategy: George Armstrong Custer. The problem was that Custer wasn't available due to that pesky court-martial. Sheridan was not going to let that stand in his way. Working behind the scenes he got the balance of Custer's sentence remitted for this campaign. (At the time Custer had about two more months to serve.) Therefore, a week after the Battle of Beecher's Island, Sheridan finally succeeded in his efforts and sent a telegram to Monroe, Michigan, summoning Custer.

As soon as he got the news Custer dropped everything, left Monroe, where he had been waiting out his sentence, and hurried back to his regiment. Sheridan planned for three columns to hit the Indians. Col. George W. Getty was to move east from the District of New Mexico with six troops from the 3rd Cavalry and two companies from the 27th Infantry. Maj. Eugene A. Carr — with seven troops from the 5th U.S. Cavalry, four troops of the 10th Cavalry and one troop of the 7th Cavalry — was to operate to the south, towards Antelope Hills and the head of the Red River.

The third column and main striking force consisted of the other 11 troops of the 7th Cavalry, five infantry companies, and the 19th Kansas Cavalry, which had not yet arrived when the campaign began. This force was under the command of Lt. Col. Alfred Sully. Sheridan planned to personally join the column and Custer commanded the 11 troops of the 7th Cavalry. Getty's and Carr's columns were to act as beaters to force the hostiles into the Canadian and Washita river valleys while Sully and Custer's troops would be the primary strike force.

Sully and Custer had established Camp Supply, a depot on the North Canadian River, and waited for the 19th Kansas Cavalry to arrive when on November 21, Sheridan arrived. On his way to Camp Supply he had crossed the trail of a war party heading north toward the Kansas settlements. Custer was ordered not to wait for the 19th Kansas Cavalry, but to instead take his 7th Cavalry and follow the trail Sheridan had found. To find the hostiles Custer was given four civilian scouts, Ben Clark, Moses E. "California Joe" Milner, Raphael Romero, and Jack Corbin, along with a dozen Osage guides.

Custer left early on November 23; however, a blizzard covered the trail he was to have followed. Custer persevered anyway and four days

181

later he found an Indian camp nestled along the Washita River. Custer proved himself to be just about as hard to be convinced by his scouts, the Osages, that they had actually found the village as he would be eight years later at the Little Big Horn. He was always skeptical of what his scouts were telling him, since they had a tendency to exaggerate and sometimes tell what they thought a person wanted to hear. Afraid that the Indians would discover his presence, Custer, not waiting to reconnoiter, attacked at dawn on November 27 using the hours between the time the scouts had convinced him they had found the village and dawn to make preparations for the attack.

Custer was right to be concerned about the possibility of being discovered. On November 26 a Kiowa war party, the same party whose trail Custer followed to Black Kettle's village, on their arrival had reported that they had spotted a cavalry trail pointing in the direction of the Washita River valley. In a council of elders it was decided to disregard the warning because they thought that the soldiers would not be foolish enough to attack in the teeth of a Plains winter, not to mention the Plains blizzard that had just blown itself out.

Custer, since he had 800 men, decided to divide the regiment into four more or less equal parts so that he could surround the village and attack from all four directions, leaving the Indians with no easy escape route. Maj. Joel Elliott, Custer's second in command, was given Troops G, H, and M, being instructed to move behind the hills to the east, swing around and charge upstream from the northeast. Capt. William Thompson was instructed to take B and F Troops, cross the river, move behind the bluffs and strike the village from the south in conjunction with Maj. Elliott. Capt. Edward Myers was to take Troops E and I and follow Thompson, deploying in the woods west of the village. Meanwhile, Custer with a special corps of sharpshooters, scouts, and Troops A, C, D and K would attack from the north, making a direct attack upon the village. (Benteen, with H Troop, was also given the assignment to secure the Indians' pony herd, a mission that he accomplished with a certain amount of flair. Benteen was an extremely competent soldier despite his extremely obnoxious personality and personal behavior when he wasn't in a fight.)

Before moving into their attack positions the men discarded their overcoats and haversacks at their final camp site; these were placed under guard by a single squad of troopers. Custer's supply train had been left even further behind under an equally light guard.

The battle actually began before Custer was able to make the signal to attack, when Maj. Elliott's battalion was discovered and an Indian immediately opened fire upon it. "Let 'er rip!" Custer shouted, and the band began playing "Gary Owen" or at least as much of it as they could before the saliva in their instruments froze, making it impossible to play them at all, but it sufficed for the purpose.

Once the battle began the Indians resisted the attack as best they could. Half-naked and still half-asleep, warriors and anyone else who could carry a weapon popped out of the teepees and opened fire on the soldiers. In their haste to get away, nude Indians, male and female and of all ages, plunged into the freezing water of the Washita River. Children were trampled under foot by the horses. One Indian woman attempting to escape with a captive white child, a small boy, was surrounded by several soldiers, whereupon she pulled out a knife that she plunged into the boy's stomach. She was immediately killed by the soldiers.

The sharpshooters on foot and Custer's four mounted companies hit the village, striking the village's defenders first at the river. He galloped to a knoll south of the river to direct the rest of the fight as the Cheyenne warriors resisted fiercely trying to protect their women and children. What Custer was attacking turned out to be the 51 lodges of the village of Black Kettle, a peace chief; the same chief whose village had been destroyed in the 1864 Sand Creek Massacre.

It was the search for gold and silver in Colorado which had ignited the fuse that led to the Battle of Sand Creek, if it could be called a battle. The butchery that had occurred there became better known as a massacre and eventually led to President Ulysses S. Grant's Peace Policy, which for a variety of reasons also failed.

Black Kettle, when the Colorado gold and silver rush began in 1858 and 1859, brought hundreds of white men to Colorado, sought peace or at least some form of more or less peaceful co-existence. But indiscriminate hostility by the whites and calls for the extermination of all Indians eventually led to the Sand Creek Massacre. In 1864 Black Kettle managed to convince one soldier, Maj. E.W. Wynkoop, commander of Fort Lyon, of his peaceful intentions. Wynkoop organized a peace conference between Black Kettle and other chiefs with the governor of Colorado; for organ-

Prisoners from Black Kettle's Camp, captured by General Custer in his winter attack at the Battle of the Washita, are shown moving through the snow on their march to captivity at Camp Supply, Oklahoma (sketch by Theodore R. Davis, Library of Congress, Prints and Photographs Division).

izing the conference Wynkoop was recalled because he had "violated his orders."

Before Wynkoop was recalled on November 2, 1864, he had given Black Kettle assurances that the Sand Creek area, about 30 miles from Fort Lyon, would be a safe area for his band to camp. Wynkoop told Black Kettle that his people would be protected by his, Wynkoop's, soldiers as long as they remained peaceful. Wynkoop's replacement, Maj. Scott Anthony, reiterated the promise of safety. Therefore, in good faith, Black Kettle established his camp there. His camp included about 100 lodges. Also present were 10 lodges of Arapaho under the leadership of Chief Left Hand. Altogether the camp at Sand Creek included about 700 men, women, and children. Only about 200 could be considered able bodied warriors.

Col. J.M. Chivington, a former Methodist preacher and somewhat experienced volunteer officer, having helped turn back the Confederate invasion of Arizona and New Mexico, arrived at Fort Lyon towards the end of November at the head of 600 men of the 3rd Colorado Volunteer Cavalry Regiment, a 90-day militia unit raised expressly for the purpose of fighting Indians and who were nearing the end of their term of enlistment. As soon as Chivington arrived he and Maj. Anthony, with 100 of his own men, marched for Sand Creek, arriving on November 29, 1864.

The fighting began when the Colorado cavalry attacked sometime between dawn and daylight. Chivington and Anthony's men appeared to be attacking from all sides. As the "soldiers" advanced women, children, and unarmed old men were killed, the survivors running in terrified panic for the creek.

Left Hand, the Arapaho chief, was killed in the first burst of gunfire. The firing lasted for four hours with Chivington reporting between 300 and 400 Indians killed, most of them being those women, children, and old men. When those who were left alive had fled, the lodges were looted and burned and the horses and mules were gathered together. Then as a final outrage the bodies of the dead were mutilated, with more than 100 scalps being taken. A few weeks later these scalps were exhibited between acts at a Denver theater.

Finally, when the full horrors of what had happened at Sand Creek were revealed, protests were heard from all over the country. Including among them were those of Kit Carson, mountain man, scout, and Indian fighter. He called what happened at Sand Creek the actions of "a coward, or a dog." Four years later the Sand Creek Massacre, no longer called a battle, was condemned by a special commission that included members of both houses of Congress and at least three Army generals who agreed: "It scarcely had its parallels in the records of Indian barbarity."

In its final report the commission called for the government to adopt policies of moderation and conciliation. What the government did do was to pay the survivors of Black Kettle's band a large amount of money in reparations. But, money and words were little compensation for the Cheyenne. Black Kettle headed south with what remained of his followers, still seeking peace; a search that ended at the Washita.

The Cheyenne never forgot or forgave the wanton butchery at Sand Creek and they continued a campaign of terror — attacking stage coaches, killing everyone on board. They also raided towns, killed cattle, and chopped down telegraph poles.

Finally in 1865 a peace commission sought to bring fighting to an end but no major chief "touched the pen." The commission tried again the next year at Fort Laramie. The Indians were told that the government only wanted to keep the Bozeman Trail open. They were purposely not told that this treaty proposed new roads and forts to protect travelers upon those new roads. The sudden arrival of Col. Henry Carrington and 600 soldiers of the 18th U.S. Infantry Regiment revealed the truth.

The war, in which the Sioux joined the Cheyenne, continued until 1868, when the Indians finally accepted the next proposed treaty, which called for the evacuation of Forts Phil Kearney, Reno, and C.F. Smith, as well as the abandonment of the road. The peace was nothing more than a truce and its end marked the beginning of the road that led to the Little Big Horn.

Just a week prior to Custer's attack, Black Kettle had met with Army officers and confessed that he had no control over the actions of his young warriors who had definitely participated in raids upon the Kansas settlements; as a matter of fact, it had been the trail of the war party returning from such a raid into Kansas that had passed through after the blizzard that had led Custer straight to Black Kettle's village. Ironically, Black Kettle returned to his village just the day before Custer's attack.

Within 10 minutes Custer's troopers possessed the village (their attack killing Black Kettle, his wife, and at least one other chief) but had to spend the bulk of the morning wiping out pockets of resistance while the Indians sought to escape down the valley. There was a delay in the attack made by Myers and Thompson. This delay created a gap through which many of the Indians fled to safety. Maj. Elliott, and a party of soldiers, including the regiment's sergeant major and 18 others, all volunteers, set off in pursuit of one of these groups. Several parties of Cheyenne warriors converged to rescue the fugitives. They cut Elliott and his party off from the rest of the regiment and killed them all. Meanwhile, no one in the rest of the 7th Cavalry knew where Elliott had gone or what had happened to him.

When Elliott and his detachment had set off in pursuit of those Indians, he had yelled: "Here goes for a brevet or a coffin!" At least one biographer of Custer has castigated Elliott as a "glory hunter" for this behavior, something that Custer was also accused of being. In the final analysis, a glory hunter spins the thread of his own fate and what finally happens is generally their own responsibility, though oftentimes they have a tendency to take others with them. Custer, even though Benteen blamed him for Elliott's death, really bears very little responsibility for it. As it was, the death of Elliott would haunt Custer for the rest his life, with the mostly undeserved stigma that Custer had abandoned him to his fate.

It was not until the sun was high in the sky and it began to get warm that the last shot of the battle was fired. There were a number of dead and dying Indians upon the ground. Those who had escaped had fled to the tall timber downstream. Those woman and children who remained were taken prisoners. Custer kept the Osage scouts from killing them out of hand. In addition, he ordered his own troopers not to fire on any of the remaining fugitives who could be seen running away. None of the prisoners included any of the warriors; they had neither given quarter nor had they asked for any.

Custer has achieved his redemption. He had won by his persistence in tracking the enemy and once he had found them by striking at once, splitting his regiment into four parts to attack from four different directions. In order to do this he choose not to make any reconnaissance and eventually this came back to haunt him, in spades. Sheridan found out about Custer's success when the civilian scout, California Joe Milner, arrived at Camp Supply with the news on November 29.

By mid-morning numbers of hostile warriors began appearing along the hillsides surrounding the remains of Black Kettle's village. Lt. Edward Godfrey conducted a private scout and was the first person to observe the existence of additional villages downstream, which he immediately reported to Custer. Questioning some of the 53 women and children he had taken captive, Custer learned that the valley for a distance of 10 miles down stream sheltered the winter camps of many bands of Cheyenne, Kiowa, Arapaho, and Comanches. Godfrey also reported gunfire from down the valley and suggested that it might be the missing Elliott. Once the gunfire from Custer's attack had begun, scores of warriors from the villages downstream mounted their ponies and raced west. It was these warriors who intercepted Elliott and his men.

Elliott had dismounted his men, who lay down in the high grass, forming a circle. The besieging Indians scorched the area where Elliott went to ground with both bullets and arrows. The Indians continually crept closer until with a final rush they killed all of their opponents.

By noon hundreds of warriors from these camps surrounded Custer in Black Kettle's plundered village. Custer established a defensive perimeter and proceeded to destroy the contents of the village and slaughter most of the 875 Indian ponies captured in the assault. Custer spared enough to remount those of his soldiers who had lost their animals and to mount his prisoners. When the slaughtering of the ponies began the Indians attempted to rescue them but were driven back by two troops led by Captain Benteen.

Custer could probably have fought his way through the Indians since, although numerous, their numbers did not appear overwhelming. However, Custer was encumbered with his wounded and prisoners, the Indians could have inflicted further casualties on his men, and his supply train was back on the trail and was only lightly protected. The Indians had found the overcoats and haversacks that Custer's men had left at the previous night's camp, forcing the squad guarding them to abandon them. In addition, Quartermaster James Bell reported running a gauntlet of fire to bring back badly needed reserve ammunition.

In addition, Custer was still completely ignorant of the location or the fate of Maj. Elliott and his detachment. The threat posed by the Indians ringing the hilltops had made an attempt at a search for Elliott and his men practically impossible, although at least one attempt was actually made. Capt. Myers and his troop were sent on a scout down river. Upon his return he reported that he had moved down river about two miles without sighting any sign of Maj. Elliott or his detachment.

Custer decided that the safety of the regiment had to come before that of Elliott and his missing troopers, who for all he knew might have made their own escape, and that it was time to go. At all likelihood by the time Custer made his decision to leave the battlefield Elliott and his men were already dead.

Custer decided he had to extricate himself from this situation, without any further loss, if possible. He therefore mounted his regiment and as dusk approached with his band playing and flags waving he advanced down the river. This move had the immediate effect he wanted, since the Indians quickly abandoned their positions upon the hilltops and returned to their villages to defend their families. Once it was fully dark he turned around and slipped out of the valley, arriving back at Camp Supply on December 2.

Thus the Battle of the Washita confirmed that Sheridan's strategy had been correct. Custer's losses included Maj. Elliott and Capt. Louis Hamilton dead, along with the 19 enlisted men who had followed Elliott. In addition, three more officers and 11 enlisted men had been wounded.

The Cheyenne, according to Custer, had lost 103 warriors killed, an early example of the body count. This figure had to include at least some women and children. The Indians have claimed ever afterward that this count was grossly exaggerated. They claimed that only 14 warriors were actually killed along with 17 women and children. However, the real loss to the Indians lay in the dead ponies, along with the destruction of food, shelter, and other possessions.

Custer, however, was castigated for the appearance of repeating what had happened at Sand Creek. But an objective comparison of what happened at Sand Creek and what happened at the Washita makes it clear that these two events were quite different.

First of all, Chivington knew where Black Kettle was and specifically targeted him and his village, even though Black Kettle was where he was at Sand Creek because he had been promised safety and had been guaranteed protection. In addition, there appears to have been no evidence that any of his people were involved in hostilities against citizens of Colorado at that time.

Regarding Custer, he didn't know whose village he was attacking until it was all over, and he had been led to Black Kettle's village because he was following the trail of a war party that had definitely been involved in depredations against white settlers. Not all, or even most, of the warriors inhabiting Black Kettle's village were anywhere near as peaceful as Black Kettle had been. Both of these things had made Black Kettle's village a legitimate target.

When the battlefield was revisited in December the idea that the Indians were blameless innocents was dealt a heavy blow. Aside from the white child prisoner known to have been killed in the attack (by an Indian woman), the remains of a white woman and her two year old son were found in the ruins of the village. The woman had been shot in the head and her son's skull had been crushed. In addition, the remains of Maj. Elliott and his men were found answering that particular mystery.

Furthermore, there had been no intentional massacre such as had occurred at Sand Creek. Once the first attack was over, no one who was not resisting the soldiers was killed or otherwise molested. Yes, women and children had been killed. But, during the fighting, like any combat situation, determining who was who as far as who were combatants and who were noncombatants was practically impossible to determine. In an Indian village under attack, combatants tended to be anyone over the age of 12, and quite a few even younger who had a weapon and knew what to do with it. In addition, what is and is not a weapon is a subject that covers a great deal of ground.

Furthermore, the deaths of Elliott and the men who died with him stirred considerable controversy within the 7th Cavalry that carried right on through to the day Custer died at the Little Big Horn close to eight years later. Custer's great enemy within the 7th Cavalry, Capt. Frederick W. Benteen, used Elliott's death as an excuse for the hatred he felt for his commanding officer. If Custer had gotten rid of Benteen then he would have saved himself and posterity quite of bit of trouble. Whether anyone else joined Benteen in this condemnation of Custer for "abandoning" Elliott and his men cannot really be known for certain. It is likely that most of the rank and file believed that Elliott and his men had been killed long before Custer made his decision to leave the battlefield.

If Custer cannot in all honestly be blamed for Elliott's death, and if it is acknowledged that Custer conducted his withdrawal from the Washita with considerable skill and daring, where can he be faulted? The answer to that particular question may lie in his tactics, or maybe not. Custer has been accused of violating a fundamental military principle. He chose to attack an enemy of unknown strength on a field of unknown terrain. In other words, he did not conduct an adequate reconnaissance in order to discover what might lie ahead. Custer decided to take this calculated risk because he knew that by conducting further reconnaissance he risked losing the element of surprise. Essentially he did the same thing for the same reasons at the Little Big Horn.

Already Custer had done what everybody else had failed to do, find and then successfully attack a hostile Indian village. To hold onto the element of surprise he gambled that it was an isolated village. He lost the gamble but won anyway. If it hadn't been for Elliott's sudden bid for glory he would have gotten away with practically no losses at all, and those casualties he did have can only be described as light to moderate. By attacking when he did Custer obtained the psychological edge.

His experiences during the Battle of the Washita fixed his style of Indian fighting. As noted, he made just about the same gambles at Little Big Horn and lost, big time.

CHAPTER NOTES

Introduction

1. As related in Gregory J.W. Urwin's *Custer Victorious* (pp. 72–74) and Tom Carhart's *Lost Triumph: Lee's Real Plan at Gettysburg — and Why it Failed* (pp. 187–189).

2. According to Jeffry D. Wert's *Custer: The Controversial Life of George Armstrong Custer* (pp. 101–103).

3. As noted in the frontispiece (or foreword) of Eric Wittenberg's *Glory Enough for All: Sheridan's Second Raid and the Battle of Trevilian Station*.

Chapter 1

1. As recorded in *Sheridan: The Life and Wars of General Phil Sheridan* by Roy Morris (p. 206).

2. As recorded in *Sheridan: The Life and Wars of General Phil Sheridan* (p. 188) and *Gray Ghost: The Memoirs of Col. John S. Mosby* (pp. 226–228).

3. As recorded in *Personal Memoirs of U.S. Grant* (pp. 397–398).

4. As recorded in *Sheridan: The Life and Wars of General Phil Sheridan* (p. 225).

5. As noted in *Under Custer's Command: The Civil War Journal of James Henry Avery*, compiled by Karla Jean Hasby, edited by Eric Wittenberg.

6. According to *Ranger Mosby* by Virgil Carrington Jones.

7. As related in James J. Williamson's memoir, *Mosby's Rangers: The Operations of the 43rd Battalion of Virginia Cavalry from its Organization to the Surrender.*

8. As related in *Custer and His Times: Book Three*, edited by G.J.W. Urwin and Roberta E. Fagin.

9. According to Williamson's *Mosby's Rangers.*

10. As noted by Wert in his book *Mosby's Rangers* (pp. 213–214, 215 and 217).

11. As reported by Mosby in his memoir *Gray Ghost* when he quoted Confederate newspaper accounts (pp. 235–236).

Chapter 2

1. According to historian Gordon C. Rhea in his foreword to Wittenberg's *Glory Enough For All.*

2. Samuel J. Martin's *Kill-Cavalry: The Life of Union General Hugh Judson Kilpatrick* relates how the raid failed when Kilpatrick lost his nerve. Kilpatrick intended to rescue Union prisoners held in various prisons in and around Richmond. A secondary objective called for the capture and execution of Confederate President Jefferson Davis and his cabinet, along with the burning of Richmond. Although Union President Abraham Lincoln and Secretary of War Edwin M. Stanton approved the raid, it is not known whether Lincoln knew about what was planned for Davis, his cabinet, and the city of Richmond (pp. 168–172).

3. Urwin, in *Custer Victorious*, related how the command of the Cavalry Corps, Army of the Potomac, was reorganized in the aftermath of Buford's death and the removal and transfer of both Kilpatrick and Pleasonton (pp. 124–127).

4. The story of this campaign is told by Thomas Lewis in *The Shenandoah in Flames: The Valley Campaign of 1864* and Wert's *From Winchester to Cedar Creek: The Shenandoah Campaign of 1864.*

5. As Wert put it in *From Winchester to Cedar Creek*, these troops were undermanned, poorly armed, and seriously demoralized (p. 111).

Chapter 3

1. As noted in *General Phil Sheridan: War Memoirs* (p. 255).

2. Averell's failure to pursue Early's forces is noted in *From Winchester to Cedar Creek* (pp. 132–133) and *The Shenandoah in Flames* (pp. 124–125).

3. Sheridan himself, on his own initiative, had organized and conducted the only pursuit of the fleeing Confederate Army of Tennessee after the Battle of Missionary Ridge at Chattanooga, as noted in *Sheridan: The Life and Wars of General Phil Sheridan* (p. 147).

4. Averell related what happened in his collection of official reports and other records that he submitted to support his request for a court of inquiry into his removal from command of his cavalry division, which was never granted.

5. Wert in *From Winchester to Cedar Creek* felt that Sheridan was basically correct in his view of Averell's conduct in the aftermath of the Battle of Fisher's Hill. Wert stated that in his opinion, Averell had been much more interested in rounding up the spoils after the success of Crook's attack at Fisher's Hill than in driving a beaten enemy straight into the ground (p. 132).

6. What happened next was recorded in Urwin's *Custer Victorious* (pp. 195–196).

7. The story of this incident was taken from Sanford's *Rebels and Redskins* (p. 283).

8. What happened next was illustrated in *Brother Against Brother: Time-Life Books History of the Civil War* (p. 395).

Chapter 4

1. Morris amply reveals Sheridan's chagrin at what happened in *Sheridan: The Life and Wars of General Phil Sheridan* (pp. 204–205) along with Sheridan's own account in *General Philip Sheridan: Civil War Memoirs* (pp. 355–356).

2. As related in Kidd's memoir *A Cavalryman with Custer* (p. 289).

3. As noted in *A Cavalryman with Custer* (p. 289).

4. How Jubal Early's army was saved is recorded in Wert's *From Winchester to Cedar Creek* (pp. 133–134) and Lewis's *The Shenandoah in Flames* (p. 125).

Chapter 5

1. As noted in *Personal Memoirs of U.S. Grant* (p. 397).

2. Mosby maintained in his debate with A.E. Richards, contained in the *Southern Historical Society Papers, Vol. 27*, that he was answerable to and reported only to General Lee and no one else, including the commander of the Valley District, where he conducted most of his operations.

3. As noted in both Wert's *Mosby's Rangers* and Williamson's *Mosby's Rangers*.

4. As noted in Mosby's memoir *Gray Ghost* (pp. 221–222).

5. Mosby provided this defense of his command in the *Southern Historical Society Papers, Vol. 27*.

6. Wert, in *From Winchester to Cedar Creek* (pp. 151–153), presents a version of events as outlined in the newspaper article quoted in *Gray Ghost* (p. 236).

7. This description was provided in Wert's *Mosby's Rangers* (pp. 216, 218).

8. Her testimony can be found in Urwin and Fagin's *Custer and His Times: Book Three*.

9. This newspaper account also appears in *Gray Ghost* (p. 236).

Chapter 6

1. As noted in Kidd's *Recollections of a Cavalryman* and *A Cavalryman With Custer*. His letters were collected and published in *One of Custer's Wolverines: The Civil War Letters of General James H. Kidd, 6th Michigan Cavalry Regiment*, edited by Wittenberg.

2. This letter was cited in *The Custer Story: The Life and Letters of General George A. Custer and His Wife Elizabeth*, collected and edited by Marguerite Merington (pp. 115, 123).

3. This is recorded in Urwin and Fagin's *Custer and His Times: Book Three*.

4. This letter was cited in *Under Custer's Command: The Civil War Journal of James Henry Avery*.

5. Bean's account is contained in Urwin and Fagin's *Custer and His Times: Brook Three*.

6. As mentioned in Wert's *Mosby's Rangers* (pp. 215, 218).

7. Once again as mentioned in Wert's *Mosby's Rangers* (pp. 215, 218).

8. This statement appears in Wert's *Mosby's Rangers* (p. 215).

9. Dr. Buck's statement is included in Urwin and Fagin's *Custer and His Times: Book Three*.

Chapter 7

1. As noted in Wert's *From Winchester to Cedar Creek* (p. 145).

2. The summons to this meeting and its aftermath were described in Urwin's *Custer Victorious* (p. 193).

3. This letter is included in *Life and Letters of Charles Russell Lowell*, collected, edited, and supplementary text by Edward W. Emerson.

4. As noted in Urwin and Fagin's *Custer and His Times: Book Three*.

5. As noted in Urwin and Fagin's *Custer and His Times: Book Three*.

Chapter 8

1. As noted in *Sheridan: The Life and Wars of General Phil Sheridan* (p. 226).

2. Mosby's reprisal was described in his memoir, *Gray Ghost* (p. 237), in Williamson's *Mosby's Rangers* (p. 248), and Wert's *From Winchester to Cedar Creek* (pp. 153, 154-155) and *Mosby's Rangers*.

3. As related in *Sheridan: The Life and Wars of General Phil Sheridan* (p. 227) and *From Winchester to Cedar Creek* (p. 154).

Chapter 9

1. The description of Custer's uniform is taken from Urwin's *Custer Victorious* (pp. 57-58).

2. See *The Custer Story* edited by Marguerite Merington (pp. 115, 123).

3. As noted by Urwin in *Custer Victorious* (pp. 11-17).

4. As Urwin scathingly noted in *Custer Victorious*. Urwin seems to have considered Van de Water's book to be nothing more than a totally undeserved act of libel and character assassination. When I first read this book as a high school student who was interested in history it turned all of my previous conceptions about Custer on their ear and I was unable to reconcile my perceptions of Custer until more modern and objective scholarship about Custer eventually became available (pp. 15-16).

Chapter 10

1. This introduction was included in the Bantam Domain abridged edition of Kidd's memoirs under the title *A Cavalryman with Custer*.

2. Those letters were collected, edited, and published as *One of Custer's Wolverines*.

3. According to Utley in his introduction to *A Cavalryman with Custer* (pp. xiv-xv).

4. As related in *Recollections of a Cavalryman* and *A Cavalryman with Custer*.

5. His account has been taken verbatim from *The Seventh Michigan Cavalry of Custer's Wolverine Brigade*.

6. Edited by Marguerite Merington, a close personal friend of Elizabeth Bacon Custer, in *The Custer Story* (pp. 115, 123).

7. Published by Whittaker as *A Complete Life of General George A. Custer*.

Chapter 11

1. The information upon which this comparison was based can be found in Urwin's *Custer Victorious* and Martin's *Kill-Cavalry*.

2. According to Urwin's *Custer Victorious* (pp. 69-70).

3. Carhart, in *Lost Triumph* (pp. 127-134), has put this interpretation forward, as does Stephen Z. Starr in *The Union Cavalry in the Civil War* (p. 438).

4. Once again according to Carhart in *Lost Triumph* (pp. 187-244).

5. Which Martin points out in *Kill-Cavalry* (pp. 54, 55–56, 62, 92–96, 99, 124–125).

6. The Annie Jones investigation was noted in both D.A. Kinsley's *Custer: Favor the Bold; A Soldier's Story* (pp. 192–195) and Dr. Thomas P. Lowry's *The Story the Soldiers Wouldn't Tell: Sex in the Civil War* (pp. 154–155).

7. The biographer was Samuel J. Martin in his book *Kill-Cavalry*.

8. According to Martin in *Kill-Cavalry* (pp. 168–172).

9. Don Graham records his statement in *No Name on the Bullet: A Biography of Audie Murphy* (p. 59).

10. As noted by Martin in *Kill-Cavalry* (pp. 189–190).

11. According to David Evans in his book *Sherman's Horsemen: Union Cavalry Operations in the Atlanta Campaign*.

12. As Martin points out in *Kill-Cavalry* (pp. 204, 218, 226).

13. Martin, in *Kill-Cavalry*, describes both of these incidents (p. 225).

14. This incident was described by Kinsley in *Custer: Favor the Bold; A Soldier's Story* (pp. 283–284).

BIBLIOGRAPHY

Bissland, James. *Blood, Tears, and Glory: How Ohioans Won the Civil War.* Wilmington, Ohio: Orange Fraser Press, 2007.

Breihan, Carl W. *Great Lawmen of the West.* South Yarmouth, Mass.: Curling Publishing, 1953, 1978.

Carhart, Tom. *Lost Triumph: Lee's Real Plan at Gettysburg—And Why It Failed.* New York: Berkley Caliber, 2005.

Catholic Biblical Association of America. *The New American Bible.* Nashville, Camden and New York: Thomas Nelson, 1969.

Donovan, Jim. *Custer and the Little Big Horn: The Man, The Mystery, The Myth.* Stillwater, Minn.: Voyager Press, 2001.

Early, Jubal Anderson. *Autobiographical Sketch and Narrative of the War Between the States, with Notes by R.H. Early.* Philadelphia and London: J.B. Lippencott, 1912.

Editors of American Heritage, narrative by Eugene Rachlis in consultation with J.C. Ewers. *Indians of the Plains.* New York: Harper and Row, 1960.

Editors of Time-Life Books. *Brother Against Brother: Time-Life Books History of the Civil War.* New York: Prentiss Hall, 1990.

Emerson, Edward W. *Life and Letters of Charles Russell Lowell.* Port Washington, New York, London: Kennikat Press, 1907.

Evans, David. *Sherman's Horsemen: Union Cavalry Operations in the Atlanta Campaign.* Bloomington and Indianapolis: University of Indiana Press, 1997.

Graham, Don. *No Name on the Bullet: A Biography of Audie Murphy.* New York: Penguin Group, 1989.

Grant, Ulysses S. *Personal Memoirs of U.S. Grant.* New York: Barnes and Noble Books, 1885, 2003.

Gray, John S. *Centennial Campaign: The Sioux War of 1976.* Norman: University of Oklahoma Press, 1988.

_____. *Custer's Last Campaign: Mitch Boyer and the Little Bighorn.* Lincoln: University of Nebraska Press, 1991.

Isham, Asa B. *Seventh Michigan Cavalry of Custer's Wolverine Brigade.* New York, Huntington, W. Va.: Town Topics, 2000.

Jones, Virgil Carrington. *Ranger Mosby.* Charlotte: University of North Carolina Press, 1944.

Kidd, James H. *A Cavalryman with Custer.* New York: Bantam Books, 1991.

_____. *Recollections of a Cavalryman.* Ionia, Mich.: Sentinel Printing, 1908.

Kinsley, D.A. *Custer: Favor the Bold; A Soldier's Story.* New York: Promontory Press, 1967, 1968, 1988.

Korn, Jerry, and the Editors of Time-Life Books. *The Civil War: Pursuit to Appomattox; The Last Battles.* Alexandria, Va.: Time-Life Books. 1987

Leckie, Shirley A. *Elizabeth Bacon Custer and the Making of a Myth.* Norman: University of Oklahoma Press, 1993.

Lewis, Thomas A., and the Editors of Time-Life Books. *The Civil War: Shenandoah in Flames; The Valley Campaign of 1864.* Alexandria, Va.: Time-Life Books, 1987.

Longacre, Edward. *Custer and His Wolverines.* Coshohocken, Pa.: Combined Publishing, 1997.

Lowry, Thomas P., M.D. *The Story the Soldiers Wouldn't Tell: Sex in the Civil War.* Mechanicsburg, Pa.: Stackpole Books, 1994.

Macmillan Reference U.S.A. *Macmillan Information Now Encyclopedia: The Confederacy.* New York: Simon and Schuster, 1993, 1998.

Martin, Samuel J. *Kill-Cavalry: The Life of Union General Hugh Judson Kilpatrick.* Mechanicsburg, Pa.: Stackpole Books, 2000.

Merington, Marguerite, editor. *The Custer Story: The Life and Letters of General George A. Custer and His Wife Elizabeth.* The Devin Adair Company, 1950. This edition published by Barnes and Noble by arrangement with Devin-Adair Publishers, 1994.

Miller, David Humphreys. *Custer's Fall: The Native American Side of the Story.* New York: Meridian Book, previously published in a Dutton edition, 1957, 1992.

Morris, Roy, Jr. *Sheridan: The Life and Wars of General Phil Sheridan.* New York: Vintage Books, 1992.

Mosby, John S. *Gray Ghost: The Memoirs of Col. John S. Mosby.* New York: Bantam Books, 1917, 1992.

Sanford, George B. *Fighting Rebels and Redskins: Experiences in Army Life of Colonel George B. Sanford.* Edited by E.R. Hagemann. Norman: University of Oklahoma Press, 1969.

Schultz, Duane. *Over the Earth I Come: The Great Sioux Uprising of 1862.* New York: St. Martin's Press, 1992.

Sheridan, Philip H. *General Philip Sheridan: Civil War Memoirs.* New York: Bantam Books, 1888, 1991.

Simson, Jay W. *Crisis of Command in the Army of the Potomac: Sheridan's Search for an Effective General.* Jefferson, N.C.: McFarland, 2008.

Sklear, Larry. *To Hell with Honor: Custer and the Little Big Horn.* Norman: University of Oklahoma Press, 2003.

Southern Historical Society Papers, Vol. 27. Richmond, Va., January to December 1899.

Starr, Stephen Z. *The Union Cavalry in the Civil War.* Baton Rouge: Louisiana State University Press, 1976–1985.

Tey, Josephine. *The Daughter of Time.* New York: Pocket Books, by arrangement with Macmillan, 1951, 1977.

Trudeau, Noah Andre. *Gettysburg: A Testing of Courage.* New York: Harper Collins, 2002.

Urwin, Gregory J.W. *Custer Victorious.* London and Toronto: Associated University Presses, 1983.

_____, and Roberta E. Fagin, editors. *Custer and His Times: Book Three.* Little Bighorn Associates, 1987.

Utley, Robert M. *Custer and the Great Controversy: The Origin and the Development of a Legend.* Pasadena, Calif.: Westernlore Press, 1980.

_____. *Frontier Regulars: The United States Army and the Indian, 1866–1890.* New York: Macmillan, 1973.

United States. War Department. *The War of the Rebellion: A Compilation of Official Records of the Union and Confederate Armies.* 128 volumes. Washington, D.C.: U.S. Government Printing Office, 1880–1901.

Van de Water, Frederick F. *Glory Hunter: A Life of General Custer.* New York: Bobbs-Merrill, 1934.

Whittaker, Frederick A. *A Complete Life of General George A. Custer.* New York: Sheldon, 1876.

Williamson, James J. *Mosby's Rangers: The Operations of the 43rd Battalion of Virginia Cavalry from Its Organization to the Surrender.* New York: Sturgis and Walton, 1904.

Wittenberg, Eric J. *Glory Enough for All: Sheridan's Second Raid and The Battle of Trevilian Station.* Washington, D.C.: Brassey's. 2001.

Wittenberg, Eric, editor. *One of Custer's Wolverines: The Civil War Letters of*

General James H. Kidd, 6th Michigan Cavalry. Kent, Ohio: Kent State University Press, 2000.

_____, editor. *Under Custer's Command: The Civil War Journal of James Henry Avery.* Compiled by Karla Jean Husby. Kent, Ohio: Kent State University Press, 1999.

Wert, Jeffry D. *Custer: The Controversial Life of George Armstrong Custer.* New York: Simon and Schuster, 1996.

_____. *From Winchester to Cedar Creek: The Shenandoah Campaign of 1864.* New York: Simon and Schuster, 1987.

_____. *Mosby's Rangers.* New York: Simon and Schuster, 1990.

INDEX